Constitutional Law, Religion and Equal Liberty

During the 20th century, many countries embarked on a process of constitutional secularization by which the role of religion gradually became limited. Yet, by the late 20th century, and increasingly following the end of the Cold War, this development began to be challenged. This book examines the return of religion in constitutions through the concept of constitutional desecularization. It places this phenomenon in the context of the constitutional memory of the countries in which it has taken place and critically examines it against the development and standards of constitutionalism as the prevailing constitutional legal and political theory. Central to this analysis is the impact of constitutional desecularization on the regulation of equality in liberty, that is, both the regulation of constitutional rights and the scope for equality of those who are granted such rights. The book argues that equal liberty forms an essential part of constitutionalism as a theory, and that constitutionalism therefore entails a continuous development towards expanding it. The first and second parts of the book present a conceptual framework for the study of constitutional desecularization. The third part presents and analyzes three cases of constitutional desecularization in Afghanistan, Iran, and Iraq. The book will be of interest to researchers and policy-makers interested in constitutional history and theory, and the role of religion in law and its compatibility with human rights.

Azin Tadjdini is an Associate Human Rights Officer at the UN Office of the High Commissioner for Human Rights.

Routledge Research in Constitutional Law

Series Editor: David Marrani

This series features thought-provoking and original scholarship on constitutional law and theory. Books explore key topics, themes and questions in the field with a particular emphasis on comparative studies. Where relevant, titles will engage with political and social theory, philosophy and history in order to offer a rounded analysis of constitutions and constitutional law.

Available titles in this series include:

Constitutional Acceleration within the European Union and Beyond
Edited by Paul Blokker

Philosophy, Obligation and Law
Bentham's Ontology of Normativity
Piero Tarantino

Constitution-making and Human Rights in the Sudans
Edited by Lutz Oette and Mohamed Abdelsalam

Constitutional Politics and the Judiciary
Decision-making in Central and Eastern Europe
Edited by Kálmán Pócza

EU Law, Fundamental Rights and National Democracy
Eduardo Gill-Pedro

Constitution-making and Human Rights in the Sudans
Edited by Lutz Oette and Mohamed Abdelsalam Babiker

Constitutional Law, Religion and Equal Liberty
The Impact of Desecularization
Azin Tadjdini

For more information about this series, please visit: www.routledge.com/Routledge-Research-in-Constitutional-Law/book-series/CONSTLAW

Constitutional Law, Religion and Equal Liberty

The Impact of Desecularization

Azin Tadjdini

Routledge
Taylor & Francis Group
LONDON AND NEW YORK

First published 2020
by Routledge
2 Park Square, Milton Park, Abingdon, Oxon OX14 4RN

and by Routledge
52 Vanderbilt Avenue, New York, NY 10017

Routledge is an imprint of the Taylor & Francis Group, an informa business

British Library Cataloguing-in-Publication Data
A catalogue record for this book is available from the British Library

Library of Congress Cataloging-in-Publication Data
A catalog record has been requested for this book

ISBN: 978-0-367-18864-1 (hbk)
ISBN: 978-0-429-19951-6 (ebk)

Typeset in Galliard
by Deanta Global Publishing Services, Chennai, India

MIX
Paper from responsible sources
FSC® C013056

Printed and bound in Great Britain by
TJ International Ltd, Padstow, Cornwall

"The entire history of social improvement has been a series of transitions, by which one custom or institution after another, from being a supposed primary necessity of social existence, has passed into the rank of a universally stigmatized injustice and tyranny. So it has been with the distinctions of slaves and freemen, nobles and serfs, patricians and plebeians; and so it will be, and in part already is, with the aristocracies of colour, race, and sex".

John Stuart Mill, Utilitarianism

To my parents

Contents

Acknowledgments

The seeds of this book were planted in August 2011, when I began as a research fellow at the Department of Public and International Law at the University of Oslo. Its subsequent growth would not have been possible without the support and encouragement of many people to whom I owe my most sincere gratitude.

I am deeply thankful to my supervisors Kirsten Ketscher, Inger-Johanne Sand, and Eivind Smith for their belief in the project and for the freedom they provided me in my pursuit of it. I am indebted to Henrik Palmer Olsen for his comments on early chapters, and to the dissertation committee, Benedikte Moltumyr Høgberg, Frances Raday, and Mikael Rask Madsen, for their positive and generous engagement with the project.

I am thankful to the Faculty of Law and the Department of Public International Law for hosting me, and to everyone who contributed with comments, conversations and advice on law and life: Cecilia Bailliet, Stein Evju, Andrea Grønningsæter, Anne Hellum, Ingunn Ikdahl, Henning Jakhelln, Markus Jerkø, Anine Kierulf, Julia Køhler-Olsen, Kirsten Sandberg, Knut Vikør, and Tone Linn Wærstad. Further, I am grateful to Bård Sverre Tuseth for his helpful guidance in the world of libraries and online databases, and to Ine Marie Ausland, Guro Frostestad, Kjetil Frantzen, Elise Koppang Frøjd, Øyvind Henden, and Shima Høegh-Omdal Saatchi for their administrative and technical support. I deeply value the company and conversations of my friends and co-fellows on the sixth floor of Domus nova: Lars Arnesen, Eugenia Blücher, Aled Delwyn-Fisher, Alexandra Gran, Nora Leerberg, Mollie, Anders Sondrup, Anniken Sørlie, and Øystein Skotheim.

Thanks are also due to Alison Kirk and Emily Summers at Routledge for shepherding this project through, and to Jayanthi Chander and the team at Deanta for the copy-editing.

I also owe great thanks to New York Law School that hosted me the academic year 2013/2014, during which I learned to think about law in ways that I had not before. I thank Wojciech Sadurski, Michèle Finck, Anne Dienelt, Isabelle Lassée, Emmanuel De Groof, and Michael Riegner for their comments on early chapters. I am grateful to my friend Jacob Weinrib, for his humble enthusiasm and good wit, his abundant sharing of his knowledge, and for helping me make sense of my own project.

Finally, my greatest debt in every way is to my parents, whose lives took an unexpected turn as a result of constitutional desecularization, the phenomenon at the heart of this book. They have encouraged whatever odd enthusiasms I have had, and provided me with their time and everything else. This book is a record of their efforts.

Part I

Conceptualizing the issue

1 Constitutional but not constitutionalism

1.1 The politicization of religion and its way into the constitution

In 1979, the Islamic revolution in Iran not only replaced a king with an ayatollah; more significantly, it also replaced the Constitution of 1906–1907 with a new Constitution that, for the first time in the country's history, established Iran as a theocracy and an "Islamic Republic" – a constitution that ideologically entrenched religion in unprecedented ways, most notably as the justification for political authority and governance, as *the* source of legislation, as a limitation on rights, and as a justification for a hierarchical categorization of people based on their opinion and beliefs. It also radically changed the justice system and the judiciary, introduced new categories of crimes, and re-introduced long-abolished crimes, punishments, and criminal procedures, all in the name of the official state religion. The 2001 international war against the Taliban in Afghanistan brought in a new government and in 2004 introduced a new Constitution that replaced the Taliban's constitutional void that had ruled in the period 1996–2001. The Constitution of 2004 also replaced the previous 1987 Constitution, and established Afghanistan as an "Islamic Republic" in which Islam was made a source of legislation and a criterion for rights, and where religion strengthened its institutional role, including in the judiciary. The invasion of Iraq in 2003 removed Saddam Hussein from power and also replaced the Ba'ath party's Constitution of 1970 with a new Constitution in 2005, making Iraq a federal state for the first time, drawn largely along, and reinforcing, ethnic and religious lines, and establishing Islam as a source of legislation. While the three previously mentioned regime changes and subsequent constitutional changes took place through revolution or war, in Hungary, the 2010 elections took place within the existing constitutional framework, yet the result can in some ways be viewed as analogous to that of a regime change. The political party Fidesz, having obtained a two-thirds majority, amended the existing constitution 12 times in ways that removed the existing checks and balances before adopting an entirely new Constitution.[1]

1 Gábor Halmai, Kim Lane Scheppele and Miklós Bánkuti, "Hungary's Illiberal Turn: Disabling the Constitution", *Journal of Democracy* [2012] 23:3 138.

The new Constitution, amounting to what one commentator has called a "one-party constitution" came into force in 2012, and entrenched religious language in ways unprecedented in the Constitution preceding it, departing from the celebrated constitutional development after the fall of the Berlin Wall.[2] Within the framework of the explicitly secular Turkish Constitution of 1982, that had been built on Atatürk's 1923 Constitution, Turkey, under the rule of the AK Party and President Erdogan, has seen a rise in religious rhetoric in political discourse, as well as in the educational system, overlapping also with constitutional amendments in 2017 that turned the parliamentary system of the country into a strong presidential system. In Russia, notwithstanding the secular character of the current Constitution of 1993, the State has established a strong tie with the Orthodox Church, in ways that can qualify as a religionization of constitutional practice, where Orthodoxy is used as a source of national ideology, and legislation has been passed that increasingly restricts fundamental rights.[3] A rather curious expression of the close tie between Church and State came after the declaration of independence of the Orthodox Church of Ukraine, following which the head of the Russian Orthodox Church described the Russian President as "a miracle of God". For someone who made his career in the Soviet secret police a few decades earlier, such a 180-degree shift in status can indeed be described as miraculous. In India, the explicitly secular Constitution has for decades faced challenges from Hindu political movements, challenges that have only exacerbated since the 2014 elections and the coming to power of the Bharatiya Janata Party, which in rhetoric and policy has reinforced the language of religious nationalism.[4] In Israel, the status of the state as a "Jewish State" has long been the subject of political debate. The debate reached new heights in 2018 when the Knesset passed the "Basic Law: Israel as the nation state of the Jewish People", whereby the right to self-determination is held to be a right exclusive to the Jewish people. Under this Basic Law, the "state views the development of Jewish settlement as a national value and will act to encourage and promote its establishment and consolidation". Less comprehensive, but still significant is the development in North Carolina in 2013 when, despite the famous establishment clause of the US Constitution, legislators introduced a resolution declaring that the state has the right to declare an official religion.[5]

2 Gábor Attila Tóth, *Constitution for a Disunited Country: On Hungary's 2011 Fundamental Law* (Central European University Press, 2013).

3 Alexey Krindatch, "Changing Relationships between Religion, the State, and Society in Russia", *GeoJournal* [2006] 26.

4 Gino Battaglia, "Neo-Hindu Fundamentalism Challenging the Secular and Pluralistic Indian State", *Religions* [2017] 8:10 216; Yogendra K. Malik and Dhirendra K. Vajpeyi, "The Rise of Hindu Militancy: India's Secular Democracy at Risk", *Asian Survey* [1989] 29:3 308.

5 Known as the "Defense of Religion Act of 2013", the resolution came as a response to a lawsuit by the American Civil Liberties Union that charged that Rowan County in North Carolina violated the First Amendment by opening 97% of its meetings with Christian prayers. http://ncleg.net/sessions/2015/Bills/House/PDF/h348v0.pdf (accessed 29 March 2019).

What are the constitutional implications of a strengthening of the role of religion in the constitution? And how does this kind of constitutional development compare to the core values of constitutionalism, encompassed in the idea of equal liberty? This book centers on the relationship between two features of modern constitutionalism: equal liberty and constitutional secularity. What are the implications for the former when there is a change of the latter?

"Constitutions", says the political theorist Hanna Pitkin, "are made, not found".[6] In making a constitution, its drafters make a political choice about the fundamental values the legal order should recognize and aim to further, as well as about the values upon which policies in that society should be made. Equal liberty is one such value. The degree of its constitutional entrenchment is a political choice. Similarly, the degree of establishment or nonestablishment of religion in the constitution is a political choice.

The object of this book is the constitutional transformation, whereby religion, leaving aside the significant difficulty of defining "religion" in the first place, is granted a more prominent role in a contemporary constitution compared to its role in the preceding constitution of the same country. Given the political and legal character of a constitution, it may in this regard be more precise to speak of religion as a "constitutional language", rather than simply calling it "religion". For ease of reference, but to the detriment of accuracy, I call this particular form of constitutional development, "constitutional desecularization". Constitutional desecularization pertains in this regard, to a legal and political process, and involves the introduction of norms external to constitutionalism into constitutions, in ways that undermine the core constitutive norms of constitutionalism itself, by introducing a particular religio-political ideology into the framework of the constitution.

In light of the use of religion by political movements prior to the constitutional change, the constitutional place of religion in the context of constitutional desecularization is arguably distinct from its role in earlier forms of confessional constitutions. Rather, this constitutional transformation involves an alteration of basic principles of the constitution and a radical departure from the constitutional past of the countries where it takes place. I seek to highlight the implications of this transformation on equal liberty as one of the constitutive elements of constitutionalism and of international human rights law, the idea that each individual is of equal moral worth and has rights to equal liberty and to be treated as an equal.[7]

More than simply representing a religionization of the constitutional sphere, and despite popular justifications and appeals to "people", "culture", or "nation"

6 Hanna Pitkin, "The Idea of a Constitution", *Journal of Legal Education* [1987] 37:2 167.

7 Some commentators describe equal liberty as the core of the notion of human dignity. For a comprehensive theory of human dignity as a theory of public law, see Jacob Weinrib, *Dimensions of Dignity: The Theory and Practice of Modern Constitutional Law* (Cambridge University Press, 2016) 61–67.

that commonly have been put forward to justify the coming into being of such constitutions, constitutional desecularization as a transition, or rather a *transformation*, appears in hindsight and, for some, already in foresight, as a more or less calculated decision towards an illiberal consolidation of political authority, to the detriment of individual rights, political participation, and government accountability.[8] In short, this form of religionization of the constitutional sphere is not so much an issue of religion as such but is about an expansion of the area for discretion exercised by political authority and a narrowing of the scope of equal liberty, facilitated through the use of religious rhetoric in the constitutional order.[9]

References to religion in constitutions and of religion as a constitutional language are invoked in constitutions to justify political authority, as well as privileges for certain groups, claims, norms, and actors.[10] From this perspective, this transformation can be understood as forming part of the shifts between exclusive and inclusive constitutional developments that have accompanied constitutional history across time and place, under various names. Inclusive constitutional developments, as understood here, have been developments towards legal orders that seek to, at least at the formal level, broaden the scope of individuals that are considered as not only subject to political authority but also considered as establishing that authority and able to hold it accountable. By contrast, exclusive constitutional developments have been developments towards legal orders that expand the scope of individuals who are excluded from such agency using various forms of justifications, both religious and non-religious.

We can therefore view this constitutional development as a competing development to that of the leading paradigm in both constitutional theory and in binding law. It is contrary to the development of constitutionalism as a political theory and a normative ideal, and to international human rights law as binding law, where both theory and law recognize fundamental rights, and equality with

8 One may in this connection note the names of the military operations in Afghanistan ("Operation Enduring Freedom") and in Iraq ("Operation Iraqi Freedom").

9 This phenomenon can also be interpreted as a form of what has been described as "corporatism", whereby religion or religious rhetoric and groups claiming such rhetoric, constitute a "corporative group" that exercise pressures on constitutionalism's central feature of equal liberty. For a rich account of corporative groups and corporatism as pressure on the consolidation of democracy, see Carlos Santiago Nino, "Transition to Democracy, Corporatism, and Presidentialism with Special Reference to Latin America" in Douglas Greenberg and others (eds), *Constitutionalism and Democracy: Transitions in the Contemporary World* (The American Council of Learned Societies Comparative Constitutionalism Papers, 1993).

10 Constitutional law deals with concrete constitutional norms. References to religion therefore perform a constitutional function in the distribution of power and rights. Whether such references reflect religious doctrinal content is less interesting for the purpose of constitutional law. For example, many constitutions establish an official state religion, yet the role of this state religion differs on how the constitutional norms are further designed, interpreted, and implemented in practice. The interpretation of references to religion or religious law is therefore, in a constitutional context, primarily a task of constitutional interpretation, ultimately exercised by those tasked to do so, rather than an exercise in theology, and their interpretation as constitutional norms may not necessarily reflect their theological interpretation.

respect to such rights, as constitutive elements of the constitutional order, whose guarantee cannot depend on the goodwill or benevolence of the State.

The point of departure in this book is the following question – what do such transformations entail as a matter of constitutional law – seen, not simply in isolation with respect to specific constitutions, but in the light of the constitutional history of the country where they occur? Beyond the strengthening of the role of religion and religious language, these transformations more importantly change the direction of the constitutional memory in countries subject to it, a constitutional transformation that breaks with its own constitutional past, including the achievements of its own past, notwithstanding the past's shortcomings. They can be identified as forming part of the recurrent phenomenon of developments towards what have been characterized as populist and fundamentalist legal orders that privilege certain groups and undermine the human rights of individuals who are precluded from being equals. In light of the limitations on equal liberty, constitutional desecularization may be regarded as a constitutional expression of populism, which at its core rejects pluralism.[11] What makes the shift represented by constitutional desecularization distinctive is that it takes place in countries that have, at some point in their constitutional memory, embarked on a process towards constitutionalism with certain achievements in that process, and where this constitutional transformation leads to a change in direction through the replacement of a constitution with a new one where the strengthened the religious language actively removes central features of previous constitutional achievements. In this regard, one may note the surprising, yet frequently encountered presumption that equates the past constitutions with the past *political* order, even when these two are not overlapping. As a result, the choice to strengthen religious references may reflect a rejection of the previous political order, rather than a rejection of constitutional secularity based on legal considerations. While falling short of a historical account of the constitutional history of the countries that are the subject of this book, I highlight some of the main features of the constitutional past of each in order to show *from what* the contemporary constitutional transformation is a change.

The examples described in the beginning of this chapter have been seen as part of the broader phenomenon of resurgence of political religion and religious rhetoric in governance.[12] However, constitutional desecularization is particular in the sense that the resurgence is translated and culminates in a change not only of politics and political discourse, but of the constitutional legal framework. The difference is not insignificant. Given the change of the constitution, we are not only

11 Jan Werner Müller, *What is Populism?* (University of Pennsylvania Press, 2016).

12 See for example, Scott Thomas (ed), *The Global Resurgence of Religion and the Transformation of International Relations: The Struggle for the Soul of the Twenty-First Century* (Palgrave MacMillan, 2005); Ran Hirschl, *Constitutional Theocracy* (Harvard University Press, 2010); Richard Antoun and Mary E. Hegland (eds), *Religious Resurgence: Contemporary Cases in Islam, Christianity, and Judaism* (Syracuse University Press, 1987); Mark Janis and Carolyn Evans (eds), *Religion and International Law* (Martinus Nijhoff Publishers, 1999).

dealing with a "resurgence of religion" or "religious revival", but with the *constitutional change* or *constitutional transformation* of such resurgence or revival, and the implications of these constitutional transformations on central features of constitutionalism in constitutions that have in the past laid the foundation for these features to be achieved. While democratic institutions still had to develop more fully, the normative framework established under some of the past constitutions would, to a considerable extent for their own time, establish the foundation for continued development towards the standards of constitutionalism. We are thus speaking of a transition from a situation where the problem could be identified as primarily one of the practice of an otherwise defendable constitution, to a situation where the problem has become the normative constitutional framework itself. The significance of the constitutional politicization of religion is not merely of theoretical interest, but has practical implications on the conduct of governance, on the rule of law, on individual rights, and on society in general. In this book, I study only one aspect of constitutional desecularization, limited to the implications of this transformation on equal liberty, exemplified with examples from the Afghan, Iranian, and Iraqi constitutional experience.

At this stage, some may already object that neither the legal systems in general nor the constitutions of the cases examined in this book qualify as legal systems or as constitutions. This objection is based on the common assumption that law matters only if it matches reality. Against this, one may argue that constitutions do matter, even when they may not have all the same functions as they would have in a democratic setting with a high degree of rule of law. Tom Ginsburg and Alberto Simpser have addressed the question of why and in which ways constitutions matter in authoritarian systems, identifying four categories of functions that such constitutions perform.[13] Constitutions can first function as an *operating manual*, describing how the government is to function, setting out the power division, and establishing the conditions under which opposition can exist. A second function is the *billboard function*, the constitution as an information provider to potential and actual uses. Although the constitution in some contexts may be the least important document in a legal system, this does not imply that it has no political importance, as it will signal ideological legitimacy to particular voices. When the promises in constitutions are not accurate signals of policy but instead pure fiction, we arrive the third function – the constitution as *window-dressing*. Window-dressing thus presumes that the text in itself is unproblematic and that the problem lies in the constitution not being respected or taken seriously. Finally, the *blueprint function* denotes the constitution as describing things not as they are, but as they might be. Steven Levitsky and Lucan Way point out that electoral authoritarian regimes – those that hold regular elections, but not necessarily on an even playing field – may help extend regime survival, as they contribute to the endurance of a political system by facilitating the consolidation

13 Tom Ginsburg and Alberto Simpser (eds), *Constitutions in Authoritarian Regimes* (Cambridge University Press, 2014) 5–10.

of political power.[14] Equally important is the force constitutions can have in shaping social norms and public preferences. In the area of equal liberty, a constitution that significantly limits the scope of equality can, over time, influence the perception of equality among people under its jurisdiction. Constitutions thus matter, including the authoritarian ones and those in states with a weak rule of law, since they provide important clues into regime practices and priorities and as they structure discourse and provide a political idiom. By setting the terms of political discourse, constitutions can define what are acceptable acts, as opposed to unacceptable acts, legitimizing one set and delegitimizing others.

Elements of the constitutional transformation by which religion comes back with force in the constitution compared to the role it had before, have been analyzed through different lenses. There are several studies on the *why* of such constitutional transformations, explaining the contributing factors and events, be they social, political, or economic, leading up to the transformation in specific countries.[15] Similarly, studies have addressed the procedural *how* of such transformations, mostly explaining the constitutional drafting processes.[16] Elements of this constitutional transformation have received considerable attention from the perspective of "constitutional theocracy", "politicization of religion", "strong religion", and as "democratic backsliding".[17] In cases where the religion in question is Islam, the constitutional transformation is sometimes conceptualized as

14 Steven Levitsky and Lucan Way, *Competitive Authoritarianism: Hybrid Regimes After the Cold War* (Cambridge University Press, 2010) 9–11.

15 Said Arjomand and Nathan Brown (eds), *The Rule of Law, Islam and Constitutional Politics in Egypt and Iran* (SUNY Press, 2013); Ran Hirschl, *Constitutional Theocracy* (Harvard University Press, 2010); Alessandro Ferrari and James Toronto (eds), *Religions and Constitutional Transitions in the Muslim Mediterranean* (Routledge, 2018); Rainer Grote, Tilmann Röder and Ali El-Haj (eds), *Constitutionalism, Human Rights and Islam After the Arab Spring* (Oxford University Press, 2016); Eugene Cotran and Adel Sherif (eds), *Democracy, the Rule of Law and Islam* (Kluwer Law International, 1999).

16 See, for example, Andrew Arato, *Constitution Making Under Occupation: The Politics of Imposed Revolution in Iraq* (Columbia University Press, 2009).

17 Recent contributions on this topic include Jean Cohen and Cécile Laborde (eds), *Religion, Secularism and Constitutional Democracy* (Columbia University Press, 2015); Susanna Mancini and Michel Rosenfeld (eds), *Constitutional Secularism in an Age of Religious Revival* (Oxford University Press, 2014); Gabriel Almond, Scott Appleby and Emmanuel Sivan (eds), *Strong Religion: The Rise of Fundamentalism Around the World* (Chicago University Press, 2013); Frances Raday, "Constitutional Secularism Vindicated: Constitutionalism and Secularism in an Age of Religious Revival: The Challenge of Global and Local Fundamentalisms", *Cardozo Law Review* [2009] 30:6 2769; Ran Hirschl, *Constitutional Theocracy* (Harvard University Press, 2010); Ran Hirschl, "The Political Economy of Constitutionalism in a Non-Secularist World" in Tom Ginsburg (ed), *Comparative Constitutional Design* (Cambridge University Press, 2012); Rudi Teitel, "Critique of Religion as Politics in the Public Sphere", *Cornell Law Review* [1993] 78:5 747; András Sájo, "Preliminaries to a Concept of Constitutional Secularism", *International Journal of Constitutional Law* [2008] 6:3 605; Lorenzo Zucca, *A Secular Europe: Law and Religion in the European Constitutional Landscape* (Oxford University Press, 2012).

constituting a particular form of constitutionalism – referred to as "Islamic constitutionalism" – and is either defended or rejected as such.[18]

Despite their differences, existing approaches to this constitutional transformation often share two presumptions. One is a dichotomy between "secular" and "religious" constitutions. The second, and related, presumption, is the generalization of "religious constitutions", where the categorization of constitutions is based on the contemporary identity of the constitution, without taking into account the constitutional past of each case, making the constitutions appear rather static in their identity. As such, we may find the constitutions of, for example, Iran, Pakistan, Norway, and Israel under the category "religious constitutions", despite the significantly different constitutional lines of the modern historical development of each with respect to the features of constitutionalism. Similarly, the term "Islamic" or "Muslim" constitutions are often applied rather non-critically to describe constitutions in Muslim majority countries, ranging from Indonesia to Afghanistan, regardless of the role that the constitution grants religion. In brief, the simple fact of the self-proclaimed "religiousness" of the constitution or the majority religion in a state is commonly taken at face value and as the main marker of the identity of constitution, without taking into account other features that may be more important and which may change the way we categorize constitutions and thereby also change the way we view the constitutions in general and constitutional desecularization in particular.

The first presumption described previously, which is based on the dichotomy of secular versus religious constitutions, often has the following underlying normative question: what place, if any, should religion have in the constitution of a country? This question is not an innocent question. It opens a box that over centuries, or even millennia if we speak of "constitutions" in the broad sense, has prompted heated disagreement, upheavals, political bargaining, and polarization. The return of religion to the political arena in the last few decades has put this question back on stage and made it a starting point for both policy and analytical approaches to the phenomenon.[19] On each side of the debate, we find a spectrum of arguments about whether or not religion should be included, and, if so, how it should be included, in the constitutional order of a country. On the one hand, we find positions arguing that religion should be included in the constitution because it is a symbol of national heritage, tradition, because it unites people, out of righteousness, or simply because it is the imperative will of God. On the same side of the debate, but out of a different concern, we find the argument that religion should have a place in the constitution because it places religion and

18 Rainer Grote and Tilmann Röder (eds), *Constitutionalism in Islamic Countries: Between Upheaval and Continuity* (Oxford University Press, 2012). Much of what has become a rich literature on the role of Islam in the constitution places a particular focus on whether the doctrinal teachings of Islam are compatible with, for example, international human rights law or with democracy.

19 See, for example, Michel Rosenfeld, "A Pluralist Critique of the Constitutional Treatment of Religion", in András Sájo and Sholomo Avineri (eds), *The Law of Religious Identity: Models for Post-Communism* (Springer, 1998).

religious authorities under the control of the state, as opposed to leaving them as unconstrained agents, or that religion should be included as an element of political compromise which may have a stabilizing force that may mitigate tensions in divided polities. On the other side of the debate, we find people who argue that religion should have no place in a constitution because the constitution should not privilege one religion over another, as an argument of state neutrality and non-discrimination, because religion and state should be separate, or simply out of a dislike for religion, or in the more extreme pursuit of state-sponsored atheism. These discussions continue to play out, not only in domestic contexts but also globally, given that constitution-making since the end of the Second World War has increasingly become an international phenomenon.

This book looks at constitutions as constitutions, establishing the framework that regulates political authority and its relationship with persons. My perspective is that religion in this context is but one language of constitutions, a language for the normative regulation of political authority. Religious rhetoric does not necessarily reflect religion or historical realities, and does not make a constitution "religious". One of the problems in using the category of "*religion*" to describe or analyze a constitution is that it leads to a dichotomy between religion and secularity, where secularity is presumed to equate non-religion, equal in status to that of religion, rather than representing a principle of governance.

Despite the limitation of the cases studied in this book to Afghanistan, Iran, and Iraq, the constitutional transformation as a matter of *constitutional law*, is not limited to a particular religion or to a particular region. I seek to highlight that constitutional desecularization represents more than an issue of "constitutional theocracy", whereby aspects of religion are infused in the legal and political framework. Rather, the language of religion in these transformations reflects a politicization of religion, with particular implications for equal liberty, and as such, it makes these transformations different.

To study constitutional desecularization as constitutional law also allows us to study the constitutional dimension of such transitions and to critically test the promises that justified their coming about. Bearing in mind that these constitutional transformations come about following regime changes, through revolution, war, or elections, with claims to bring about democracy, justice, and freedom, it is of interest to critically assess the extent to which the new constitution provides a realistic basis for these aims to be achieved. A quick comparison of the new constitutions with the constitutional history of each country suggests that there is surprisingly little reflective interaction with the past constitutions and their achievements with a view to remedying their shortcomings in order to achieve democracy, justice, and freedom.

This book is an argumentative contribution to the discussion of these constitutional transformations. I seek to make sense of them as a matter of *constitutional law*, as opposed to religion. The way in which religion is used in these constitutional transitions transcends the dichotomy between religious versus secular constitutions, and is arguably different from the way in which the traditional form of the confessional constitution entrenched religion. In the contemporary context, the use and interpretation of religion and the way in which it is entrenched would suggest that we are dealing with a selective reinvention of religion that is used in a particular way that limits equal liberty and as such represents an illiberal turn. Religion, in the context of constitutional desecularization, thus has a particular role, and it is this role which places the constitution at odds with equal liberty as a constitutive element of constitutionalism. The constitutional inclusion of religion may, in this connection, amount to establish what one commentator has called "autocratic legalism" or "Populist constitutionalism", whereby the language of religion and constitutionalism is used to dismantle the constitutional order.[20] In this connection, one may observe a distinction in literature's approach to this transformation, depending on whether the religion in question is Islam or not. It is surprising to note that in the cases where we are dealing with a strengthening of the constitutional role of Islam, such transformations appear to be more easily justified as "cultural" and analyzed as a particular sub-category of constitutionalism or within the framework of religious law. By contrast, other religions used in the same way are more commonly analyzed within the framework of populism or fundamentalist politics.

What I argue in this book is that the identification of the state with a comprehensive doctrine in the first place – whether this is one particular religion or a non-religious philosophy – in itself is incompatible with the notion of constitutionalism, regardless of the content of the religious or non-religious doctrine in question. The more functions the constitution gives to the comprehensive doctrine, the farther away from constitutionalism and international human rights law will the constitution place itself. The issue is therefore not the *type* of comprehensive doctrine, nor its interpretation, but the constitutional adoption of such a doctrine in the first place.

In this connection, I wish to add two things to the already rich literature on the topic. One is methodological and the other is substantial. First, by placing the topic within a discussion of constitutionalism, this study problematizes the often-encountered notion of "Islamic constitutionalism". I argue that because equal liberty as a constitutive element of constitutionalism is dependent on constitutional secularity, constitutionalism will entail secularity. Therefore, constitutionalism precludes religious sub-types or other forms of qualified constitutionalism. What is at issue is how religious language impacts *constitutionalism*, the form of state power, and the privilege of certain groups or elites and not religious values *per se*. Second, in going beyond the dichotomy of religion and secularity, yet maintaining the centrality of constitutional secularity for the achievement of equal liberty, I seek to place this form of constitutional development within the larger global constitutional landscape. If the constitutive features of modern constitutionalism are lacking in a constitutional design, this will place the constitution outside the paradigm of constitutionalism.[21] Therefore, Islamic constitutions and

20 Kim Lane Scheppele, "Autocratic Legalism", *The University of Chicago Law Review* [March 2018] 85:2 545–583.

21 On this, I follow Jacob Weinrib's unified theory on public governance and modern constitutionalism as "a fundamental innovation in governance", Jacob Weinrib, *Dimensions of Dignity: The Theory and Practice of Modern Constitutional Law* (Cambridge University Press, 2016).

"Islamic constitutionalism" cannot be justified by arguing that such constitutions may advance the values of liberal democracy. From the perspective of constitutionalism, such an argument is irrelevant, because the question is not whether constitutionalism is an instrument for the promotion of certain outcomes that can be realized in its absence. In other words, the defense of constitutionalism is not because it produces an outcome that other forms of theories are incapable of offering. Such a defense would establish a problem of verification, and the superiority of constitutionalism cannot be based on the idea that it produces better outcomes. Constitutionalism therefore cannot be defended based on an instrumental defense – that is, because it is instrumental for the achievement of good outcomes. Instead, the defense of constitutionalism must be based on its internal features and its internal logic.

1.2 Equal liberty as a constitutive element of constitutionalism

My point of departure is the idea that constitutions inform us about a legal system's normative standpoint with regard to two fundamental questions.[22] These two questions are both questions of distribution. The first is the distribution of political power, hereunder the question of what type of governance is justified and how it is justified. The second is the distribution of rights, hereunder the question of *who* can enjoy rights and the justifications for denying some persons the rights that others may enjoy.

The regulation of political authority, hereunder its relationship with persons under its authority, has been the object of a diverse collection of normative theories and practices. Since the 18th century, two features have dominated the approach to this question in law. One is constitutionalism as a normative theory, and the other is the adoption of the written constitution as a form. Because the constitution is a form, its content can reflect any normative theory and not necessarily that of constitutionalism.

The adoption of the constitutional form, and the expansion of the theory of constitutionalism and its basic features of popular sovereignty and free and equal persons as both the justification and the aim of political authority, has spread to more and more legal systems in a way that some describe as a spread of liberal constitutional democracy, at least on the normative level, and on the level of self-proclamation by most constitutions and political authorities.[23] Constitutionalism's basis in free and equal persons entails that persons exist prior

22 For a precise account on the place of these two questions in political philosophy, see Jonathan Wolff, *An Introduction to Political Philosophy* (Oxford University Press, 1996, revised ed. 2006).

23 Gregory Fox and Brad Roth (eds), *Democratic Governance and International Law* (Cambridge University Press, 2000); Tom Ginsburg (ed), *Comparative Constitutional Design* (Cambridge University Press, 2012); Dag Michalsen, *Rett en Internasjonal Historie* (Pax Forlag, 2011).

to political authority, and this is reflected in the notion of constitutional rights.[24] Constitutional rights thus have a certain function and meaning under the idea of constitutionalism.[25] This has influenced, and is in turn influenced by, international law as an additional layer claiming authority through law, no longer only as an instrument of inter-state relations, but as an instrument of intra-state relations, directly addressing the relationship between political authority and persons who fall under that authority, as well as increasingly between persons.[26]

Since 1945, international human rights law, articulating into binding norms the core of the idea of constitutionalism, has, through its system of individual rights brought international law and constitutional law into closer normative proximity.[27] In bringing international law into the internal sphere of states, international human rights law marks a radical shift in the understanding of sovereignty.[28] Sovereignty can thus be understood as having gone from primarily being

24 Locke saw sovereignty as being limited by the terms of the social contract, as opposed to Hobbes' view on sovereignty as unlimited. See Jonathan Wolff (2006) and Dag Michalsen (2011).

25 Dag Michalsen (2011) 267–289; Tom Ginsburg and Rosalind Dixon (eds), *Comparative Constitutional Law* (Edward Elgar, 2011); Aharon Barak, *Human Dignity: The Constitutional Value and the Constitutional Right* (Cambridge University Press, 2016).

26 For a long time, the discussion about the relationship between international law and the domestic constitution was dominated by the question of monism versus dualism. After the Second World War, a more pragmatic style of thinking emerged, engaged with aspects of domestic practice. Today, the discussion largely centers on developing a normative framework for thinking about the relationship between national and international law. See, for example, Mattias Kumm, "Democratic Constitutionalism Encounters International Law: Terms of Engagement", in Sujit Choudry (ed), *The Migration of Constitutional Ideas* (Cambridge University Press, 2006); Mikael Madsen, "Transnational Fields: Elements of a Reflexive Sociology of the Internationalisation of Law", *Rætferd* [2006] 29:3 114, 23–41. A related question is that of the constitutionalization of international law; see Jeffrey Dunoff and Joel Trachtman (eds), *Ruling the World? Constitutionalism, International Law, and Global Governance* (Cambridge University Press, 2009); Anne Peters, "Compensatory Constitutionalism: The Functions and Potential of Fundamental International Norms and Structures", *Leiden Journal of International Law* [2006] 19.

27 The involvement by the international community and international law since the mid-1990s in processes of state-building has led some commentators to speak of "internationalized constitution-making". See Constance Grewe and Michael Riegner, "International Constitutionalism in Ethnically Divided Societies: BosniaHerzegovina and Kosovo compared", in Armin Von Bogdandy and Rüdiger Wolfrum (eds), *Max Planck Yearbook of United Nations Law* (2011) 1–64. In setting out a policy framework for peace-building, the UN has affirmed the centrality of constitutions: "Constitution-making processes are a central aspect of democratic transitions, peacebuilding and state-building". See UN, *Guidance Note of the Secretary-General, United Nations Assistance to Constitution-Making Processes*, April 2009, 3. Efforts to standardize constitution-making are also found at the regional level. The European Commission for Democracy through Law (Venice Commission) operating under the Council of Europe, is one such example.

28 For a rich account of the intersection of constitutional ideas and international law, see Jean L. Cohen, *Globalization and Sovereignty: Rethinking Legality, Legitimacy and Constitutionalism* (Cambridge University Press, 2012).

a state-centered notion to one which bases the sovereignty of the state on the state's recognition of the sovereignty of each individual.[29] This entails the recognition of fundamental rights that are inherent and which cannot be limited by the state, and where the legal systems make the exercise of political authority accountable to all those who are subject to it.[30] Within this account, equal liberty becomes central to political legitimacy. As a result, the adoption and content of domestic constitutions are not, at least in principle, solely at the mercy of sovereign states as this notion has traditionally been understood. Through the "piercing of the sovereign veil", international human rights law and its basis in free and equal persons, bring the international order into the domestic one, and places each individual, as free and equal, at the core of the notion of sovereignty. The basis of the state is thus free and equal persons, but this freedom and equality are in turn also dependent on the state for its guarantee and legal protection. Consequently, this requires a certain constitutional configuration of the relationship between individuals and political authority.

Within this narrative, two observations can be made. One is the development towards an increased separation between the state and its use of religious rhetoric in the constitution and in political governance, a development towards what we can call "constitutional secularity". The other is the development towards an expansion of the scope of equality. While the interpretation of *who* may qualify as "equal" is subject to continuous expansion, the acknowledgment of formal equality was in itself fundamental to the idea of constitutionalism, representing a break with feudal notions of status-based rights and legal hierarchies of persons, sometimes justified in religious terms.[31]

The general direction of the development aside, constitutional developments and constitutional practice do not move in a linear direction according to the above narrative. Instead, they reflect an ongoing tension between, on the one hand, ideas and policies that embrace constitutionalism's core and constitutive idea of equal liberty, and, on the other hand, ideas and policies that seek its limit or that wholly deny it, sometimes also pursued under the heading of *constitutionalism*.[32] Because neither constitutionalism nor equality and liberty are static notions, if seeking to be compatible with the idea of

29 Ibid.

30 For an analysis tracing the changes of the concept of sovereignty, see Kristoffer Lidén and Henrik Syse, "The Politics of Peace and Law: Realism, Internationalism and the Cosmopolitan Challenge", in Cecilia Bailliet and Kjetil Larsen (eds), *Promoting Peace Through International Law* (Oxford University Press, 2015).

31 Jonathan Israel, *Radical Enlightenment: Philosophy and the Making of Modernity 1650–1750* (Oxford University Press, 2001); and by the same author, *Democratic Enlightenment: Philosophy, Revolution and Human Rights 1750–1790* (Oxford University Press, 2011); Dag Michalsen, *Rett en Internasjonal Historie* (Pax Forlag, 2011) 267–272.

32 Jan Werner Müller provides an insightful account of these tensions in 20th-century Europe and the link between political thought and transitions to ideological extremes. See Jan Werner Müller, *Contesting Democracy: Political Ideas in Twentieth-Century Europe* (Yale University Press, 2011).

constitutionalism, constitutional developments must reflect an ongoing constitutional approximation towards the standards of constitutionalism. Many, if not all, jurisdictions have experienced constitutional developments that at certain points in time represent a back-sliding to the ongoing constitutional approximation and commitment to constitutionalism, its constitutive elements, and its central values.[33] Such constitutional developments and deviations from the standards of constitutionalism take various forms and use various constitutional languages. The subject of this study is one such type of constitutional development.

Equal liberty is the acknowledgment of persons as equal with respect to having constitutional rights. With the emergence of the idea of constitutionalism, equality became a foundational value in constitutional context.[34] Equality has, over time, been subject to democratization, in the sense that its scope has expanded to include more and more persons and fewer grounds for exclusions.[35] Yet, we find a number of examples in modern constitutional history where constitutions have departed from this standard and returned to establishing a system of legal hierarchies based on previously abolished statuses and through the adoption of new distinctions, whether on the basis of religious or non-religious justifications.

In using the notion "equal liberty", this book refers to a framework "in which people stand in relations of equality to others".[36] Elizabeth Anderson calls this "democratic equality", by which she refers to an equality that creates conditions in which persons make claims on one another in virtue of their equality, not their inferiority to others. In terms of the development of constitutionalism and constitutional developments guided by constitutionalism, there has been a move towards an expansion of the notion of equality, most clearly seen in the development of international human rights law.

To understand the relationship between constitutional design and equal liberty, it can be helpful to recall how egalitarian political movements have historically

33 Steven Levitsky and Lucan Way, *Competitive Authoritarianism: Hybrid Regimes After the Cold War* (Cambridge University Press, 2010) offers an empirical account of the use of elections by autocracies that engage in democratic abuse. See also Tom Ginsburg and Alberto Simpser (eds), *Constitutions in Authoritarian Regimes* (Cambridge University Press, 2014) analyzing different functions that constitutions have in nondemocratic systems. For an account of totalitarian states in Europe in the 20th century, see Dag Michalsen, *Rett en Internasjonal Historie* (Pax Forlag, 2011) 325–331.

34 Some commentators view not only equal liberty as a value, but constitutionalism as such as a set of values, or a "mindset", in Martti Koskenniemi's terms. Although they do not provide binding legal norms, Koskenniemi argues that these values invite to serious normative considerations for public law. Martti Koskenniemi, "Constitutionalism as Mindset: Reflections on Kantian Themes about International Law and Globalization", *Theoretical Inquiries in Law* [2006] 8:1 9–36.

35 Dag Michalsen (2011) 267–287.

36 Elizabeth Anderson, "What is the Point of Equality", *Ethics* [1999] 109:2 287–337.

conceived of their aims and the systems they have opposed. Inegalitarianism bases social order on a hierarchy of human beings, ranked according to intrinsic worth, and therefore granted different degrees of rights or none at all. Inequality refers not so much to distribution of goods as it does to relations between superior and inferior persons. These are what Iris Young identifies as the faces of oppression: marginalization, status hierarchy, domination, exploitation, and cultural imperialism.[37] These unequal social relations generate and were thought to justify inequalities in the distributions of freedoms, resources, and welfare. This is the core of inegalitarian ideologies. By contrast, equal liberty asserts the equal moral worth of people and repudiates distinctions of moral worth based on birth or social identity or on inherited social status, race, gender, genes, religion, sexual orientation, or ethnicity. Egalitarians base claims to social and political equality on the fact of universal moral equality.[38]

The social condition of living a free life is that one stand in relations of equality with others. Since equal liberty is a *relational theory* about how individuals stand in relation to one another and towards political authority, it is therefore central to democratic theory. Historically, one of the achievements of egalitarian movements was to vindicate an understanding of citizenship that includes the right to participate as an equal in civil society as well as in government affairs.[39] A group that is excluded from or segregated within the institutions of civil society or from participating in government affairs, or that is subject to discrimination on the basis of ascribed social identities, has been relegated to second-class citizenship, even if its members enjoy some rights. To be able to function as an equal involves not just the ability to effectively exercise political rights, but also to participate in various activities of civil society more broadly. It requires the capability to effectively access education and work, and it entails the right to political participation, including the conditions needed for that, such as freedom of expression and freedom of association.

Because it is a theory and not law, constitutionalism does not *per se* make legally binding obligations for constitutional design. International law, by contrast, sets minimum standards that are legally binding. Traditionally, international law has said little about domestic constitutions. There are nevertheless two ways in which international law influences constitutions. One is through international human rights law, which concerns the relationship between the state and individuals, and therefore directly addresses a constitutional matter. The other more procedural way is through the international community's increased involvement

37 Iris Young, *Justice and the Politics of Difference* (1990) quoted in Anderson, ibid. 312.

38 Anderson, ibid. 313.

39 Anderson, ibid. 317.

in constitution-making.[40] Efforts to standardize constitution-making are also found at the regional level.[41]

In addition to forming a constitutive element of constitutionalism, equality and nondiscrimination are also fundamental principles of international human rights law, and they are essential to the enjoyment of all human rights. Each of the core human rights treaties explicitly protect equality and prohibit both *de jure* and *de facto* discrimination.[42]

In its preamble, the UN Charter states that the peoples of the UN "reaffirm faith in fundamental rights, in the dignity and worth of the human person, in the equal rights of men and women and of all nations large and small".[43] Article 1(3) of the Charter brings equal liberty and non-discrimination into the purpose of the UN in establishing that the purpose is "promoting and encouraging respect for human rights and for fundamental freedoms and for fundamental freedoms for all without distinction as to race, sex, language, or religion".

The Universal Declaration of Human Rights (UDHR) elaborates this further in Article 1 which affirms that "all human beings are born free and equal in dignity and rights", and Article 2(1) which makes it clear that no status can justify exemption from rights protection:

> Everyone is entitled to all the rights and freedoms set forth in this Declaration, without distinction of any kind, such as race, colour, sex, language, religion, political or other opinion, national or social origin, property, birth or other status. Furthermore, no distinction shall be made on the basis of the political, jurisdictional or international status of the country or territory to which a person belongs, whether it be independent, trust, non-self-governing or under any other limitation of sovereignty.[44]

40 See for example, the 2009 Guidance Note of the UN Secretary-General, which sets out a policy framework for peace-building, and affirms the centrality of constitutions. "Constitution-making processes are a central aspect of democratic transitions, peacebuilding and state-building". See, UN, Guidance Note of the Secretary-General, United Nations Assistance to Constitution-Making Processes, April 2009, 3. See also, Grewe and Riegner (2009).

41 The European Commission for Democracy Through Law (the Venice Commission), created in 1990 after the fall of the Berlin Wall, and operating under the Council of Europe, is tasked to help members bring their legal and institutional structures in line with what is understood to be "European standards". See Resolution 90(6) "On a Partial Agreement Establishing the European Commission for Democracy Through Law", adopted by the Committee of Ministers, 10 May 1990.

42 These principles are elaborated in the International Covenant on Civil and Political Rights and the International Covenant on Economic, Social and Cultural Rights as well as in subsequent conventions, including the Convention on the Elimination of All Forms of Discrimination Against Women, and the Convention on the Elimination of Racial Discrimination.

43 Charter of the United Nations, 24 October 1945, 1 UNTS XVI, Preamble.

44 Article 7 of the UDHR furthermore recognizes that: "All are equal before the law and are entitled without any discrimination to equal protection of the law. All are entitled to equal

Under international human rights law, discrimination has been defined as:

> any distinction, exclusion, restriction or preference which is based on any grounds such as race, colour, sex, language, religion, political or other opinion, national or social origin, property, birth or other status, and which has the purpose or effect of nullifying or impairing the recognition, enjoyment or exercise by all persons, on an equal footing, of all rights and freedoms.[45]

The principle of non-discrimination and equal liberty require an active obligation on the part of the State to eliminate conditions that cause or contribute to perpetuating discrimination.[46]

Moreover, the prohibition against discrimination in Article 26 of the International Covenant on Civil and Political Rights (ICCPR) is not limited to the rights contained in the convention. This means that the right not to be discriminated against is a free-standing right and its application is not confined to the rights in the covenant. As interpreted by the UN Human Rights Committee: "Article 26 provides that all persons are equal before the law and are entitled to equal protection of the law without discrimination on any of the enumerated grounds" and "When legislation is adopted by a State party, it must comply with the requirement of article 26 that its content should not be discriminatory".[47] Based on the constitutive character of equality and non-discrimination in international human rights law, as well as the idea of constitutionalism, these rights are understood as foundational rights or foundational values.[48]

To measure a constitution against the standards of constitutionalism and international human rights law implies less weight on a state-centered paradigm of constitutions. This approach is related to that proposed, for example, by Mattias Kumm, for whom international law and constitutional law function within an "integrative basic conceptual framework for a general theory of public law".[49]

---

protection against any discrimination in violation of this Declaration and against any incitement to such discrimination".

45 Human Rights Committee, *General Comment No. 18* (1989) para. 7.

46 Human Rights Committee, *General Comment No. 18* (1989).

47 Human Rights Committee, *General Comment No. 18* (1989) para. 12.

48 Kirsten Ketscher, for example, argues that because of their character of foundational values, equality and non-discrimination contribute to the establishment and interpretation of law, regardless of whether they are codified or not. Ketscher applies the notion "grunnrettigheter" (in Danish) about the foundational norm that articulates the protection of dignity, liberty, equality, and fellowship between persons. Kirsten Ketscher, *Socialret: Principper, Rettigheder, Værdier* (Karnov Group, 2008) 105 and 108.

49 Mattias Kumm, "The Cosmopolitan Turn in Constitutionalism: On the Relationship between Constitutionalism in and beyond the State", in Jeffrey Dunoff and Joel Trachtman (eds), *Ruling the World? Constitutionalism, International Law and Global Governance* (Cambridge University Press, 2009) 263–264.

Under this approach, constitutions, as well as international law, can and should be measured against an independent standard of "constitutionalism".[50] Domestic constitutional orders must therefore open up to international human rights law. Under this approach, the constitution must be justified to those it seeks to govern, but this justification must meet a standard of constitutionalism that is not limited by the will of the demos.[51]

To objections about the legitimacy of such an approach, one may agree with Kumm that these are not more "radically distinct" than questions of legitimacy that arise under a strictly domestic and state-centric approach. For both approaches, Kumm identifies four criteria, derived from the commitment of human beings as free and equal, that constitute the matrix of sources of normative legitimacy. These are: (1) a formal principle of legality and respect for law; (2) a jurisdictional principle of subsidiarity, which may allocate jurisdiction either to more or less remote levels of governance; (3) a procedural principle of due process, which means democracy inside the state and good governance at the international level; and (4) substantive principles of respect for human rights.[52]

While international law traditionally, and in accordance with the doctrine of non-intervention in internal affairs and the horizontal paradigm of equal states, has been primarily concerned with inter-state relations, international human rights law has since 1945 concerned itself with the internal space of states. Therefore, "two leading systems exist today for protecting the fundamental rights of individuals. Constitutional law and [international] human rights law".[53]

Both international human rights law and constitutional law perform the same function of limiting what governments may do to persons within their jurisdiction. In limiting government power, there is therefore something inherently constitutional about international human rights law.[54] International human rights law is in this sense a form of internationalized constitutional law, and it is a critical part for rejecting the "traditional, horizontal paradigm of international law based

50 Vicki Jackson and Mark Tushnet (eds), *Comparative Constitutional Law* (Foundation Press, 2006) 243–267.

51 Mattias Kumm (2009) ibid. 268.

52 Mattias Kumm (2009) ibid. 268–277.

53 Gerald Neuman, "Human Rights and Constitutional Rights: Harmony and Dissonance?" *Stanford Law Review* [2003] 55:5 1863–1864.

54 Stephen Gardbaum, "Human Rights and International Constitutionalism", in Jeffrey Dunoff and Joel Trachtman (eds), *Ruling the World? Constitutionalism, International Law and Global Governance* (Cambridge University Press, 2009) 237. Or in the words of Bardo Fassbender, "The UN Charter is a constitution in the clothes of a treaty, because no other garment was available in 1945": Bardo Fassbender, "Rediscovering a Forgotten Constitution: Notes on the Place of the UN Charter in the International Legal Order", in Jeffrey Dunoff and Joel Trachtman (eds), *Ruling the World? Constitutionalism, International Law and Global Governance* (Cambridge University Press, 2009) 133.

on the sovereign equality of states, and replacing it with a more vertical constitutionalist or public law paradigm".[55]

In addition to international human rights law having the same justification as constitutionalism, there are other arguments for justifying international human rights law as a standard for domestic constitutions. Arguing for a "complementary constitutionalization" of international law, Anne Peters points out that the increased externalities of democratic decisions taken within polities; the increase in problems seen to require a transnational solution; and an increase in executive branch power justify international law's assumption of the constraining functions of constitutional law.[56]

1.3 Outline of further study

This book's perspective on the particular constitutional transformation represented by constitutional desecularization is from the intersection of constitutional secularity and equal liberty. In making this choice, I seek to highlight the centrality of these two features within the theory of constitutionalism and to accentuate the legal implications for equal liberty when religion's role is strengthened in the constitution. In doing so, the aim is to place the discussion within a constitutional law narrative.

I proceed through an elaboration in two general steps. The first consists of providing an account of equal liberty as a constitutive element of constitutionalism and constitutional secularity as a principle of governance. This entails a particular qualification for how we understand modern "constitutionalism". The second step consists of presenting the experience of constitutional desecularization in Afghanistan, Iran, and Iraq, by highlighting how some of the general features of the new constitutions alter the regulation of equal liberty, in particular, through a study of the rights to freedom of thought, expression, and political participation.

Chapter 2 builds on the initial conceptualization made earlier in this chapter, on how religion is used as constitutional and political language. In this regard, I critically review an approach to "Islamic Constitutionalism" often found in the literature, and ask the question whether such constitutions do in fact fall under the paradigm of constitutionalism. I furthermore proceed with conceptualizing desecularization as a constitutional reflection of political Islam which, as such, can also be framed as a form of fundamentalism. Finally, Chapter 2 examines how both religion and non-religious ideologies function as

55 Gardbaum, ibid. 237.

56 Anne Peters, "Compensatory Constitutionalism: The Functions and Potential of Fundamental International Norms and Structures", *Leiden Journal of International Law* [2006] 19 580.

a constitutional external aim that preclude equal liberty as a constitutive feature of constitutionalism.

Part II examines the development of constitutionalism into modern constitutionalism, as well as various forms of constitutional developments. Chapter 3 examines some of the central features of constitutionalism, in particular, equal liberty and how this feature leads to a particular conception of both sovereignty and constitutional rights, including in the way that constitutional rights can be limited. It proceeds with an account of constitutional secularity as a principle of governance that enables equal liberty. The chapter presents an overview of the development of constitutional secularity as an idea, as well as its development in constitutional arrangements in practice.

Part III proceeds with the specific case studies of the constitutions of Afghanistan, Iran, and Iraq. Chapter 4 looks at the modern constitutional past of the three countries, and in particular on the recent political changes that prompted the constitutional changes. The chapter highlights some of the main features of the de-secularized constitutions, including the form of government and the restraining principle, which represent two significant elements of the way in which equal liberty is limited in these constitutions. Chapter 5 proceeds with analyzing three rights in particular: the right to freedom of thought or belief; the right to freedom of expression; and the right to political participation. The chapter begins with an overview of these rights as features of modern constitutionalism and their entrenchment in international human rights law, before looking at elements of these rights under the de-secularized constitutions of Afghanistan, Iran, and Iraq. I end with some final observations in Chapter 5.

The reason for measuring de-secularized constitutions against the standards of constitutionalism is three-fold. First, constitutionalism is, despite the lack of consensus as to its precise content, the dominant paradigm for the regulation of political authority and for the drafting of contemporary constitutions.[57] Second, and linked to the importance of constitutionalism, most constitutions would claim adherence to the standards of constitutionalism.[58] The third reason is to

57 Lorraine Weinrib, "Constitutional Conceptions and Constitutional Comparativism", in Vicki Jackson and Mark Tushnet (eds), *Defining the Field of Comparative Constitutional Law* (Foundation Press, 2006) 23–81; Jeffrey Dunoff and Joel Trachtman (eds), *Ruling the World? Constitutionalism, International Law, and Global Governance* (Cambridge University Press, 2009); Jon Elster and Rune Slagstad, *Constitutionalism and Democracy* (Cambridge University Press, 1988); Mattias Kumm, "The Cosmopolitan Turn in Constitutionalism: On the Relationship between Constitutionalism in and beyond the State", in Jeffrey Dunoff and Joel Trachtman (eds), *Ruling the World? Constitutionalism, International Law and Global Governance* (Cambridge University Press, 2009).

58 The Afghan and Iraqi constitutions and *travaux préparatoires* articulate a commitment to constitutionalism. See Hannibal Travis, "Freedom or Theocracy: Constitutionalism in

challenge the dominant view in scholarship which tends, when dealing in particular with Islamized constitutions, to apply the terminology "Islamic constitutionalism", without problematizing what constitutionalism entails beyond its institutional features and as an instrument of power limitation.[59]

Afghanistan and Iraq", *Northwestern University Journal of International Human Rights* [2005] 4:3 1–52; by contrast, the origin of the Iranian Constitution of 1979 expresses opposition to the idea of constitutionalism: *Discussions in the Assembly for Revision of the Constitutional Draft* (1979). See also Eva Rakel, *Power, Islam, and Political Elite in Iran: A Study on the Iranian Political Elite From Khomeini to Ahmadinejad* (Brill, 2009).

59 This view is found, for example, in Noah Feldman, "The Democratic Fatwa: Islam and Democracy in the Realm of Constitutional Politics", *Oklahoma Law Review* [2005] 58 1–9; Noah Feldman, *The Fall and Rise of the Islamic State* (Princeton University Press, 2008); Rainer Grote and Tilmann Röder (eds) (2012); Ran Hirschl, *Constitutional Theocracy* (Harvard University Press, 2010); Intisar Rabb, "'We the Jurists': Islamic Constitutionalism in Iraq", *University of Pennsylvania Journal of Constitutional Law* [2008] 10:3 527–579; Bruce Rutherford, "What do Egypt's Islamists Want? Moderate Islam and the Rise of Islamic Constitutionalism", *Middle East Journal* [2006] 60:4 707–731; Mohammed Fadel, "Judicial Institutions, the Legitimacy of Islamic State Law and Democratic Transition in Egypt: Can a Shift toward a Common Law Model of Adjudication Improve the Prospects of a Successful Democratic Transition?" *International Journal of Constitutional Law* [2013] 11:3 646–665; Clark Lombardi, "Can Islamizing a Legal System Ever Help Promote Liberal Democracy? A View from Pakistan", *University of St. Thomas Law Journal* [2010] 649–691; Clark Lombardi, "Designing Islamic Constitutions: Past Trends and Options for a Democratic Future", *International Journal of Constitutional Law* [2013] 11 615–645; Clark Lombardi and Nathan Brown, "Do Constitutions Requiring Adherence to Shari'a Threaten Human Rights? Egypt's Constitutional Court Reconciles Islamic Law with the Liberal Rule of Law", *American University International Law Review* [2006] 21 379–435.

2 Beyond the secular/religious divide

2.1 Religion as a constitutional language

The political utility of religion is not new nor is the fact that political actors would appeal to religion as one of many means to secure power. While earlier political authority would make general references to deities, more sophisticated theories on religion as an ideology were developed in the late Middle Ages. In the 1500s, Machiavelli observed that it was fundamental to the ruler's success that he "appear to be religious", for religion was a useful instrument of social control.[1] Hobbes, whose main issue is political control, advocates a state religion or political religion in order to facilitate political stability, and proposes the subordination of the church to the state.[2]

Contemporarily, the spread of religious ideologies in the 1970s and 1980s can be viewed as what one commentator has called a "conscious manipulation of conservative or illiberal religion by state elites, both religious and non-religious actors", or what other commentators have called "selective reinvention of tradition".[3] But while political religion has become a powerful force in a number of countries, it has not necessarily resulted in a constitutional change. In some countries, the influence is political and social.[4] In other countries, it has led to legal changes, but not to constitutional change. In a few countries, it has resulted in a complete constitutional transformation.

Because of the name and rhetoric of these constitutions, one may sometimes be led to think about them as a particular constitutional phenomenon that is culturally founded. This book challenges the assumption that what drives these

1 Frederick Whelan, *Hume and Machiavelli: Political Realism and Liberal Thought* (Lexington Books, 2001); Marcela Cristi, *From Civil to Political Religion: The Intersection of Culture, Religion and Politics* (Wilfrid Laurier University Press, 2001) 95.

2 Leo Strauss, *The Political Philosophy of Hobbes: Its Basis and Its Genesis* (University of Chicago Press, 1963) 74.

3 Scott Hibbard, *Religious Politics and Secular States: Egypt, India and the United States* (Johns Hopkins University Press, 2012) 248.

4 For an account of the political and social influence of political Islam, see Karima Bennoune, *Your Fatwa Does Not Apply Here: Untold Stories From the Fight Against Muslim Fundamentalism* (Norton and Company, 2015).

constitutional transformations is culture or religion. Rather, the motives, stakes, and processes are political and the issues are legal and constitutional, not religious or cultural. In short, when religion is brought into the constitution, it becomes a political ideology, not a theological matter.

The perspective of this book is that conceptualizing this constitutional development as a matter of *religion* is inaccurate for making sense of these constitutional transformations. Instead, I propose to conceptualize this as an expression of a constitutional language that limits equal liberty. Religion is both a marker of cultural identity and it can be an instrument of politics. It is important to know when it is the first and when it is the second. This conceptualization has two important implications for the analysis. First, it focuses on the *legal nature* of the constitution, rather than on its proclaimed religiousness. The concept and content of Islamic law are therefore of less interest for the purposes of analysis. The conflicts of such constitutions with international human rights law and the standards of constitutionalism is not primarily a problem of religion, but a problem of *law*. This means that the solution does not lie in going from conservative or illiberal doctrinal interpretations of religion to liberal interpretations, but rather concerns precluding religion as a principle of governance.

The significance of this constitutional transformation lies, in other words, not so much in the use of religion as such, but in the use of religion as a constitutional language that limits equal liberty. Therefore, constitutions that apply non-religious ideologies to limit equal liberty have more in common with constitutions using religious language to limit equal liberty than they have with secular constitutions that comply with the standards of constitutionalism. In this connection, the division of constitutions into secular versus religious may therefore not necessarily be a helpful way of categorizing constitutions.

Nonetheless, a rich literature has emerged that does precisely that, taking the religious claim of a constitution as a main marker of its identity, which also has led to the creation of the notion of "Islamic constitutionalism". This has prompted the question of whether the constitutional transformation represented by a strengthened role of religion would still fall under the paradigm of constitutionalism. According to some commentators, it does. Ran Hirschl's continuum of constitutionalism, for example, would encompass most constitutions.[5] If we start from the far end of the continuum going from left to right, on the left end, Hirschl places constitutional systems that establish some form of separation between religion and state. At the most extreme end, he places atheism or proactive elimination of religion. Next, he establishes *laïcité* or assertive secularism. Closer to the middle of the continuum is secularism-as-neutrality,

5 Hirschl applies "constitutionalism" as a general category to classify and study constitutions and their relationship to religion. Ran Hischl, *Constitutional Theocracy* (Harvard University Press, 2010).

which emphasizes an impartial stance towards religious creeds. Near the center, we find soft, formal separation. Next is weak religious establishment – the formal, mainly ceremonial designation of state religion. To its right, is *de facto* establishment. And further down the line, we find varying degrees of constitutional theocracy. This part begins with "selective accommodation", where the general law is secular, but jurisdictional autonomy is granted religious communities. Next are religious jurisdictional enclaves and secular jurisdictional enclaves. At the extreme end, we find mixed systems of religious law and general legal principles. Yet, as one commentator points out, one may question whether it is possible that many national jurisdictions, far from being easily plotted along the continuum, rather approximate several or many points along the continuum, depending on the issue and one's perspective.[6] One may also question his account's near equation of *constitutionalism* with *constitutions.*

2.1.1 "Islamic constitutionalism"

Although the constitutional transformation that is the subject of this book can be observed across time and place, one may get the impression that there is something particular when *Islam* is involved, reflected in and perpetuated by a growing literature on "Islamic constitutionalism". Given the widespread resurgence of Islamic political movements in the last decades, such transformations have largely been associated with the Middle East, and, for some, even as exclusive to "Islam". Since particularly the 1990s, and in the context of the adoption of the current Afghan and Iraqi constitutions, vast literature has emerged on the topic of the compatibility of Islam and human rights.[7] Some of these approaches place considerable weight on the "religious" claim of the constitutions, leading to an emphasis on various aspects of religious law or the history of religion and religious law, and less, or no, consideration of how religion performs a particular constitutional function when entrenched in the constitution. Other approaches, while recognizing the political dimension of religion in these developments, nevertheless still emphasize the "religious" aspect and the relationship between state and religion in the constitution. Separately, but still related to this approach is

6 Paul Babie, "Religion and Constitutionalism: Oscillations along a Continuum", *Journal of Religious History* [2015] 39:1 131.

7 Raja Bahlul, "Is Constitutionalism Compatible with Islam?" in Pietro Costa and Danilo Zolo (eds), *The Rule of Law: History, Theory and Criticism* (Springer, 2007) 515–542. See also, Mashood Baderin, *International Human Rights and Islamic Law* (Oxford University Press, 2003); Andrew March, *Islam and Liberal Citizenship* (Oxford University Press, 2009); Clark Lombardi, "Designing Islamic Constitutions: Past Trends and Options for a Democratic Future", *International Journal of Constitutional Law* [2013] 11 615–645; Nimer Sultany, "Against Conceptualism: Islamic Law, Democracy and Constitutionalism in the Aftermath of the Arab Spring", *Boston University International Law Journal* [2013] 13 435–449; Intisar Rabb, "'We the Jurists': Islamic Constitutionalism in Iraq", *University of Pennsylvania Journal of Constitutional Law* [2008] 10:3 527–579.

that of "clash of civilisations", which, despite being subject to criticism, remains an influential idea and presumption that underlies many debates.[8]

Part of this debate, which is not limited to the case of Islam, has called for a reconsideration of the model of constitutional secularity, which dominated much of both theory and constitutional developments in the 20th century. The model of constitutional secularity is challenged by arguments pointing to the similarities between law and religion, and that lawmaking is justified on religious grounds because law's legitimacy is derived from shared moral norms.[9] The conception of law as embracing the community's good and its expression of public virtue implies that the political, under such an approach, is equated with the religio-moral consensus.[10] It is in this context that the notion "Islamic constitutionalism" has emerged. Yet what "Islamic constitutionalism" would entail is unclear. When encountered in literature, it often covers significantly different constitutions and ideas, from the theocratic constitution of Iran to the largely secular constitution of Indonesia. It is distinct from constitutional Islam, even though the distinction is often absent in discussions, where "constitutions" and "constitutionalism" are used interchangeably. Some commentators seek to trace a theory of "Islamic constitutionalism" in the history of Islamic law.[11] Others argue that given the lack of clarity of the theory, one should rather examine how the idea of "Islamic constitutionalism" is given substance by Islamic political actors in a specific context.[12]

While the notions such as "Islamic constitutionalism", often together with "the Muslim world" and "the Muslim community", have come to occupy the field, they have also come to face criticism for being an invention that collapses all of the diversity found in the population and legal orders originating in countries from Indonesia to Morocco.[13] The common usage of the term "Muslim" rather than other identifiers to characterize individuals shifts the frame of the debate to one in which religion and identity are constructed as one, also in the constitutional arena. In doing so, Islam becomes the distinguishing feature, above any other features, leading to a taxonomy that erases the diversity of legal systems,

8 Samuel Huntington, *The Clash of Civilizations and the Re-making of the World Order* (Simon and Schuster, 2002).

9 See, for example, Michael Perry, "Why Political Reliance on Religiously Grounded Morality is not Illegitimate in a Liberal Democracy", *Wake Forrest Law Review* [2001] 36 217.

10 Rudi Teitel, "Critique of Religion as Politics in the Public Sphere", *Cornell Law Review* [1993] 78:5 753.

11 See, for example, Mohammed Fadel, "Judicial Institutions, the Legitimacy of Islamic State Law and Democratic Transition in Egypt: Can a Shift toward a Common Law Model of Adjudication Improve the Prospects of a Successful Democratic Transition?" *International Journal of Constitutional Law* [2013] 11:3 646–665.

12 Bruce Rutherford, "What do Egypt's Islamists Want? Moderate Islam and the Rise of Islamic Constitutionalism", *Middle East Journal* [2006] 60:4 707–731.

13 Fatou Sow (ed), *Gender and Fundamentalisms* (CODESIRA, 2018), quoting Saleh Bechir and Hazem Saghieh, "The "Muslim Community": A European Invention", published on openDemocracy. https://www.opendemocracy.net/conflict-terrorism/community_2928.jsp.

and leaves out an account of the particular constitutional memory and development of countries.

Given the prevalent use in literature of "Islamic constitutionalism", I will in the following sections outline some of the main normative positions in the discussion that the notion gives rise to.

Defense of "Islamic constitutionalism": the compatibility argument

The compatibility argument holds that "Islamic constitutionalism" is a form of constitutionalism, or that it is not necessarily incompatible with constitutionalism. Indeed, the very use of the notion "Islamic constitutionalism" already signals such compatibility and gives rise to the idea that this is a particular category of constitutionalism. For example, the 2005 campaign platform of the Muslim Brotherhood in Egypt stated that the Brotherhood seeks to create a "republican system of government that is democratic, constitutional, and parliamentary and that conforms with Islamic principles".[14] This position is also found in the scholarship on the topic. In his review of Islamic legal thinkers in Egypt, Bruce Rutherford argues that the conception of "Islamic constitutionalism" "shares many characteristics with classic liberalism and democracy".[15] A related argument is that "Islamic constitutionalism" may further liberal democracy.[16] Consider, for example, the approach of Ahmad Dawood and Tom Ginsburg who argue that Islamic constitutions are compatible with constitutional democracy because such constitutions can advance basic values of liberal democracy.[17] This view begins by identifying some advantageous outcome and argues that religious constitutions or Islamic constitutions are conducive to its realization. Different commentators focus on promoting different kinds of outcomes. Some, for example, argue that the inclusion of a greater role for religion in a constitution may contribute to the realization of human rights and rule of law or that it may contribute to political stability, popular legitimacy, and support of the constitution. What unifies these approaches is the view that religious or Islamic constitutions can be justified because of the good results that they may potentially bring.

The defense of "Islamic constitutionalism" through the compatibility argument invokes constitutionalism and proposes an interpretation of "Islamic constitutionalism" as a version of it. However, while the argument or presumption of compatibility is invoked, it is rarely analyzed. Instead, references to

14 Referenced in Bruce Rutherford, "What do Egypt's Islamists Want? Moderate Islam and the Rise of Islamic Constitutionalism", *Middle East Journal* [2006] 60:4 716.

15 Ibid.

16 See, for example, Abdulaziz Sachedina, *Islam and the Challenge of Human Rights* (Oxford University Press, 2009); Sayed Khatab and Gary Bouma, *Democracy in Islam* (Routledge, 2007).

17 Ahmad Dawood and Tom Ginsburg, "Constitutional Islamization and Human Rights: The Surprising Origin and Spread of Islamic Supremacy in Constitutions", *University of Chicago Public Law & Legal Theory Working Paper* [2014] 477.

constitutionalism are presented without critical scrutiny of what constitutionalism entails beyond its institutional features.

Defense of "Islamic constitutionalism": the rejection of universalism argument

Another defense of "Islamic constitutionalism" is based on a rejection of constitutionalism's universal validity. While the first type of defense presumes that constitutionalism, democracy, and human rights are universal and that "Islamic constitutionalism" is compatible with that or that it can help achieve such values, the second type of defense by contrast rejects the universality of constitutionalism, sometimes together with a rejection of the universal validity of human rights as well. It is an approach that upholds the paradigm of the "clash of civilizations",[18] and is based on static notions of "the West" and "Islam" and their binary divide. This reifies Samuel Huntington's notion of immutable inter-cultural fault lines that delimit the contemporary moment. This view does not recognize that clashes about constitutionalism and human rights that exist within societies can be more determinative as those that are presumed to exist between societies or civilizations.[19] This argument is proposed both by those upholding the "clash of civilizations" idea, the "East–West" binary, and political actors on the far right where fundamentalist-inspired claims that invoke notions of culture and religion support this vision. The underlying presumption is the same: that demands for the universality of human rights law and human rights values come more naturally, or are local to, the Western international legal academy than similar demands emanating from within other regions.[20]

Critique of "Islamic constitutionalism": from within a religious framework

Within Islamic legal thought, the discussion about the degree to which religion should influence governance has existed at least since the 10th century.[21] The positions found in the contemporary context can therefore be said to be based on a historical line of similar ideas, while they at the same time are shaped by the contemporary reality of statehood and modern constitutions. The argument found among these commentators is that Islam is entirely compatible with a separation

18 For Huntington, this is a proof of the West's superiority, for Islamists, this is a proof of Islam's superiority. The basic global divide envisaged is, however, roughly the same.

19 For an account that highlights the intra-cultural conflicts, see Karima Bennoune, "Remembering the Other's Others: Theorizing the Approach of International Law to Muslim Fundamentalism", *Columbia Human Rights Law Review* [2010] 41 635–698.

20 Ann Elizabeth Mayer, "Universal versus Islamic Human Rights: A Clash of Cultures or a Clash with a Construct?", *Michigan Journal of International Law* [1994] 15 307–379.

21 Ira Lapidus, "The Separation of State and Religion in the Development of Early Islamic Society", *International Journal of Middle East Studies* [1975] 6:4 363–385.

of religion from political governance.[22] One may call this a religion-based argument for a secular constitution. The Egyptian Islamic scholar, judge, and faculty member of *al-Azhar*, Abd-al Raziq, argued against an Islamic notion of government, stating "Islam is a religion, not a state, a message, not a government".[23] In 1925, Abd-al Raziq published a 1925 essay on "Islam and the Foundations of Political Power",[24] where he argued, based on sources of Islamic law, that Islam should have no role to play in political life. To the extent it indirectly affects politics, it should remain within the confines of individual morality.

A contemporary version of a similar line of thought is put forward by An-Na'im, who argues that there is no such thing as objectively applying or objectively enforcing religious law, as it is always interpreted through human agency.[25] Therefore, some degree of coercion with respect to the adherents of the dominant religion is inevitable.[26] An-Na'im's argument is that *Shari'a*, with some exceptions, is compatible with most international human rights norms. However, *Shari'a*, he argues, must be accepted by individual Muslims, not imposed by the State. Therefore, to ensure freedom and security for Muslims, a separation between Islam and the State is necessary.

While a discussion of the compatibility between religion and human rights may be interesting from a theological perspective, it is insufficient for the purposes of understanding the role of religion in a constitution. Moreover, the discussion does not look at the constitution as such but focuses more on the theological interpretations of religious law. This perspective seems to equate and conflate "religion" with "religion in the constitution". Yet, while the discussion is seemingly theological, it also contains a normative dimension, as its conclusions are sometimes used to support policy decisions and normative conclusions that are put forward during constitutional drafting processes, about whether or not religion should be included in a constitution – the idea being that if Islam or Islamic law is or can be compatible with human rights, then its inclusion is a good thing. The theoretical frameworks that the literature has brought to this phenomenon have, at the same time, blinded us to the second dimension of this phenomenon: by overemphasizing "religion", the constitutional dimension

22 Abdullahi Ahmed An-Na'im, *Islam and the Secular State: Negotiating the Future of Shari'a* (Harvard University Press, 2008). See also, James J.H. Burns (ed), *The Cambridge History of Medieval Political Thought 350–1450* (Cambridge University Press, 1988) 333ff.

23 Souad Ali, *A Religion, Not a State: Ali abd-Al Raziq's Islamic Justification for Political Secularism* (University of Utah Press, 2009).

24 Abd-al Raziq, "Al-Islam wa-usul al-hukm" (1925) referenced in Abdelilah Belkeziz, *The State in Contemporary Islamic Thought: A Historical Survey of the Major Muslim Thinkers of the Modern Era* (I.B. Tauris, 2009).

25 Abdullahi Ahmed An-Na'im, *Islam and the Secular State: Negotiating the Future of Shari'a* (Harvard University Press, 2008) 10–11 and 282–283.

26 For a study of state religion and violation of the religious rights of those who adhere to the state religion, see Jeron Temperman, "The Neutral State: Optional or Necessary? A Triangular Analysis of State-Religion Identification, Democratisation & Human Rights Compliance", *Religion and Human Rights: An International Journal* [2006] 1:3 284–286.

is left largely underassessed. Constitutions, surely, are very particular documents. When placed in a constitution, what does religious language entail, beyond the fact that it is "religious"?

From the perspective of constitutionalism, the concept of "religious constitutions" or "religious constitutionalism" clashes with the very concept that they purport to explicate. These conceptions proceed first by identifying or presuming the kinds of beliefs and actions that make up a good or valuable life, and then enlisting the coercive authority of the state to bring them about. The illiberalism of these conceptions comes into conflict with the liberal commitments of the concept to the freedom and equality of each individual, as they compel individuals to conform to a particular conception of life.[27] These conceptions violate equality by elevating not only a religion, but the State's interpretation of that religion, into a standard that individuals are forced to follow. As such, the state religion becomes a means of control, which expands State authority over individual autonomy. If a constitution subordinates freedom and equality to a particular conception of life, as interpreted by the State, then the idea stands in opposition to the very rights that modern constitutionalism seeks to secure.[28] In his account on human dignity as forming the organizing idea of public law, Jacob Weinrib rejects the view that human dignity concerns the relationship between an individual and some particular end – whether religious or philosophic – to which his or her thoughts and actions must conform and that the state would be justified in coercively enforcing.[29] Instead, the concept of human dignity concerns the equal right of each person to freedom. As such, this concept of human dignity is a constitutive element of constitutionalism, and the exercise of public authority. As free, each person has the right to determine the purposes that he or she will pursue. As equal, each person has a duty to pursue his or her purposes in a manner that respects the right of others to freedom. As a result, the basis and boundaries of public coercion must be reconsidered: "Any exercise of public authority – indeed, public authority itself – would have to be justified in terms of its fidelity to the equal right of each person to freedom". The implications of the right of each person to equal freedom both justify and direct the authority of the public institutions that together comprise a legal system.[30]

Therefore, a constitution that imposes a particular conception of life that is articulated in religious terms will in this regard not be any different from a constitution that articulates such a conception in non-religious terms. Both will provide the State with a mechanism of control and by consequence reduce equality and liberty of individuals.

27 Jacob Weinrib, *Dimensions of Dignity: The Theory and Practice of Modern Constitutional Law* (Cambridge University Press, 2016) 37–75.

28 Ibid.

29 Ibid. 7 and 120.

30 Ibid. 8.

2.1.2 Political Islam and constitutional desecularization

An often-encountered assumption of scholarship studying "Islamic constitutions" is that the use of religion in these constitutions reflects a cultural or religious legal heritage, often pointing to Islamic law and its historical development since the second century of Islam.[31] This assumption, therefore, largely takes the constitutional references to religion and claims of being "religious" at face value and treats religious references as part of a narrative of Islamic law and the development of Islamic legal history. The parallel often drawn is that between Islamic constitutions and confessional states as they developed in Europe.

The powerful belief system that sees Islamic constitutions and re-Islamized constitutions as a re-connection to values and traditions for nations liberated from foreign influence is shared by many. As a result, dissenting views, in particular those advocating secular options, are easily dismissed as inauthentic, elitist, or foreign-influenced, and little attention is paid to the fact that the instrumentalization of religion also carries a significant external aspect.

As a *religion*, Islam is a monotheistic religion, with its sources, theology, rituals, and a legal body.[32] It is also a religion with different schools of thought, yet without a central authority that decides what is and what is not Islam or Islamic law. Islamic legal science, *fiqh*, was created only from the second Islamic century onwards, as Islamic law needed to develop into a legal system with the conquering of new territories and new legal questions arising.[33]

By contrast, *political Islam*, a political ideology, is composed of systematic ideas about how to govern and organize society.[34] What makes this ideology particular is its identification with Islam as a religion. Or, as articulated by the founder of the Islamic Republic in Iran, "My religion is my politics, and my politics is my religion".[35] The source and exercise of political authority are thus justified through religious language. Characteristic to political Islam as an ideology is its claim that a just and ideal society must be based on the *Shari'a*. For Islamists, understood here as those who believe in political Islam as an ideology, there is no distinction between Islam as a religion and political Islam, since religion is politics

31 For this reason, part of scholarship on contemporary use of Islam and Islamic law in the legal context often includes discussions on their historical development.

32 Knut Vikør, *Mellom Gud og stat. Ei historie om islamsk lov og rettsvesen* (Spartacus Forlag, 2003); Knut Vikør, "The Origins of the Shari'a", in Peri Bearman and Rudolph Peters (eds), *The Ashgate Companion to Islamic Law* (Taylor and Francis, 2010).

33 *Fiqh* embodies the study of the sources of Islamic law and the methodology for deriving norms from these sources. Although the history of Islamic jurisprudence is marred by a polarization of interests between the government and legal scholars, *fiqh* has, to some extent, remained a theoretical discipline, developed by individual jurists and not internalized by the legislative machinery of government. As the expansion of Islam progressed, the need for regulation emerged historically. For a comprehensive account, see Knut Vikør, ibid.

34 Frédéric Volpi, *Political Islam: A Critical Reader* (Routledge, 2011).

35 Khomeini, "Islamic Government" translated to English, in Hamid Algar (ed), *Khomeini: Islam and Revolution* (Mizan Press, 1981).

and politics is religion. There is, in other words, no distinction drawn between faith and political governance. This understanding is paradoxically shared by many of Islam's critics who fail to draw a distinction between political Islam and Islam as a religion.[36]

One may view the rise of political Islam in connection with the fall of the Ottoman Empire following the First World War.[37] The Ottoman Empire was justified through reference to the historical notion and institution of the Islamic caliphate.[38] Following the fall of the Ottoman Empire, a secular, Turkish nation state was established, and the caliphate was formally abolished by the Turkish National Assembly on 3 March 1924.[39] Shortly afterwards, in 1928, the Muslim Brotherhood was established in Egypt, marking the beginning of modern political Islam.[40] The aim of the Muslim Brotherhood, beginning as a political movement, was to reestablish the caliphate, not in its historical symbolic form, but as an ideal form, as an expression for Islam's universal ambitions and Islam's political dimension.[41] The great political breakthrough of political Islam as an ideology was the Islamic revolution in Iran in 1979, which for the first time also crystallized political Islam into a constitutional form.

Among the central political ideologists of political Islam we find Hassan al-Banna (1906–1949), the founder of the Muslim Brotherhood; Sayyid Qutb (1906–1966); Sayyid Abu'l-A'la Mawdudi, founder of the political party *Jamaat-e-Islami* in British India in 1941; and Ruhollah Khomeini (1903–1989), founder of the Islamic Republic of Iran in 1979. The perspective of political Islam is universal, in the sense that it is not premised on the existing borders of modern states. The contemporary notion of the historical term, *Ummah*, reflects its universal aspirations.[42] The ideology of political Islam justifies itself through the religion of Islam, and sees itself as the only correct interpreter of that religion. It is not only an ideology involving political governance as understood in the modern context, but it includes the governance of all aspects of human existence, including aspects that under a modern constitutional democracy are established as spheres of personal autonomy, guaranteed through constitutional rights, where the state cannot interfere beyond its obligation to protect.

The ideology of political Islam contains also an aspect of elite-governance in conflict with the idea of popular sovereignty as a constitutive element of

36 Sørensen (2015) 329.

37 Joel Beinin and Joe Stork, *Political Islam* (University of California Press, 1997).

38 On the origin of the idea of the Caliphate and its historical development, see Knut Vikør, *Ei Verd Bygd på islam: Oversikt over midtaustens historie* (Det norske samlaget, 2010). See also Noah Feldman, *The Fall and Rise of the Islamic State* (Princeton University Press, 2008).

39 Abolishment of the Caliphate Law of 3 March 1924. Andrew Mango, *Atatürk* (John Murray Publishers, 1999).

40 Sørensen (2015) 329.

41 Ibid.

42 Knut Vikør, *Mellom Gud og stat: Ei historie om islamsk lov og rettsvesen* (Spartacus Forlag, 2003).

modern constitutionalism. The idea of governance under political Islam purports that an Islamic elite should organize the fight for the establishment of Islamic governance. It is also elite in the sense that the rule is under God's laws, as interpreted by the elite in power.[43] The constitutional development of politicization of religion, as a product of political Islam, thus contains an inherent tension with values and ideas that are in direct opposition to those of constitutionalism and international human rights law, while at the same time employing modern features and institutions of constitutionalism.

While constitutional developments towards a strengthening of the role of religion occur also in constitutions that are already confessional, such developments do not fall under "constitutional desecularization" because such constitutions have never been subject to a process towards constitutional secularity in the first place. This would distinguish, for example, the Constitution of Pakistan from the Constitution of Iraq. The Pakistani constitutional history does not contain a similar development towards constitutional secularity. Therefore, although the role of religion has become strengthened in the Constitution of Pakistan in recent decades, it is not "de-secularized", because it never began a process towards constitutional secularity to begin with.

The impact of the increased constitutional role of religion is arguably different, and the changes more dramatic, in constitutions which have put behind a constitutional process towards secularity. It is different because such constitutions and legal systems, at least *de jure*, have adopted a number of features of constitutionalism which through the process of desecularization are subject to a halt or to reversals. Constitutional desecularization is therefore not merely or primarily an issue of an increased role of religion as such, but, more importantly, it is a transition that involves a re-configuration of the legal system as a whole.

That a constitution that is nominally, and proclaims itself to be, religious, ultimately is a secular document is acknowledged also by the political authorities that uphold them. An example that illustrates this is the constitutional crisis in Iran in January 1988, arguably resulting from the shortcomings of the 1979 Constitution. Facing the crisis, Ayatollah Khomeini – the "founding father" of the Constitution – held that the Islamic government in the form of *Velayat-e Faqih* establishing the theocratic form of government in Iran, was the most important of the divine commandments and had priority over other commandments such as prayer, fasting, and pilgrimage to Mecca.[44] In other words, a political choice was made to prioritize the form of government which has no firm basis in doctrinal Islamic law over what has been understood as the basic tenets of Islam.

Despite its use in this book, to call this particular form of constitutional transformation, "constitutional desecularization", can be a dangerous pitfall, since

43 Knut Vikør, *Mellom Gud og stat: Ei historie om islamsk lov og rettsvesen* (Spartacus Forlag, 2003).

44 Said Arjomand, *The Turban for the Crown: The Islamic Revolution in Iran* (Oxford University Press, 1988).

the notion can give the impression that there is something "religious" about the constitutions simply because they refer to religion, or something "secular" about constitutions simply because they do not refer to a religion. In this connection, one may ask how de-secularized is the de-secularized constitution? Does the application of religious rhetoric and the inclusion of clergy in the political and legal system imply that a constitution is religious? As a political and legal document, the constitution is an entirely secular document dealing with worldly issues, even in a case where it uses religious language.[45]

A constitution cannot be "religious" in the common sense of the word. Therefore, whenever a constitution establishes a religious nature for the state it does so in the form of a state-sanctioned version of religion. In doing so, the state at the same time ignores the many nuances, differences of opinion, and doubts that will always surround religion and personal faith.[46] Therefore, the constitutional establishment of religion will inevitably be a political act, and therefore no different from the establishment of any other ideology in the constitution.

As such, when used in a constitution, religion serves no different function than that of nonreligious ideologies that have been, or that are at present, constitutionally used to justify limitations on equal freedom in a way that breaks with the standards of constitutionalism.[47] Religion thus becomes a constitutional language that serves a particular function, hereunder that of limiting equal liberty through re-establishing hierarchies that have been previously abolished or reduced. Desecularization of constitutions through the use of a strengthening of religious rhetoric therefore implies the translation of religion into a constitutional language that serves a particular function. What makes religion particular is its historically intertwined relationship with political power, more so perhaps than the more recent non-religious ideologies of the 19th and 20th centuries.[48] Therefore, the use of religion in a constitutional context could suggest that the constitution builds on some form of historical heritage, which thereby may immunize it from critical scrutiny. While this may in some instances be the case, the purpose of a state religion in modern constitutions cannot be identified without examining the particularities of each constitution and placing this in the context of the constitutional memory of each country. One cannot, in other words, make the assumption that religious rhetoric in a contemporary constitution serves the same

45 A similar point is expressed by Ran Hirschl who stresses that constitutional theocracy is a political phenomenon and not a theological or judicial one. See Ran Hirschl, *Constitutional Theocracy* (Harvard University Press, 2010) 19.

46 Efraim Karsh, *Islamic Imperialism: A History* (Yale University Press, 2006) 11–12.

47 For a critical discussion of the oversimplification of the bipartite model of secular versus religious, or tripartite models (secular, religious, and hybrid), see Cole Durham, "Perspectives on Religious Liberty: A Comparative Framework", in Johan Van der Vyver and John Witte (eds), *Religious Human Rights in Global Perspective: Legal Perspectives* (Martinus Nijhoff Publishers, 1996) 1–44. See also, Arcot Krishnaswami, *Study of Discrimination in the Matter of Religious Rights and Practices,* UN Doc. E/CN.4/Sub.2/200/Rev.1 (1960).

48 Jeroen Temperman, *State-Religion Relationships and Human Rights Law: Towards a Right to Religiously Neutral Governance* (Martinus Nijhoff Publishers, 2010).

purpose as religious rhetoric has served in the past. And even if this was the case, the question arises as to whether it can be justified today.

2.1.3 The politicization of religion and fundamentalism

Much of the conventional wisdom about religious politics finds its roots in the idea that the contemporary resurgence of religion represents a popular reaction to the modernizing tendencies of the secular state – a dispute between those who seek to infuse public life with the "traditional values" of religion and a state that embodies the irreligious values of secular modernity.[49] This reinforces the distinction between secular and religious, which is reflected also in the secularization thesis discussion which predicts that modernity and economic development causes individuals to become less religious.[50] Peter Berger's *The Desecularization of the World* and Samuel Huntington's *Clash of Civilizations* thesis are examples of this. Berger introduced the notion of "desecularization" in 1999, to describe a variety of manifestations of the worldwide resurgence of religion, and to underline the vitality of religion *vis-à-vis* modernity, thereby concluding that the "secularization theory" could not be empirically supported.[51] Modernity, it seems, has facilitated also religious actors and ideas.[52] Pivotal to Berger's definition is desecularization as *counter-secularization*.

Huntington views the issue largely in religious terms, arguing that contemporary political conflicts are defined along cultural lines. Huntington's perspective, which remains influential, is that communalism, hierarchy, and an emphasis on social control are tied closely to Islamic and Asian traditions, while liberal democracy, constitutionalism, equality, and individual freedom are rooted in the Western tradition. Through an essentialist understanding of religion that de-emphasizes

49 Scott Hibbard, *Religious Politics and Secular States: Egypt, India and the United States* (Johns Hopkins University Press, 2012) 20.

50 Max Weber, *Economy and Society* (Berkeley University Press, 1978). For an expansion of the secularization thesis, see also Bryan Wilson, *Religion in Secular Society: A Sociological Comment* (Watts, 1966); Peter Berger, *The Sacred Canopy: Elements of a Sociological Theory of Religion* (Doubleday, 1967); and Mark Chaves, "Secularization as Declining Religious Authority", *Social Forces* [1994] 72:3 749–774. For a critique of the secularization thesis, see Vyacheslav Karpov, "Desecularization: A Conceptual Framework", *Journal of Church and State* [2010] 52:2 232–270. Karpov's critique problematizes the secularization thesis through an analysis of desecularization. In Karpov's perspective, secularity is not modernity dependent because secularity as an idea precedes the formation of statehood.

51 Peter Berger (ed), *The Desecularization of the World: Resurgent Religion and World Politics* (Ethics and Public Policy Center and Wm. B. Eerdmans Publishing Co., 1999).

52 Barry Rubin, "Religion and International Affairs", in Douglas Johnston and Cynthia Sampson (eds), *Religion, the Missing Dimension of Statecraft* (Oxford University Press, 1994) 20–36. Several studies have pointed to modernity as externally causing desecularization, as well as causing secularization. Jonathan Fox, *A World Survey of Religion and the State* (Cambridge University Press, 2008). See also, Jonathan Fox, "World Separation of Religion and State in the Twenty First Century", *Comparative Political Studies* [2006] 39:5 331–364.

other dimensions, the self-understanding of many religious activists reinforces the view of religious politics as an ideological conflict between competing value systems, and leaves out other considerations, including economic dimensions and the role of foreign policy. Fundamentalists commonly argue that the contemporary social ills of society are rooted in efforts to impose an alien modernity. The separation of religion from public life, including constitutional secularity, is thus inimical to their understanding of religion.[53]

In his critique of this way of understanding religious politics, Scott Hibbard points out the credence given to illiberal religious activists, and the assumption that their understanding of religious tradition is authentic, overlooking intra-communal conflicts within religious communities.[54] Relatedly, the assumption that Western civilization is defined by Enlightenment values is equally problematic. Western societies throughout the modern period have had their own debates between open and closed visions of social life, between liberal and illiberal constitutional developments.[55]

As Hibbard observes, the resurgence of illiberal religious activism after the Cold War did not arise as spontaneously as many assume.[56] Secular state actors have facilitated the resurgence of religious politics by supporting religious movements and religious division for political gain. Part of this includes the support of Islamist militancy as a means of countering Soviet influence during the Cold War.[57] The resurgence therefore cannot be ascribed to a failed modernity project, nor is it due solely to the efforts of religious revivalists. If this had simply been a matter of religion, we could ask why such transitions always involve conservative and exclusive interpretations of religion, and why such legal systems also contain seemingly paradoxical arrangements, such as exemptions from religious law in the sectors for business and tourism.[58] Religion reshapes modern politics,

53 Samuel P. Huntington, *The Clash of Civilizations and the Remaking of World Order* (New York: Simon & Schuster, 1996) 70.

54 As he points out: "ironically (…) conservative Muslims often have more in common with Haredi Jews and Evangelical Christians than they do with liberal or secular Muslims". Scott Hibbard, *Religious Politics and Secular States: Egypt, India and the United States* (Johns Hopkins University Press, 2012) 22.

55 Ibid. 23. Religious ideologies reflect not a return to tradition *per se*, but rather an ideological reconstruction of tradition for a modern context. Geertz refers to this as "re-traditionalization", quoted in Scott Hibbard (2012) 11.

56 Ibid. 20.

57 Ibid. 246, 252. The ideological transformation in the 20th century, Hibbard notes, involved the active promotion of religion by state actors as means of mobilizing popular support behind their respective claims to rule and abandoned commitments to an inclusive vision of social order in favour of exclusive religious politics. The shift was very much a part of an anti-leftist discourse within the Cold War dynamics, where conservative religion was promoted around the world because it was seen as a bulwark against the influence of leftist ideologies.

58 See Ran Hirschl, *Constitutional Theocracy* (Harvard University Press, 2010) 120. See also by the same author, "The Political Economy of Constitutionalism in a Non-Secularist World", in Tom Ginsburg (ed), *Comparative Constitutional Design* (Cambridge University Press, 2012) 164–191.

Scott Hibbard observes, but its politicization has also changed religion, in particular through the effort by political actors to promote one interpretation of religion at the expense of others.[59]

While the conceptualization and contextualization of the strengthening of religion in the constitution as an outcome of political religion have been marginalized in literature, they are not new. Peter Chelkowski and Robert Pranger apply this perspective in their survey of the dynamic interaction between ideology and power in the Middle East, as does Scott Hibbard, more recently.[60] However, one can observe that the distinction between political religion and religion has become increasingly erased in parallel with the shift towards a reduced commitment to the universalism of international law that characterizes part of the scholarship since the 1990s.

Looking at its use of religion to limit equal liberty, the similarity between this constitutional transformation and populist and fundamentalist experiences becomes clearer. Several features of the coming to power of populism identified by James M. Mallory apply equally to the transformation represented by constitutional desecularization. In the first phases, Mallory observes, populism emphasized mobilization in an "inclusionary" way, trying to broaden the set of actors in the political process while controlling them through organizations "formed, in sectoral and functional organizational structures joined at the top by interlocking sectoral elites".[61] Hibbard identifies a pattern of association of illiberal interpretations of religion with the phenomenon of right-wing populism.[62] The exclusive interpretation of religious tradition is invoked to mobilize popular sentiment along communal lines and to cultivate popular acceptance for policies supporting a hierarchical pattern of social order.[63] Hence the ills of society were typically linked to an overt secular square that had purged religion from public life or to a "liberal elite".

There are two theoretical implications of Hibbard's account. First, contemporary religious politics do not reflect a struggle between forces of progress and modernity, nor does religious revivalism represent an anti-modern traditionalism. The conflict is only defined in religious terms. Second, religions are in no way monolithic, but characterized by a variety of competing interpretations, progressive and conservative, liberal and illiberal. What is at issue is therefore a two-fold struggle: the first is a reinterpretation of a given religious tradition, while the

59 Scott Hibbard, *Religious Politics and Secular States: Egypt, India and the United States* (Johns Hopkins University Press, 2012) 245.

60 Peter Chelkowski and Robert Pranger (eds), *Ideology and Power in the Middle East: Studies in Honor of George Ienczowski* (Duke University Press, 1988).

61 James M. Malloy, "Authoritarianism and Corporatism in Latin America: The Modal Pattern", in James M. Malloy (ed), *Authoritarianism and Corporatism in Latin America* (University of Pittsburgh Press, 1977) 12.

62 Scott Hibbard, *Religious Politics and Secular States: Egypt, India and the United States* (Johns Hopkins University Press, 2012) 253.

63 Ibid.

second involves the application of these ideas to a political setting. Another pattern identified by Hibbard is the loss of ideological commitment, as political campaigns increasingly favor marketing strategies and steer clear of substantive political debate. The emphasis on social issues embodies a distracting discourse used to mobilize constituencies instead of providing for a program of governance, contributing to what Hibbard calls "competitive populism".[64]

One may therefore view this constitutional transformation not as a struggle between tradition and modernity, nor between secular elites and religious opposition, but about competing visions of life, between exclusive and inclusive visions of governance. Because of the justifications used to narrow the scope of equal liberty and the use of religion as an external aim, the transformation may be viewed as a constitutional reflection of fundamentalist movements. We can conceptualize this as fundamentalism since it reflects a state-sponsored imposition of a politicized version of religion, in a way that "controls, restricts or deters the exercise of the rights of others who may have different views or backgrounds, thereby threatening the values of pluralism and broadmindedness, which are central to democracy".[65]

While there is no clear definition of "fundamentalism", one may agree with the description provided by the UN Special Rapporteur on freedom of association and peaceful assembly, as "any movement – not simply religious ones – that advocates strict and literal adherence to a set of basic principles", which is "[a]t bottom, a mindset based on intolerance of difference".[66] In this regard, the Special Rapporteur has highlighted "political fundamentalism" as a particular form of fundamentalism, entailing "the elevation of a particular political ideology or party or State leader above others, to the extent that those holding competing ideas are limited in their ability to express competing views".[67] Similarly, Marieme Helie-Lucas identifies fundamentalism as "political movements of the extreme right, which in a context of globalization ... manipulate religion, culture or ethnicity, in order to achieve their political aims".[68] She notes that such movements

> usually articulate public governance projects, in keeping with their theocratic visions, and impose their interpretation of religious doctrine on others as law or public policy, so as to consolidate social, economic and political power in a hegemonic and coercive manner.[69]

64 Ibid. 254.

65 A/HRC/32/36, para. 9. See also, A/HRC/34/56.

66 A/HRC/32/36, para. 9. This approach is reflected in some of the theories presented in support of Islamic Constitutionalism, which emphasize that Islamic faith is based on revelation through the *Qur'an* and the *Sunnah*, and arguing that the justification of the state is the enforcement of the *Shari'a*.

67 A/HRC/32/36, para. 42.

68 Marieme Hélie-Lucas, "What is Your Tribe? Women's Struggles and the Construction of Muslimness", in Harsh Kapoor (ed), *Dossier 23–24* (Women Living Under Muslim Laws, 2001) 49.

69 Ibid. 51.

Constitutional desecularization can, through its use of religious language to limit equal liberty, be seen as a constitutional form of fundamentalism.

As such, different constitutions and constitutional developments can be understood as reflecting liberal versus illiberal views on how to organize society. Towards this end, the state's promotion of illiberal interpretations and exclusive interpretations of religion in the constitution would place the constitution in the illiberal camp by establishing an external aim for the constitution.

Under the idea of constitutionalism, the purpose of the constitution is to establish a condition upon which individuals can interact on the basis of free and equal terms. This condition is both the justification of political governance and the aim of governance. The following chapter will examine constitutional developments that disable the condition of equal liberty.

2.2 Exclusive constitutional developments and external aims

Constitutions that justify political authority and constitutional rights on the basis of something other than the condition of equal liberty establish what we, for the purpose of this book, can call an external aim.[70] We can call this an external aim because the aim for the exercise of political authority and for constitutional rights lies in something other than the condition of equal liberty.

Under constitutionalism, the justification of public authority rests on the recognition that each person has the right to interact with another on terms of equal freedom. This establishes a framework for the exercise of public authority, since the government cannot deny this right without thereby denying the justificatory basis for its own authority.[71] In order to adhere to the standards of constitutionalism, a constitution must therefore establish a duty of the government to exercise political authority in the closest possible conformity with its own ideal of equal freedom. This does not mean that equal liberty is an external aim. External aims mean that a legal system, including the constitution, is simply a tool for realizing something of value apart from it.[72] Equal liberty, by contrast, is not an external aim because it is the constitutive basis of constitutionalism and for the constitution.

External aim constitutions use the constitutional form for the achievement of an aim that is different from the justificatory basis for constitutionalism.

70 My use of "external aim" has some features in common with William Galston's "monistic constitution". Galston's "monistic constitution" refers to constitutions that use *one* ideology, whether religious or nonreligious, as an aim that the legal system should serve. See William Galston, *The Practice of Liberal Pluralism* (Cambridge University Press, 2005) 187–196.

71 Jacob Weinrib, *Dimensions of Dignity: The Theory and Practice of Modern Constitutional Law* (Cambridge University Press, 2016) 91–107.

72 Used in this sense, external aims are similar to instrumental theories. For a discussion on the distinction between instrumental and non-instrumental legal theories, see Arthur Ripstein, *Force and Freedom* (Harvard University Press, 2009) 7–11 and 255–256.

External aim constitutions differ in the type of aims they seek to achieve. Equally, the strength of the external aim may vary.

External aims can take either a religious or a non-religious form. The first two modern constitutions – the US constitution of 1787 and the French constitution of 1791 – mark a break with the confessional state and with the practice of referring to an external aim or source in the justification of public authority. In their removal of an external aim, these two constitutions were, however, exceptions in the wave of constitution-making that subsequently began.

Historically, external aims have been articulated through religious language or through religion as an external aim in itself.[73] Under such constitutions, the stated purpose of the constitution is to fulfill an aim outside of itself, such as, for example, to create a pious society in line with a divine ideal. The 20th century also saw the emergence of non-religious external aims, of which communism was the most widespread, sometimes articulated as statesanctioned atheism aimed at eradicating the role of religion in society. In this respect, there is no fundamental difference between religious and non-religious external aims, since both limit public authority through an external aim that is something different from the condition of free and equal persons. The replacement of a state religion as an external aim with a non-religious external aim will therefore not represent a development towards constitutionalism. An approximation of the legal system that brings the exercise of public authority in the closest possible conformity with its own ideal of equal freedom takes place only if the constitutional development reduces or removes the place of the external aim, be it religious or nonreligious.

2.2.1 State religions as external aims

In a confessional constitution, the state religion may amount to an external aim if the constitution establishes the state religion in a way that overrides equality in liberty as a constitutive element of constitutionalism. The way in which the state religion amounts to an external aim is if, for example, the constitution establishes religion as a criterion for legislation, for governance, for exercise of or access to constitutional rights, or as a criterion for determining the scope of rights.

A central feature of the politicization of religion in the constitution is the introduction of an external aim or a strengthening of an already existing external aim. In, for example, Afghanistan, Iran, and Iraq, the constitutional transformation resulted in a strengthening of the state religion as a constraint on legislation, referred to as the restraining principle.[74] In Iran, such a principle was found in the 1906–1907 Constitution, but had limited significance since it was limited to one

73 For an account of various forms of religious claims for governance, see Dag Michalsen, *Rett en Internasjonal Historie* (Pax, 2011) 35–336; 69–74; 85–86; and 154–160.

74 Constitution of Afghanistan (2004), Article 3; Constitution of Iran (1979) Articles 2, 3, and 4; and Constitution of Iraq (2005) Article 2(1).

provision and not institutionalized. Therefore, the restraining principle under the past constitution had largely been a dormant provision.[75] The same was the case in the past Afghan constitutions.[76] In the Iraqi context, there had never been any restraining principles in the past constitutions and the de-secularized constitution introduced this principle for the first time.

The restraining principle is a provision that provides that legislation must not contradict the official state religion. That religion is an external aim for the constitution and thus for the relationship between political authority and people is expressly stated in Khomeini's *Islamic Government*, which formed the ideological basis for the Iranian Constitution of 1979: "Islam is prepared to subordinate individuals to the collective interests of society and has rooted out numerous groups that were a source of corruption and harm to human society".[77] In the Constitution of 1979, this idea is translated into binding law through its inclusion in the lengthy Preamble, as well as in several provisions, most notably Article 2, which lays out the "system of belief" of the Islamic Republic.

2.2.2 Non-religious external aims

Some non-religious and secular constitutions can be considered as being similar to confessional states if the non-religious ideology amounts to an external aim in ways that are similar to a state confession. In such cases, the non-religious ideology will constitute an external aim.[78] Therefore, although such ideologies are non-religious, their constitutional function is similar to that of religious rhetoric.

To the extent we are speaking of secular ideologies, these are not necessarily overlapping with the notion of constitutional secularity as a principle of governance that does not in itself reflect any value judgments about beliefs. However, when secular ideologies contain value judgments about belief and its place within society, they will amount to an external aim.

One example is the communist ideologies which were translated into constitutional state atheism which again triggered measures aimed at the eradication of religion. The 1976 Constitution of Albania, for instance, provided that "the state recognizes no religion of any kind and supports and develops the atheist view so as to ingrain into the people the scientific and materialistic world-view".[79] Contemporary versions of constitutional state atheism are found in the constitutions of China, Cuba, and Vietnam. China's constitution does not explicitly establish an atheist state, but this is deduced from the position of the Communist

75 Constitution of Iran of 1906–1907, Article 2 of the Supplement of 1907.

76 See for example, Constitution of Afghanistan of 1964, Article 64.

77 Khomeini, "Islamic Government" translated to English, in Hamid Algar (ed), *Khomeini: Islam and Revolution* (Mizan Press, 1981) 89.

78 Smart discusses extensively the question of the extent to which the nature of secular world views can be considered "religious". Ninian Smart, *The World's Religions* (Cambridge University Press, 1992) 21–28.

79 Constitution of the People's Socialist Republic of Albania (1976), Article 37.

Party as the ruling party; Communist Party members have to adhere to the Party's code of atheism, in which the position is that religion will eventually die out and until that time it has to be tightly controlled.[80]

2.2.3 *External aims and limitations on equal liberty*

A common way to assess the compatibility of state religion constitutions with constitutionalism is to assess the extent to which the state religion may infringe upon the right to freedom of religion or belief. The prevalent view is that establishment is not *per se* contrary to constitutionalism and international human rights law, because the establishment of religion may not necessarily infringe upon the religious rights of those who do not adhere to the official state religion.

The problem with this way of assessing the compatibility of state religion with constitutionalism and international human rights law is that it equates the total set of human rights norms with the norms of religious freedom. The approach also presumes that the state version of the official state religion overlaps with that of the adherents of that religion. It, moreover, does not assess the other functions that a state religion may have in a constitution.

By contrast, some commentators use equality and non-discrimination considerations in their arguments against state religion.[81]

From the perspective of constitutionalism, established religion and non-religious confessional constitutions are problematic for reasons in addition to those stated previously. In defining one religion or non-religious external aim, a constitution establishes grounds for limiting equality in liberty and increases state interference with personal autonomy. Therefore, the issue is not primarily whether a constitution is religious or not, but whether there is an external aim that conditions political authority and the exercise of rights.

80 Document 19: The Basic Viewpoint and Policy on the Religious Question during our Country's Socialist Period, March 1982.

81 De Jong, quoted in Jeroen Temperman, *State-Religion Relationships and Human Rights Law: Towards a Right to Religiously Neutral Governance* (Martinus Nijhoff Publishers, 2010) 161. See also, Frances Raday, "Constitutional Secularism Vindicated (Constitutionalism and Secularism in an Age of Religious Revival: The Challenge of Global and Local Fundamentalisms", *Cardozo Law Review* [2009] 30:6 2769–2798.

Part II

Constitutional developments and the development of constitutionalism

3 The object of constitutions and constitutionalism

The way in which we assess the place of religion in constitutional developments and, in a similar vein, the extent to which it makes sense to speak of "religious constitutionalism", "Islamic constitutionalism", or any other form of qualified constitutionalism, depends in part on how we first understand "constitutionalism".

In this section, building on the distinction made earlier between constitutions and constitutionalism, this chapter identifies central features of modern constitutionalism, with particular attention paid to its constitutive elements of equal liberty and constitutional secularity. How does constitutionalism justify political authority, and what is the relevance of constitutional secularity in this regard?

Political authority and its relationship with individuals have taken various forms and justifications throughout history, reflected in constitutions embodying different political theories. Constitutions can therefore reflect a number of political theories, of which constitutionalism is but one. Similarly, constitutional developments in the same country can over time reflect the same political theory or go from one theory to another. Therefore, not all constitutions will at all times reflect the standards of constitutionalism. The aim of this chapter is to distinguish the particular way in which political authority and its relationship with individuals is justified under the theory of constitutionalism through its basis in equal liberty. In light of this standard, we can better understand the particularity of the constitutional developments, including how the politicization of religion in such developments alters some of the basic features of constitutionalism.

At a basic level, the object of constitutions can be described as the justification and regulation of political authority and the relationship between this authority and people within its jurisdiction, whether descriptively or normatively.[1] In articulating this relationship, the constitution defines the status of individuals, the conditions for who can exercise political authority, and the rights and duties of each. The question of what a "constitution" is gained importance in the aftermath of the French Revolution, separating theorists who pursued a normative orientation from theorists adopting a more sociologically oriented disposition.[2]

1 Dario Castiglione, "The Political Theory of the Constitution", *Political Studies* [1996] 33 417–435.

2 Chris Thornhill, *A Sociology of Constitutions: Constitutions and State Legitimacy in Historical-Sociological Perspective* (Cambridge University Press, 2011) 8.

The specific conception of political modernity that marked the Enlightenment processes held that the possession of a formally prescribed and written constitution was a hallmark of progressively realized or enlightened modern societies.[3] For normative analysis, the constitution comprises a body of norms that prescribes legal conditions for the public use of power. For sociological inquiries, on the other hand, constitutions are observed as evolving through multilevel historical processes. Therefore, from a descriptive and sociological understanding of constitutions, the adoption of modern constitutions beginning with the American and French constitutions, do not form points of categorical discontinuity in the legal normative history of modern society, because legal arrangements before this period can also be classified as constitutions.[4]

Similarly, if we understand constitutional law as normative ideas about political authority and its relationship to individuals, then an account of constitutional developments would not be limited to the study of modern constitutions, with the meaning of constitutions adopted from the 18th century onwards. It could instead begin with the legalization and regularization of power and politics. In the 4th century BC, Herodotus' "constitutional debate", which is thought to present the earliest theoretical account of the question of the best form of government, provides a debate about the merits and shortcomings of monarchy, oligarchy, and democracy, reportedly held prior to the accession to the throne by Darius.[5] Aristotle's political theory in the 3rd century BC identified six types of constitutions, classified into right or ideal constitution or government, and wrong or perverted form of government.[6] For Aristotle, aristocracy belonged to the first group, together with kingship and polity. Democracy was included as one of the "wrong" constitutions, together with tyranny and oligarchy, while the mixing of two extreme "wrong" constitutions would result in a moderate "right" constitution.[7]

3.1 Constitutionalism as a normative ideal and as a process

With the developments of the ideas of constitutionalism in the 17th century, a particular standard emerged for constitutional norms, and thus for the exercise of political authority and governance.[8] Under this theory, the exercise of political authority had to meet certain conditions. The justification of politi-

3 Ibid. 9.

4 Ibid. 10.

5 Herodotus Histories III. For an analysis, see Patrick Brannan, "Herodotus and History: The Constitutional Debate Preceding Darius' Accession", *Traditio* [1963] 19 427–438.

6 See entry "Aristotle's Political Theory" in *Stanford Encyclopedia of Philosophy*. https://plato.stanford.edu/entries/aristotle-politics/.

7 Ibid.

8 Stephen Holmes, "Constitutions and Constitutionalism", in Michel Rosenfeld and Andras Sájo (eds), *The Oxford Handbook of Comparative Constitutional Law* (Oxford University Press, 2012) 189–216.

cal authority in free and equal individuals indicates a closer distance between the ruler and the ruled and can be said to mark the start of the development towards constitutional democracy, although similar ideas had been articulated earlier. Constitutionalism thus is a theory of governance that establishes a certain standard for the exercise of power and for the rights and duties of people. In the absence of constitutionalism, constitutional norms remain norms that merely regulate or describe the exercise of political authority independent of any standard, and can create systems of absolute power, tyranny, aristocracy, a feudal system, or majority rule without the protection of minority rights. Constitutionalism, as understood here, is a normative ideal and a historical project with specific achievements to its credit.

Therefore, under the theory of constitutionalism, equal liberty, popular sovereignty, and accountability are closely linked. The exercise of political authority will only be accountable towards those persons it considers "equal", but the recognition of equality in itself is central to constitutionalism. Consider, for example, constitutions that throughout history have excluded women, persons based on the color of their skin, minorities of different kinds, and those without property from the exercise of rights on terms of equal freedom. In such legal systems, political authority can impose obligations on some persons who are not able to hold the exercise of political power accountable. The development of constitutional norms towards equality and accountability reflects a development in political theory from theories that exclude persons based on factors such as their gender, faith, opinion, wealth, profession, status, ethnicity, or color towards their inclusion as equals.[9]

3.1.1 Central features of constitutionalism

"Constitutionalism" is neither understood nor applied in a unified way. A rather minimal definition is provided by *The Oxford Handbook of Law and Politics*: "Constitutionalism is the constraining of government to better effectuate the fundamental principles of the political regime".[10]

9 While 20th-century constitutionalism had the state at its core, constitutionalism in the 21st century involves both state and non-state actors, with evolving understandings of responsibility beyond the state. This evolving conception has been informed by international law, where international human rights covenants, the expanding jurisdiction of various international criminal tribunals, universal jurisdiction, and the way that these inform constitutional law and the normative commitment of states add to the concept of constitutionalism. Ruti Teitel, "Transitional Justice and the Transformation of Constitutionalism," in Tom Ginsburg and Rosalind Dixon (eds), *Comparative Constitutionalism* (Edward Elgar, 2011) 57–76.

10 Keith Whittington, "Constitutionalism", in Gregory Caldeira, Daniel Kelemen and Keith Whittington (eds), *The Oxford Handbook of Law and Politics* (Oxford University Press, 2008) 281–299 .

From this minimal definition, we can divide the approaches to constitutionalism into two.[11] One approach regards constitutionalism as what is expressed through constitutional norms, in a constitution adopted by a constituent power. This understanding of constitutionalism equates, to a large extent, *constitutions* with *constitutionalism*. Under this view, no distinction is made between what is constitutional law on the one hand, and what is political theory on the other. This understanding of constitutionalism is process-centered, since it gives more attention to constitutions as being the product of the constituent power. One may in this sense say that this approach is more value-neutral as it places less attention on the content and justification of the constitution; in other words, on the political theory of the constitution. Central to this approach are questions such as whether the constitutional drafting process is valid, whether the constituent power is elected according to a certain standard, etc. This view is closely related to what one commentator calls the "democratic statist" notion of constitutionalism, and what some refer to as constitutionalism in the "minimal sense". It is a view that, moreover, is based on a state-centered perception of sovereignty.[12] Much of the literature on the revival of religion in constitutional developments builds on this understanding of constitutionalism, and as a result, it contains limited discussion on the content of constitutionalism.

A second approach considers constitutionalism as a political theory, which sets a minimum standard for the *content* of constitutions as norms regulating governance.[13] Under this view, constitutionalism does not refer to the fact of simply having a constitution adopted by a constituent power, but to having a "particular kind of constitution, however difficult it may be to specify its content".[14] In emphasizing that there is a distinction between constitutions and constitutionalism, some commentators speak of "constitutions without constitutionalism" to describe the state of constitutional law at particular times and places.[15] It reflects the idea that constitutions and constitutionalism are separate notions, and that the mere fact of having adopted the former need not reflect the achievement of

11 Mattias Kumm makes a closely related distinction between two forms of understanding constitutionalism: "democratic statist" notion of constitutionalism and "practice conception" of constitutionalism. See Mattias Kumm, "The Best of Times and the Worst of Times: Between Constitutional Triumphalism and Nostalgia", in Petra Dobner and Martin Loughlin (eds), *The Twilight of Constitutionalism?* (Oxford University Press, 2010) 201–219.

12 Erik Kuhonta, "Towards Responsible Sovereignty: The Case for Intervention", in Donal Emmerson (ed), *Hard Choices: Security, Democracy, and Regionalism in Southeast Asia* (Walter H. Shorenstein Asia-Pacific Research Center Books, 2008) 292–314.

13 See, for example, Martin Loughlin, "What is Constitutionalism?" in Petra Dobner and Martin Loughlin (eds), *The Twilight of Constitutionalism?* (Oxford University Press, 2010) 48 and 55.

14 Gerhard Caspar, "Constitutionalism", *University of Chicago Occasional Paper*, No. 22 [1987] 5.

15 H.W.O. Okoth-Ogendo, "Constitutions without Constitutionalism: An African Political Paradox", in Douglas Greenberg, S.N. Kartz, B. Oliviero and S.C. Wheatley (eds), *Constitutionalism and Democracy: Transitions in the Contemporary World* (Oxford University Press, 1993).

the latter.[16] This understanding of constitutionalism is offered, for example, by Martin Dobner and Petra Loughlin who also point out the influence of the idea of constitutionalism on constitutional design:

> Under its influence, modern constitutions have established a set of governmental institutions that provide the necessary conditions for the realization of a democratic Rechtstat. Such constitutions constrain politics by legal means, structure power relations comprehensively, help normatively to integrate societies, and offer a practical account of legitimate democratic rule within the state.[17]

This view of constitutionalism is sometimes called constitutionalism in the rich, maximal sense, or the "practice conception of constitutionalism".[18] What distinguishes this understanding from the first one is that a constitution that comes into place according to a legitimate process may still fall outside the framework of constitutionalism because of its content – because of the way in which it justifies political authority and its relationship with individuals. It is this understanding of constitutionalism that forms the premise of this book, and that forms a standard against which to measure constitutional desecularization.

While the concept of constitutionalism leaves room for a variety of different ways of establishing and organizing political governance, it nonetheless does establish a minimum framework. On the basis of the development of the theory of constitutionalism, it is to some extent possible to describe some of the features that are central to constitutionalism. While there are divergent views on the substantive features of constitutionalism, one may nonetheless identify some of these, including the rule of law, separation of powers, checks and balances, free and fair elections, judicial independence, and constitutional rights and their justiciability.[19] In addition to the substantive aspects of constitutionalism, Dieter Grimm identifies five functional features of constitutionalism:[20]

16 Ibid. 65; Nathan Brown, *Constitutions in a Nonconstitutional World* (State University of New York Press, 2002).

17 Dobner and Loughlin (2010) xi.

18 Kumm (2010).

19 For example, when speaking of the "three-faceted concept" of constitutionalism that entails the protection of human rights, the imposition of limitations on governmental powers, and adherence to the rule of law, Michel Rosenfeld sets out substantive features of constitutionalism. Michel Rosenfeld, "Modern Constitutionalism as Interplay between Identity and Diversity", in Michel Rosenfeld (ed), *Constitutionalism, Identity, Difference, and Legitimacy: Theoretical Perspectives* (Duke University Press, 1994) 27–28. Similarly, Mark Tushnet stipulates that "constitutionalism" is applicable only when some substantive requirements are satisfied. Mark Tushnet, "Authoritarian Constitutionalism", *Cornell Law Review* [2015] 100:2 391–461; Jacob Weinrib, *Dimensions of Dignity: The Theory and Practice of Modern Constitutional Law* (Cambridge University Press, 2016) 137–175.

20 Dieter Grimm, "The Achievement of Constitutionalism", in Petra Dobner and Martin Loughlin (eds), *The Twilight of Constitutionalism?* (Oxford University Press, 2010) 9.

1. The constitution in the modern sense is a set of legal norms that emanate from a political decision, rather than some pre-established truth
2. The purpose of these norms is to regulate the establishment and exercise of public powers, as opposed to a mere modification of a pre-existing public power
3. The regulation is comprehensive in the sense that no extra-constitutional bearers of public power and no extra-constitutional ways and means to exercise this power are recognized
4. Constitutional law finds its origin with the people as the only legitimate source of power. The distinction between constituent power and constitutionalized power is essential
5. Constitutional law is higher law. It enjoys primacy over other laws and legal acts emanating from governments. Acts incompatible with the constitution do not acquire legal force.[21]

Together, the functional and substantive features of constitutionalism point us towards a standard for the justification and regulation of political authority and governance.

Constitutional desecularization represents a change with respect to two features that constitute two primary concerns of constitutional law, as well as constituting two of the functional features of constitutionalism as described previously. One is the issue of political authority. For the purposes of this book, the question is limited to the role of religion in justifying or binding such authority. The other issue, which is related, is that of the relationship between political authority and individuals as well as between individuals, limited to the regulation of equal liberty in the context of constitutional rights. Before analyzing these two issues in the next chapter in relation to the particular constitutional development of politicized religion, I will discuss their status under the theory of constitutionalism. How is political authority justified under constitutionalism, and what are the grounds upon which equality between individuals can be limited?

Because constitutionalism is a political theory, an ideal, any constitutional development towards it will have to be an ongoing development. Constitutional practice, because it is practice and not ideal, needs to be in constant development towards the achievement of the ideal. The emphasis on constant reform of constitutions in order to approximate a normative standard was already articulated by Immanuel Kant, who in *Towards Perpetual Peace* describes how peace might be instituted, and he does so by determining reforms for a civil, international, and cosmopolitan constitution.[22] The achievement of peace, in which equality and freedom stand at its core, is, for Kant, the essential reason for creating and

21 Ibid.

22 Azin Tadjdini, "The Constitutional Dimension of Peace", in Cecilia Baillet and Kjetil Larsen (eds), *Promoting Peace Through International Law* (Oxford University Press, 2015) 395–415.

reforming constitutions.[23] As a prerequisite for peace, which Kant considers as being directly connected to individual liberty, a constitution must reflect all these elements. At the same time, he acknowledges that perpetual peace is an ideal that may never be attained. His theory is nevertheless intended as a guide to reach perpetual peace through constant reform of legal and political structures.

For Kant, equal liberty is one of what he identifies as the three "definite articles" needed for the achievement of perpetual peace.[24] He articulates this as a requirement that the civil constitution of every state be republican. By "republican", Kant refers to a constitution where all citizens are *free*, dependent upon common legislation, and legally *equal*. His political philosophy is one that emphasizes laws to be enacted by the consent of the governed (popular sovereignty) and which apply to all citizens accordingly. Kant's overarching aim is thus to bring about perpetual peace worldwide by means of law that secures the basic rights of individuals.

The connection between rights and form of government is a dynamic and multidimensional one. Rousseau's theory of the social contract posits that it is not possible for liberty to exist without equality, and that the two "consist of the greatest good of all".[25] Montesquieu insisted on equality as a necessary precondition for republicanism:

> Love of the republic in a democracy, is a love of the democracy: love of the democracy is that of equality. Love of the democracy is likewise that of frugality. As every individual ought to have here the same happiness and the same advantages, they ought consequently to taste the same pleasures and to form the same hopes; which cannot be expected but from a general frugality ... A true maxim is therefore, that in order to love equality and frugality in a republic, these virtues must have been previously established by law.[26]

The issue is also connected to the question of legitimacy. In political theory, the dominant approach to the idea of legitimacy has been made through reference

23 To this end, Kant proposes the adoption of a legal constitution in three stages: (1) a constitution based on the civil rights of individuals within a nation; (2), a constitution based on the international right of states in their relationships with one another; and (3) a constitution based on a cosmopolitan right. Commenting on Kant's conception of personal autonomy, Habermas notes that a religious or metaphysical justification of human rights becomes superfluous. Therefore, secularization of politics is simply the flipside of the political autonomy of citizens. Jurgen Habermas, *The Postnational Constellation: Political Essays*, Max Pensky (ed.) (2001) 127.

24 Azin Tadjdini, "The Constitutional Dimension of Peace", in Cecilia Baillet and Kjetil Larsen (eds), *Promoting Peace Through International Law* (Oxford University Press, 2015) 397–399.

25 Rousseau, *The Social Contract*, referenced in Christopher Bertram, *Rousseau and the Social Contract* (Routledge, 2004).

26 Montesquieu, *The Spirit of the Laws*, quoted in Cass. R. Sunstein, *Beyond the Republican Revival* (Yale Law Review, 1988) 97 1552.

to social contract theory. Social contract theories share a concern for arbitrary interference with one's liberty. Human beings have the right to conduct their individual lives as they deem fit because they have authority only over themselves and hence no one has authority over them. They nonetheless reserve the right to transfer that authority to others or to a political entity. A legitimate government is one to which people have transferred their right to rule themselves and to which they have consensually agreed to allow act on their behalf. While some theorists, such as Locke, leave open whether majority rule is a necessary element of democratic decisionmaking, others, such as Rousseau, bring the idea of the social contract closer to political equality in the idea that laws must be under the frequent review of the whole citizenry as it is the only way liberty can be guaranteed. Exercise of political authority must be defensible to all that are subject to it, as political equals.[27] A democratic state, in order to be fully legitimate, must not only issue laws in a procedurally correct way but also ensure that they comply with certain substantive values. For Rawls, equality is a central element of justice.[28] The account of legitimacy as political equality is fairly uncontroversial. Within the dominant contemporary political and legal theories, the concept of legitimacy is intrinsically linked with political equality.[29]

Gradually, international human rights law has recognized that among the elements that are essential in the full expression of equal and inalienable rights of all humans, is a form of government that is representative in character, in which political power is accountable to everyone. To ensure that the will of the people serves as the basis for the authority of government, international human rights law establishes a right to free and fair elections. It also guarantees universal and equal suffrage to adult citizens.[30] The guarantee of universal and equal suffrage requires that individuals must be permitted to vote on a nondiscriminatory basis. It also guarantees the right of citizens to seek political or public office, individually or as representatives of political parties or organizations, and guarantees that political parties or organizations can compete with each other on the basis of equal treatment before the law and by the authorities.

Although the principle of democratic elections was set forth in the Universal Declaration of Human Rights (UDHR) and in the International Covenant on Civil and Political Rights (ICCPR), the international community has only fairly recently addressed the issue in greater depth and posed the question of whether

27 Jacob Weinrib, "Authority, Justice, and Public Law: A Unified Theory", *University of Toronto Law Journal* [2014] 64:5 703–735.

28 Ronald Dworkin, "What is Equality? Part II: Equality of Resources", *Philosophy and Public Affairs* [1981] 10:4 283–345; John Rawls, *Justice as Fairness: A Restatement* (Harvard University Press, 2001).

29 John Rawls (ibid.); Wojciech Sadurski, *Equality and Legitimacy* (Oxford University Press, 2008). For the opposite view, see Richard Arneson, "Equality and Equality of Opportunity for Welfare", in Louis Pojman and Robert Westmoreland (eds), *Equality: Selected Readings* (Oxford University Press, 1997) 229–241.

30 ICCPR, Article 25; UN Human Rights Committee, General Comment No. 21.

there is a right to democracy under international law. While this right is not explicitly pronounced, one can conclude that such a right exists based on the interdependence of human rights, particularly the right to free and fair elections, to stand public office, to self-determination, to freedom of association, and to freedom of expression.[31,32]

3.1.2 Equal liberty as the justification for political authority

Political authority and its relationship with individuals have throughout history taken various forms. Political authority can exist within a state context and a non-state context. It can be justified in religious terms or in non-religious terms. Often, the idea that justifies political authority is also the idea that guides the justification for limitations to individual liberty.

While, in the context of constitutional law, justification for political authority can be anything, by contrast, in the context of constitutionalism, political authority is based on, and justified in, popular sovereignty and the recognition of free and equal persons, or in the words of the radical French philosopher Condorcet, "the natural equality of men" is the chief basis of men's rights.[33] What counts as free and equal has evolved over the course of constitutionalism's development, and both liberty and equality have been subject to changes in their conceptions. But the recognition of liberty and equality in itself represents a significant move from political theories that are based on hierarchies, and where liberty or certain types of liberties are reserved for particular groups or individuals.

For political authority to be legitimately exercised under constitutionalism, it must be based on free and equal persons who are both the subject of political authority and able to take part in the exercise of political authority.[34] Under such a rule, all people are subject to publicly enacted standards of behavior, subjecting individuals to common law-giving. This distinguishes constitutionalism from other theories of political authority. For example, in an autocracy, political authority is held by a single individual. In such a system, persons are bound by the law, but unable to contribute to its enactment. In an aristocracy, political authority is held by persons of a particular rank, while those excluded from these ranks are passive. Through its basis on equal liberty, the idea of constitutionalism

31 ICCPR, Articles 1, 19, 22, and 25.

32 The Treaty of the European Union 1992, Article 6(1); and the European Court of Human Rights has concluded that "democracy … appears to be the only political model contemplated by the ECHR, and accordingly the only one compatible with it". *United Communist Party of Turkey and others v Turkey*, Reports 1998-I at para. 45.

33 Quoted in Jonathan Israel, *Democratic Enlightenment: Philosophy, Revolution and Human Rights 1750–1790* (Oxford University Press, 2011) 6.

34 Jacob Weinrib, *Dimensions of Dignity: The Theory and Practice of Modern Constitutional Law* (Cambridge University Press, 2016); Anne Peters, "Compensatory Constitutionalism: the Function and Potential of Fundamental International Norms and Structures", *Leiden Journal of International Law* [2006] 19 579–610.

requires political authority to be held by a totality of adult citizens, who contribute to the creation of the laws by which they are bound. Constitutionalism is thus based on an egalitarian idea. Within this idea, what counts as "equal" has been subject to change.[35] Once it included only a portion of adult male citizens. The acknowledgment of equal liberty is nevertheless in itself significant, removing any formal boundaries for the expansion of who counts as equal. Modern constitutionalism aims to make the exercise of political authority accountable to neither the few nor to the many, but to each and every person subject to the law's authority.

Constitutionalism thus prescribes a particular form of the rule of law, connected to the source and legitimacy of constitutions. A distinctive feature of constitutionalism is the idea of constitutions as the fundamental law which simultaneously establishes the governmental system of the state and regulates the exercise of political authority within the system. Government thus derives its legitimacy and authority from the constitution. In turn, the constitution derives its legitimacy from the constituent power, which under constitutionalism rests with the people. The rule of law under constitutionalism and its principle of popular sovereignty thus presume a rule of law through democracy. This tells us something about the justification for the exercise of political authority. This does not mean, however, that anything that is law is valid. It only tells us that the law has been enacted through a democratic process. Having established this, we can move on to saying that constitutionalism cannot be reduced only to the prescription of political authority. This brings us to the aspect of content – or the standards that constitutionalism sets for the content of the acts of political authority.

While political authority and the separation of powers secure individuals from the arbitrary power of everyone else, the standards for the *content* of constitutionalism establish the justification for the exercise of such power.[36] Because the right of government to exercise political authority is based on the right of individuals to interact with one another on terms of equal freedom, government cannot deny this right without thereby denying the justificatory basis for its own authority.[37]

Some may object that this understanding of constitutionalism is overly demanding since it demands the creation of a democratic utopia, far removed from practice and pragmatic political considerations. But unlike the constitutive aspect of constitutionalism which articulates equal liberty as the basis for political authority, the exercise of political authority is a regulative aspect. It articulates the standard for assessing the extent of a legal system's adequacy and entails the duty of government to exercise political authority in the closest possible conformity

35 For a comprehensive account of the development of non-discrimination and equality in international law, see Stephanie Farrior (ed), *Equality and Non-discrimination Under International Law* (Routledge, 2015); Wouter Vandenhole, *Non-discrimination and Equality in the View of the UN Human Rights Treaty Bodies* (Insentia, 2005).

36 Jacob Weinrib, *Dimensions of Dignity: The Theory and Practice of Modern Constitutional Law* (Cambridge University Press, 2016) 59–61 and 75.

37 Ibid.

with its own ideal of equal liberty. The regulative aspect therefore calls for the ongoing approximation of a legal system towards the standards of constitutionalism. This provides us with a standard for measuring constitutional developments and assessing whether a constitutional development at any given moment constitutes an approximation or a reversal.

That constitutionalism through the regulative aspect requires governments to realize an ideal, does not, however, mean that it is an instrumental theory. For instrumental theories, the legal system is simply a tool for realizing something of value external from it.[38] While instrumental theories differ about the particular value that legal systems should pursue, they agree that if a legal system is of value, it is because it can further the realization of some valuable end, whether this end is maximal pleasure, a classless society, a pure nation, an Islamic state, Christian values, or commitment to *Hindutva*, etc. But, unlike the idea of an instrumental theory, constitutionalism is not conceivable apart from a legal system.

A constitution designed to comply with the standards of constitutionalism may still violate the regulative aspect, for example, through the imposition of arbitrary constraints on the rights of individuals. By contrast, a constitution that violates the constitutive aspect of equal liberty will fall completely outside the framework of constitutionalism. A violation of the constitutive aspect, for example, subjecting the independence of one or more persons to the arbitrary powers of others without having the right to holding them accountable, negates the rights of particular persons in their interaction with others, thereby removing the justification for political authority based on the right of each person to interact on terms of equal liberty with everyone else. The problem with, for example, the legal system under Nazism or apartheid in this connection is not that they constrained the rights of persons subject to law on grounds that the right itself did not require, but that they sought to negate the rights of particular persons in their interaction with others. Because the violation of the constitutive aspect and the regulative aspect create two different pathologies, the categorization of constitutions and their compatibility with constitutionalism is not always a matter of degree. The extent to which constitutions violate the regulative aspect would be a matter of degree. A violation of the constitutive principle, by contrast, would place a constitution outside the paradigm of constitutionalism.

This suggests that a defense of constitutionalism should not primarily be because it identifies a morally beneficial outcome, and then maintains that this structure contributes to its realization. Such a defense could also be used for constitutions that do not adhere to the standards of constitutionalism. Instead of justifying constitutionalism by appealing to benefits that could, in principle, be achieved in its absence, constitutionalism should be defended through itself.[39]

38 Ibid. 121.
39 Ibid.

3.1.3 Shift from state-centered to individual-centered sovereignty

Connected to equal liberty as a constitutive element of constitutionalism is the development in the understanding of sovereignty in both constitutional law in practice and constitutionalism as a theory. Sovereignty as a set of rules that define governance structures was in clear terms explicated in the 16th and 17th centuries.[40] The defining principle of these initial efforts, in particular by Bodin and Hobbes, to clarify the meaning of sovereignty was that there could be one, and only one, source of law, and that this source, the sovereign, was either in practice or in theory not subject to any higher authority.[41] Even if, as Hobbes admitted, divine authority or natural law existed, in practice only the sovereign could make laws.[42] There could be no earthly, external, international, or transnational actor that could negate the will of the sovereign. A political order based on sovereignty or the sovereign state can be contrasted with a society such as that of the medieval world, in which there were overlapping authority claims within the same territory. The political world in which states with defined territories and some degree of autonomy from external, especially transnational, authority – most notably the Catholic Church or the Caliphate – evolved over several hundred years.

It was, however, the religious wars in Europe that provided the motivation to develop a doctrine that could legitimate a political order populated with one, and only one, final source of authority within a given territory. For Bodin, the fundamental objective of any government must be to ensure order, and not to protect liberty. Bodin did not regard the sovereign as unconstrained. The sovereign was bound by the laws of God and nature and by custom. By contrast, Hobbes rejected even the modest constraints imposed on the sovereign. Once individuals had entered into a social contract, they could not, in Hobbes' view, challenge the sovereign.[43]

In Europe, the Peace of Westphalia, often defined as a critical moment in the development of the modern state system, de-legitimated the Catholic Church as a transnational source of authority and initiated a long period in European history in which the secular balance of power, rather than a notion of a unified

40 Stephan Krasner, "Problematic Sovereignty", in Stephen Krasner (ed), *Problematic Sovereignty: Contested Rules and Political Possibilities* (Columbia University Press, 2001) 1–23; Quentin Skinner, *Foundations of Modern Political Thought*, vol. 2 (Cambridge University Press, 1978).

41 Quentin Skinner, "The Sovereign State: A Geneology", in Quentin Skinner and Kalmo Hent (eds), *Sovereignty in Fragments: The Past, Present and Future of a Contested Concept* (Cambridge University Press, 2010) 35ff. See also, Julian Franklin (ed), *Bodin on Sovereignty* (Cambridge University Press, 1992); A.P. Martinich, *Hobbes* (Routledge, 2005).

42 Howell Lloyd, "Sovereignty: Bodin, Hobbes, Rousseau", *Revue Internationale de Philosophie* [1991] 45:179 (4) 353–379.

43 Ibid. see also Quentin Skinner, "Hobbes on Sovereignty: An Unknown Discussion", *Political Studies* [1965] 13:2 213–218.

Christendom, defined the way in which leaders conceived of, and practiced, politics.[44]

The concept of sovereignty has, through constitutionalism's basis of equal liberty, contributed to an understanding of sovereignty that is more nuanced than the traditional notion of sovereignty. We can call this an "individual-centered" notion of sovereignty. The purpose of sovereignty under the individual-centered understanding is to ensure individual rights by not allowing states to hide behind inviolable borders. This understanding of sovereignty is reflected in international human rights law. The UN Charter recognizes both forms of sovereignty – human rights as a reflection of individual sovereignty, and the classic state sovereignty principle of non-intervention. The notion of individual sovereignty implies a number of limitations for the exercise of state sovereignty. At the domestic level, it establishes certain standards for the type of interferences that the state can impose upon individuals. The shift of sovereignty to include a duty to protect individual rights reflects the inter-linkage between constitutionalism, constitutional democracy, and international human rights law.

3.1.4 Constitutional rights and limitations to equal liberty

In light of the development described in the previous section, limitations on individuals' rights are no longer the prerogative of political authority exercising sovereignty, but must be justified under both the constitutive aspect and the regulatory aspect of constitutionalism. The constitutive aspect requires that no person is excluded from having rights.[45] The regulatory aspect prescribes that limitations cannot be justified in anything but to achieve conditions for the exercise of equal liberty. Already in the framework of the 1789 Declaration on the Rights of Man and Citizens, limitations on rights could not derive from some collective good, interest, or value.[46] Instead, they should originate in the fabric of society itself, the equal liberty of all members of society.[47]

If the aim of political association is the preservation of each person's liberty, then limits to rights through law must do so in order to preserve the equal liberty itself, not some other external aim or interest. Constitutional rights under

44 For a critical perspective on the "myth" of the Westphalian moment, Pärtel Piirimäe, "The Westphalian Myth and the Idea of External Sovereignty", in Quentin Skinner and Kalmo Hent (eds), *Sovereignty in Fragments: The Past, Present and Future of a Contested Concept* (Cambridge University Press, 2010) 64ff; also see James Turner Johnson, *Sovereignty: Moral and Historical Perspectives* (Georgetown University Press, 2014) 117ff.

45 Jacob Weinrib, "Authority, Justice, and Public Law: A Unified Theory", *University of Toronto Law Journal* [2014] 64:5 703–735.

46 Ibid.

47 Chris Thornhill, *A Sociology of Constitutions: Constitutions and State Legitimacy in Historical-Sociological Perspective* (Cambridge University Press, 2011) 207–213; Jan-Werner Müller, *Contesting Democracy: Political Ideas in Twentieth Century Europe* (Yale University Press, 2011).

constitutionalism are therefore based on two presuppositions. Firstly, that rights specify the demarcated spheres of action between persons, as opposed to boundless freedom. Secondly, that these demarcations which define rights can only be determined by law.

In the context of constitutionalism, there is a duality in the relationship between government and rights since freedom and equality form the basis for political authority. Rights are therefore, on the one hand, the foundation for political authority, and on the other hand, political authority is under the duty to guarantee rights. Since the mid-20th century, the content of these rights is increasingly informed and supplemented by international human rights standards, making the idea of universal rights to a large extent legally binding. In the modern constitutional paradigm, individual rights are not merely subject to guarantee by domestic constitutions, but also by international law, in particular, international human rights law, and in some cases, by regional mechanisms, including regional courts.[48] In some legal systems where the rights have been able to develop over time, they are further strengthened through their institutionalization. In other societies, the constitutional entrenchment of the rights forms a first and significant step.

Legal hierarchies of persons based on their status have historically been a common feature of legal systems. Different justifications, both religious and non-religious, have been put forward for the unequal distribution of rights. The American and French revolutions of 1776 and 1789 can in this regard be interpreted as rights revolutions. The revolution represented a break from a system in which the power of the state was limited by bearers of privileged office. In detaching rights from feudal privilege, constitutional rights gave formal expression to the principle of individual integrity in legal standing.

Based on the previous matters, we can highlight two particular features that characterize constitutional rights as they have developed under the idea of constitutionalism, and which will have a bearing on the type of limitations that are compatible with constitutionalism. The first is the connection between constitutional rights and form of government. By acknowledging, at least on a theoretical level, the free and equal status of persons, and by bringing this idea into the justification for political authority, constitutionalism connects the concept of rights to the exercise of political authority. Since the exercise of political authority is justified by the free and equal status of persons, constitutionalism prescribes a system of political authority and governance that is based on equal liberty. Therefore, a form of government that does not establish conditions for equal liberty, including political equality, will not only represent a system with limitations

48 Stephen Gardbaum, "Human Rights as International Constitutional Rights", *The European Journal of International Law* [2008] 19:4 749–768. By the same author, see also Stephen Gardbaum, "Human Rights and International Constitutionalism", in Jeff Dunoff and Joel Trachtman (eds), *Ruling the World? Constitutionalism, International Law and Global Government* (Cambridge University Press, 2009).

to constitutionalism, but under such a system, the conception of rights will differ from that of constitutionalism.

The second feature concerns more directly the type of limitations that the political authority can decide on. Since political authority under the idea of constitutionalism is based on free and equal persons, limitations on constitutional rights cannot be used to alter this condition.

Constitutional rights establish limits to the exercise of political authority. In a democratic system of government, where decisions are the result of majority decisions, constitutional rights ensure rights with which the majority cannot interfere. This has implications for the structure of limitations. How can the state justifiably limit constitutional rights when such rights are the basis for the justification of the state itself? In other words, limitation of constitutional rights must be based on the justification for the state itself.

Constitutional rights concern the freedom and equality of persons both towards the state and towards other persons. The justification for limitations to constitutional rights can therefore be found on two levels, one vertical (towards the state) and the other horizontal (towards other persons).[49] On a horizontal level, limitations concern the sphere of autonomy and freedom that a person has in relation to the state. A limitation to a constitutional right defines this sphere of personal autonomy. It can do so with respect to the rights of all persons, or to particular groups of persons. On a vertical level, because the exercise of one person's freedom may come to interfere with another person's freedom, constitutional rights must be limited to ensure the upholding of a condition of free and equal persons. Since constitutionalism creates a system of rights protection in which all persons can enjoy their freedom by acting in consistency with the freedom of others, then there must be limits on the rights. The two different levels require different justifications for rights limitations. In a modern system of constitutionalism, the structure of rights limitation bridges the horizontal and vertical aspect of constitutional rights. The structure can be described as a two-step structure. Rights are, in general, stated in a broad manner, which may give the impression that constitutional rights are absolute and signal the importance of the sphere of personal autonomy and freedom in a vertical sense towards the state. In other words, there are limited grounds for justifying limitations to rights on the vertical level. By contrast, the horizontal level presents us with more justifications for limiting rights, since the exercise of rights may come to interfere with others. The second step in modern constitutionalism is increasingly dominated by some form of proportionality principle.

The modern constitutional rights theory that has developed after the Second World War draws a fundamental distinction between the scope of the constitutional right and the extent of its protection.[50] The scope defines the content

49 Ibid.

50 Aharon Barak, *Proportionality: Constitutional Rights and Their Limitations* (Cambridge University Press, 2012) 19–44.

of the right by marking the right's boundaries. The extent of its protection prescribes the legal limitations on the exercise of the right within its scope by defining the justifications for the right's limitation. Based on this distinction, the modern theory of constitutional rights is said to be based on a two-stage analysis. In the first stage, the constitutional right's scope is determined. This involves a determination of the right's content and the drawing of the right's boundaries. In the second stage, one determines whether constitutional justifications exist to limit the realization of the right through sub-constitutional legislation. Modern constitutional theory thus distinguishes between the determination of the right's scope and the determination of the right's limitations. The distinction emphasizes the considerable weight that modern constitutional law grants to individual rights by requiring a justification each time a limitation is made.

The distinction also highlights the difference between the constitutional level that determines the scope of the right and the sub-constitutional level that establishes limitations, reflecting the distinction between the constituent body and the legislative body. In a constitutional democracy, this provides the individual or the minority with a layer of protection against a possible tyranny of rights by the majority.

The distinction is manifested in international human rights law, which offers general rights, and in the next step allows for limitations on rights, either through general limitation clauses or through specific ones.

Because rights under constitutionalism can be limited only to the extent they interfere with other rights, limitations must be based on an exercise of weighing, rather than set rules. In modern constitutional law, the principle of proportionality has emerged as a main tool for limiting constitutional rights.[51]

With its origin in German administrative law, the proportionality principle began to be applied by the Federal Constitutional Court in the late 1950s and has spread over the succeeding decades to many constitutional regimes around the world, at domestic levels, as well as regional and international mechanisms, including the Human Rights Committee and the European Court of Human Rights. The proportionality principle determines whether the means employed by the authorities to promote its conflicting public policy objectives are justified.

Different courts apply different formulae for the principle of proportionality, but its essence converges. One example of its content of this principle is the one articulated by the Supreme Court of South Africa:

> The limitation of constitutional rights for a purpose that is reasonable and necessary in a democratic society involves the weighing up of competing values, and ultimately an assessment based on proportionality … There is no absolute standard which can be laid down for determining reasonableness

51 Mattias Kumm, "The Best of Times and the Worst of Times: Between Constitutional Triumphalism and Nostalgia", in Petra Dobner and Martin Loughlin (eds), *The Twilight of Constitutionalism?* (Oxford University Press, 2010) 201–219.

> and necessity. Principles can be established, but the application of those principles to particular circumstances can only be done on a case by case basis. This is inherent in the requirement of proportionality, which calls for the balancing of different interests. In the balancing process, the relevant considerations will include the nature of the right that is limited, and its importance to an open and democratic society based on freedom and equality; the purpose for which the right is limited and the importance of that purpose to such a society; the extent of the limitation, its efficacy, and particularly where the limitation as to be necessary, whether the desired ends could reasonably be achieved through other means less damaging to the rights in question.[52]

While this section has examined some of the features of modern constitutionalism, the next section continues by examining the relationship between the constitutional role of religion and these features.

3.2 The development towards constitutional secularity in theory and practice

3.2.1 Constitutional secularity as a principle of governance

Constitutional secularity is a principle of governance, and entails the absence of religion or religious rhetoric as a criterion for governance, including as a criterion for constitutional rights.[53] Some describe secularity in terms of "separation between religion and state", in which case "constitutional secularity" would entail a constitution whereby religion and state are separated. For the purposes of this book, however, the notion of separation is not entirely precise, since we are not speaking of "separation" and strictly speaking, we are not speaking of "religion" either. We are not speaking of separation, because on the basis of constitutional secularity, the state may still interfere in religious matters in the same way in which the state may interfere in other matters. We are not speaking of "religion", because the constitution as a framework for governance is ultimately a secular and political document, and every reference to religion as a consequence gains a political status. Thus, religion, whenever referenced in a constitution, becomes a language of politics and a language of law.

Constitutional secularity, understood as a principle of governance that entails the non-bindingness of religion on governance, is not new. The approaches to constitutional secularity can be divided into three levels. One is at the level of theory or ideas. The second is at the level of domestic constitutional norms. The third is through international law.

52 S.v Makwanyane (1995) 3 SA 391, para. 104.

53 I'm here referring to the absence of religious rhetoric as an *explicit* normative criterion for constitutional rights.

Constitutional secularity as a principle of governance does not require agnostic, atheist, or non-religious background assumptions. It is a notion that assumes that political authority is not justified or limited on the basis of religion or religious discourse. Constitutional secularity is thus a principle of governance that entails the non-bindingness of religion on public authority.

"Secularity", for lack of a clear definition, has entailed a wide range of understandings and approaches in scholarship. It is sometimes used interchangeably with the words "secularism", "secular", and "*laïcité*".[54]

Not being in itself a political theory, or a theory of justice or of legitimacy, constitutional secularity as a principle of governance is a normatively dependent concept.[55] It therefore needs to rest on a normatively substantive theory on what renders constitutional arrangements legitimate. The normatively dependent theory that constitutional secularity is dependent on for the purposes of this book is that of constitutionalism, understood as a theory whereby the exercise of political authority and its relationship with persons rests on the recognition of each individual as free and equal.

Being a normatively dependent theory, constitutional secularity will not by itself result in constitutionalism, as is clear from the many examples of constitutional design throughout time. Constitutional secularity is not an all-encompassing constitutional theory but must be combined with other elements. We can, therefore, have a number of secularity constellations: secular pluralism; secular monism; secular democracy; secular autocracy; secular totalitarianism; secular republicanism; secular communism, etc. However, not all these constellations are compatible with constitutionalism. What distinguishes secularity from nonsecularity as an element of these constellations is its non-preferentialism towards religion as a principle of governance, and not, as is sometimes perceived, that it is value neutral.[56]

54 For an overview, see Sindre Bangstad, *Sekularismens ansikter* (Universitetsforlaget, 2009) 25–50. See also, Barry Kosmin, "Contemporary Secularity and Secularism", in Barry Kosmin and Ariela Keysar (eds), *Secularism and Secularity: Contemporary International Perspectives* (Taylor Francis, 2007).

55 I borrow the term "normatively dependent concept" from Rainer Forst. See Rainer Forst, "The Justification of Human Rights and the Basic Right to Justification: A Reflexive Approach", *Ethics* [2010] 120:4 711–740.

56 Some commentators use the notion "neutrality" about secularity. For a general discussion and problematization of secularity as neutrality, see Lorenzo Zucca, *A Secular Europe: Law and Religion in the European Constitutional Landscape* (Oxford University Press, 2012) 97–111. The argument that secularity in itself is a *value* that ensures diversity and pluralism, was expressed by the Constitutional Court of South Africa, in *Minister of Home Affairs and Another v Fourie and Another; Lesbian and Gay Equality Project and Others v Minister of Home Affairs and Others*. The landmark decision from 2005, penned by Justice Albie Sachs, in ruling that same-sex couples had the right to marry, highlighted the constitutional value of secularity as a value that ensures pluralism and diversity. For Sachs's own explanation and contextualization of the decision, see Albie Sachs, *The Sacred and the Secular: South Africa's Constitutional Court Rules on Same-Sex Marriages* [2013] Ray Distinguished Lecture. Available at: http://law-apache.uky.edu/wordpress/wp-content/uploads/2014/01/8-Sachs.pdf.

Frances Raday poses the question of whether constitutionalism necessarily must be secular.[57] Raday begins by underlining that secularity in this context is a principle of governance, not a matter of belief. Her argument is that secular constitutionalism guarantees a public space for equal participation by those of religious belief and non-belief alike, and private space for matters, including religious matters, into which the state may not enter. Raday's approach is thus to illustrate the benefits of constitutional secularity by contrasting it with alternative principles of governance.

However, constitutional secularity as a necessary element of constitutionalism can also be approached from another angle. Instead of arguing that secular constitutionalism is essential for human rights and equal liberty, one can argue that human rights are articulations of the standards of constitutionalism. This requires a reconceptualization of our thinking of human rights. Instead of thinking of human rights as an external aim that requires secular constitutionalism for its realization, we can argue for constitutional secularity through constitutionalism itself. Constitutional secularity applies both to the constitutive aspect of constitutionalism and to its regulative aspect. Constitutionalism must be secular because it is based on the idea of free and equal persons. This constitutive aspect of constitutionalism precludes any form of external aim, whether religious or non-religious, as justification for political authority and thus for a constitution. The value of constitutional secularity for the achievement of constitutionalism is therefore not secularity as such, but constitutionalism, which is secular.

Raday identifies two themes from the critique against secular human rights which we also can apply to the context of constitutionalism. The first is the thesis that there is symmetry between religious and secular values as eschatological ideologies where secularism is yet another competitor on the ideological map. The second is the thesis that there is a threat to peace resulting from secular intolerance.

Both these critiques can be rebutted simply by responding to the question of what constitutional secularity is. Discussions on secularity often do not distinguish between various categories of secularity, but talk about secularity as one. In this connection, it can be helpful to distinguish between three different categories of secularity: societal secularity, sometimes referred to as secularization, political secularity, and constitutional secularity.

Societal secularity refers to the degree of religiosity in people's lives, the degree of personal religiosity regardless of the place for religion that the legal order prescribes. Analysis of societal secularity will therefore be through descriptive studies.

Political secularity refers to either descriptive or normative accounts of the extent to which religion has or should have in the political discourse and the

57 Andras Sajo asks the same question. See Andras Sajo, "Constitutionalism and Secularism: The Need for Public Reason?" *Cardozo Law Review* [2008–2009] 30.

political life of a society.[58] The degree of political secularity is thus independent of the place of religion in the constitutional framework.

Constitutional secularity refers to normative or descriptive accounts of the extent to which religion is prescribed or should be prescribed by the constitution. It is under constitutional secularity that it becomes relevant to pose the question of the extent to which religion serves, or should serve, as a justificatory principle for political authority and as a regulatory principle. Based on the previous matters, constitutional secularity becomes distinctively different from the broader category of "secularism", which, in all its vagueness, usually refers to levels of religiosity and the influence of religious institutions in society in general.[59,60] "Secularism" can thus refer to and be used about a number of things.[61]

The degree of secularity and the way of thinking about secularity varies both within the three categories as well as between them. The level of political secularity is likely to reflect the level of societal secularity, since the use of religious rhetoric in political argumentation is unlikely to be effective unless there is a certain degree of religiosity in society. Over time, religious rhetoric in politics, especially if also translated into the system of schools and education, may nonetheless influence the degree of societal religiosity as well. But neither political secularity nor societal secularity necessarily reflect the level of constitutional secularity, since this is a principle of governance and not a matter of belief. This would explain how a state may be constitutionally secular, yet have a high degree of religiosity in both society and in politics. Conversely, a confessional state with an active state religion need not necessarily reflect a religious population. The point here is that neither of these forms of secularity automatically entails the other. A polity could be constitutionally secular, while civil society could be quite religious, and political society may use religious rhetoric to justify their claims and policies.

58 For a comprehensive account of political secularity, see Cohen (2013). Cohen identifies four levels on which religion and state can be disconnected within the idea of what she terms "political secularism". These include the secularism at the level of legitimacy, at the level of justification of public law and policy, at the level of power and jurisdiction and at the level of recognition-endorsement. Cohen's argument is that religious legitimacy tends to be grounded in religious truths, transcendent sources, unquestionable authorities, and meta-social guarantees, while democratic legitimacy and constitutional authority must be immanent, reflexible, fallible, and contestable by those subject to it. See also John Rawls, *Political Liberalism* (Columbia University Press, 1993) and Jürgen Habermas, *Between Facts and Norms: Contributions to a Discourse Theory of Law and Democracy* (MIT Press, 1996).

59 The term, "secularism" was coined by George Jacob Holyoake around 1846. The content of Holyoake's "secularism" was not antireligious, although some interpreted it that way. The French term *laïcité* was coined in the 1870s. See Sindre Bangstad, *Sekularismens Ansikter* (Universitetsforlaget, 2009).

60 Koselleck, *The Practice of Conceptual History: Timing History, Spacing Concepts* (Stanford University Press, 2002).

61 For an overview of the history of the concept of "secularism", see Sindre Bangstad, ibid. 28–49; and Barry Kosmin, "Contemporary Secularity and Secularism", in Barry Kosmin and Ariela Keysar (eds), *Secularism and Secularity: Contemporary International Perspectives* (Taylor Francis, 2007).

Constitutional secularity is thus a distinct phenomenon. Constitutionalism as a specific normative political project entails constitutional secularity in order to ensure equal liberty of individuals.

That a number of modern constitutional states started out as confessional states could suggest that constitutional secularity is not a precondition for constitutionalism. However, that would be to conflate constitutionalism as a theory and constitutional developments in practice. In the following, I will present the development of constitutional secularity as an idea, before moving on to an overview of the extent to which constitutional secularity has been reflected in constitutional developments.

3.2.2 Constitutional secularity as an idea

Throughout much of human history, religion has been closely aligned, or fused, with political authority and law. Historically, political leaders have been even more important than theological ones in influencing the institutionalization of religion.[62] At the same time, this close alignment has been subject to challenge and critique for both principled and pragmatic reasons for almost the same period of time. Some commentators propose the origins of the separation between political authority and religion to as early as Babylonia 3,500 years ago.[63] Others point to the Byzantine period.[64] Yet others trace it to the Protestant Reformation and subsequent development during the Enlightenment processes.[65]

A prevalent strand in literature, which continues to shape a widespread assumption, is one that links secularity with developments in Europe from the 16th century and onwards, particularly the Reformation and the following religious wars and subsequent Enlightenment processes.[66] From this narrative, some commentators draw the conclusion that secularity – in all its forms – is a colonial or imperialist phenomenon when it appears outside the Western hemisphere. This has sometimes also led to a normative conclusion about secularity as a principle of governance. Charles Taylor's much-referenced account of secularity, for example, is based on the idea that modern secularity is a result of internal developments within European Christianity, and must be understood

62 Robert Barro and Rachel McCleary, "Which Countries Have State Religions?" *The Quarterly Journal of Economics* [2005] 120:4 1332.

63 Marcel Gauchet, *The Disenchantment of the World: A Political History of Religion* (Princeton University Press, 1997).

64 J. Herrin, *Byzantium: The Surprising Life of a Medieval Empire* (Princeton University Press, 2008); Paul Babie, "Synthesis or Separation? Church, State and Marriage in Byzantine Law", *Journal of Law and Religion* [2010] 26:2 585–594.

65 Ran Hirschl, *Constitutional Theocracy* (Harvard University Press, 2010) 35.

66 Charles Taylor, *A Secular Age* (Belknap Press of Harvard University Press, 2007); Talal Asad, *Formations of the Secular: Christianity, Islam, Modernity* (Stanford University Press, 2003).

in light of a Christian context.[67] Put differently, Christianity is thus viewed as a necessary historical prerequisite for secularity.[68]

However, the development of secularity does not need to be reduced to a narrative that sees secularity as arising out of Christianity, bearing in mind the problem represented by a monolithic understanding of "Christianity" in this regard. Instead, we can view the development of constitutional secularity as a narrative of conflicting ideas and rivalry within societies, between authority justified in religion and authority justified in non-religious terms. This understanding of conflicting ideas and rivalry that exist *within* societies, stands in contrast to Taylor's account, as well as that found in what has been known as "clash of civilization" theories, which divide the world into different spheres based on religion or culture, rather than a world where ideas and influences travel across places and change over time.[69]

One may in this connection, distinguish between accounts that trace the development of the *term* "secular" and accounts that trace the phenomenon and *idea*, regardless of the terminology. In other words, the existence of the idea or practice of separation between religion and political authority is not limited or reduced to the development of the term "secular".

The *idea* that governance should be separated from religion can be traced long back in history. Sophisticated theories later developed both within a religious framework and outside a religious framework. In the 12th and 13th centuries, theories arguing for the separation of religion and governance were articulated within the framework of the three monotheistic religions. Maimonides (1138–1204), Averroes (Ibn Rushd) (1126–1198), and Thomas Aquinas (1225–1274) merged Aristotelian Greek philosophy with Jewish, Islamic, and Christian thought, respectively.[70] Averroes' *The Decisive Treatise* from the 12th century provides a justification for the emancipation of science and philosophy from official theology, and has been considered a precursor to modern secularity, influencing Renaissance thought in Italy.[71] Similarly, classical republican theory rejected

67 Ibid. 31. See also Peter Berger, who argues that secularity was part of the Jewish-Christian tradition from its beginning. Peter Berger, *The Sacred Canopy: Elements of a Sociological Theory of Religion* (Doubleday, 1967).

68 Charles Taylor, *A Secular Age* (Belknap Press of Harvard University Press, 2007).

69 Rejecting the "clash of civilizations", the UN Special Rapporteur in the field of cultural rights points instead out that "there is a clash within each civilization between those who champion human equality and universal human rights and those who do not, sometimes due to fundamentalist or extremist ideology". A/HRC/34/56, para. 31.

70 Moshe Halbertal, *Maimonides: Life and Thought* (Princeton University Press, 2014); Anfinn Stigen (1983).

71 Averroes, *The Decisive Treatise* (Brigham Young University, 2002). Dante's *Divine Comedy* includes Averroes in a rather favourable role, see Stigen, *Tenkningens historie* (Ad Notam Gyldendal, 1993).

a role for religion in the political deliberation process and is therefore a clear expression of a theory of constitutional secularity.[72]

The Reformation in Europe, while not being the origin of constitutional secularity, nevertheless marks a shift in the development towards constitutional secularity as a paradigm. Luther's objection to the status and powers of the Catholic Church led him to repudiate every claim by the ecclesiastical authorities to exercise any jurisdiction over temporal affairs.[73] His central belief about the Church was that since the Church is nothing but a *congregation fidelium*, it cannot properly be said to possess any separate jurisdiction at all. Luther's theological premises committed him to both attacking the jurisdictional powers of the Church and filling the power vacuum this created by mounting a corresponding defense of the secular authorities.[74] If the Church was nothing more than a *congregation fidelium*, his argument went, it follows that the secular authorities must have the sole right to exercise all coercive powers, including the powers over the Church.

The Reformation was, however, a far less radical departure from the theocratic constitution and confessional governance. As was the case with the theories of Maimonides, Averroes, and Aquinas in the 12th century, the theoretical justification of the Reformation was based on theological premises, arguing for constitutional secularity with the help of religious rhetoric and based on religious sources. Constitutional secularity was, in other words, championed from within a religious framework.

By contrast, some of Luther's contemporaries and predecessors, including Machiavelli (1469–1527), Marsiglio of Padua (1275–1342), and Dante (1265–1321) mounted much more radical critiques of the religious system of governance and did so from outside the religious framework. In his critique of the Church's power, Marsiglio of Padua suggested that all coercive power must be secular by definition, and thus that the Church could not be regarded as jurisdictional authority at all.[75] Similarly, in *De Monarchia*, published in the early 13th century and later banned by the Catholic Church in 1538, Dante condemns the theocratic conception of power elaborated by the Church.[76]

The idea of constitutional secularity understood as a principle of governance – the idea that political authority ought to be justified in non-religious terms in order to be legitimate – is thus separate from, and precedes the idea of constitutionalism and its translation into modern constitutional developments. This

72 J.G.A. Pocock, *The Machiavellian Moment, Florentine Political Thought and the Atlantic Republican Tradition* (Princeton University Press, 1975); Cass Sunstein, "Beyond the Republican Revival", *Yale Law Journal* [1988] 97 1539–1590.

73 Quentin Skinner, *Foundations of Modern Political Thought*, vol. 2 (Cambridge University Press, 1978) 14.

74 Ibid. 15.

75 Cary Nederman, *Community and Consent: The Secular Political Thought of Marsiglio of Padua's Defensor Pacis* (Rowman and Littlefield Publishers, 1995).

76 Dante Germino, *Machiavelli to Marx: Modern Western Political Thought* (University of Chicago Press, 1972).

would imply that constitutional secularity did not begin with the emergence of constitutionalism, but rather that constitutionalism included the idea of constitutional secularity in its theory of governance, together with a number of other features.

We have previously seen the approach to constitutional secularity as an *idea*. Part of the literature traces constitutional secularity from the historical development of the *term*, as opposed to the existence of *ideas* of secularity regardless of the terminology being used. Charles Taylor, for example, in arguing that secularity comes from a Judeo-Christian tradition bases his argument on the word's terminological origin.[77]

In social sciences, particularly up until the 1980s, secularity was closely linked to an understanding of modernity,[78] the idea being that modernization would lead to secularity, formulated as the *secularization thesis or theory*.[79]

In terms of public law theories and constitutional developments, constitutional secularity dominated both the theory of public law and the practice in constitutional developments in the 20th century. However, critiques and challenges towards the secular order increased towards the end of the century and in particular with the fall of the Berlin Wall. Since the 1990s, there has been an increased scholarly attention to the compatibility of religion with human rights and constitutionalism both at the national level and at the international level. Part of this scholarship has sought to provide a theoretical justification for the inclusion of religion in constitutional design. This has also been reflected in policy changes and the adoption of, or support for, constitutions with a stronger religious language, based on arguments such as constitutionalism not being "one size fits all", or that constitutionalism does not require constitutional secularity as long as fundamental rights are respected.[80]

3.2.3 Constitutional secularity in constitutional developments

In the practice of constitutional law, the general constitutional development has been one which develops towards equal liberty as a constitutive element of constitutionalism, and a reduction of what were once self-evident legal hierarchies of personhood justified through references to religion and to non-religious ideologies. The development towards equal liberty has also entailed a development

77 Taylor argues that "secular" is a Christian concept that has to be understood in light of a Christian text.

78 Peter Berger, *The Sacred Canopy: Elements of a Sociological Theory of Religion* (Doubleday, 1967).

79 For an overview of the origin of the theory and subsequent approaches, see William Swatos and Daniel Olson (eds), *The Secularization Debate* (Rowman and Littlefield Publishers, 2010).

80 An example of such an approach to reject constitutional secularity is found in Michael Perry, "Why Political Reliance on Religiously Grounded Morality is not Illegitimate in a Liberal Democracy", *Wake Forrest Law Review* [2001] 36 217.

towards constitutional secularity and has been integral to the development of constitutionalism. Translated into constitutional norms, constitutional secularity overlaps in time with the consolidation of states. The modern constitution reflects a consolidation of the state based on national, rather than religious identity.[81] Constitutional secularity has come to mean that some of the functions of religious authorities are taken over by the state, are privatized, or are left to the individual's autonomous sphere.[82] Constitutional secularity also presumes and allows for a public–private divide, where religion or faith are considered as individual matters belonging to the private sphere. Constitutional secularity is thus an integral part of constitutionalism, as it is a condition for equal liberty.

At the same time, there are a number of constitutional developments that seek and have sought the reversal of both equal liberty and constitutional secularity. Take, for example, the confessional South African constitutions under apartheid, which established and legitimized a hierarchy of persons based on skin color and ethnicity.[83] Another example is the departure from the Weimar Constitution by the National Socialist Party in Germany and its replacement by the program of *Gleichschaltung* whereby parts of the population were deprived of personhood altogether.[84]

While the idea of constitutional secularity has existed for a long time, it was with the modern constitutions adopted in the 18th century and the US and French constitutions that the idea of constitutional secularity was translated into a legally binding, normative framework for the State. Prior to this, constitutional secularity existed primarily as a normative theory, as an idea.[85] Both the US and French constitutions established a new political system that differed fundamentally from the one they had replaced, and both revolutions and subsequent constitutions sought to put an end to the absolutism of the post-feudal state.[86] This was also

81 András Sájo, "Preliminaries to a concept of constitutional secularism", *International Journal of Constitutional Law* [2008] 6:3/4 605–629.

82 Ibid. 609.

83 See, for example, the 1983 Constitution of South Africa, in its Preamble and Articles 52(1) a, and 100(1) ii, ix, and xii, and the Persons of Colour Act enacted under the constitution. Christian denominations, in particular the Dutch Reformed Church, openly supported racial segregation. See Miranda L. Joetgen, "Learning from Mistakes of the Past: Christianity, Apartheid and Social Movement Framing", *Bridge/Work* 2:1, article 6. In describing the legal system of the South African apartheid, David Dyzenhaus applies the notion "wicked legal systems", referring to legal orders in which law "is used as the instrument of an immoral political ideology". David Dyzenhaus, *Hard Cases in Wicked Legal Systems: Pathologies of Legality* (Oxford University Press, 2010).

84 David Dyzenhaus, ibid.

85 Some commentators articulate the shift represented by the American and French revolutions as a shift that turned philosophy into law. See Michel Rosenfeld and Andràs Sajó (eds), *Oxford Handbook of Comparative Constitutional Law* (Oxford University Press, 2012) 8; Giovanni Sartori, "Constitutionalism: A Preliminary Discussion", *American Political Science Review* [1962] 56:4 860.

86 Dieter Grimm, "The Achievement of Constitutionalism", in Petra Dobner and Martin Loughlin (eds), *The Twilight of Constitutionalism?* (Oxford University Press, 2010) 5.

reflected in changes in the use of "constitution" as a notion. Whereas before the 18th century, "constitution" was usually used to describe the state of a country, after the 18th century, this use of the word no longer held true.[87] The shift from a mere descriptive notion of "constitution" to "constitution" used in a normative sense implied that it took more to qualify as a "constitution" than used to be the case. A concrete articulation of the shift is found in the French Declaration of the Rights of Man and Citizens of 1789, which in Article 16 stipulates that "a society in which the guarantee of rights is not ensured, nor a separation of power is worked out, has no Constitution". Constitutionalism would therefore come to represent a particular form for the justification, legitimacy, and power of government and its relationship with people under its jurisdiction.

3.2.3.1 Confessional and non-confessional states

The first two modern constitutions, the American and French, mark a break with the confessional state. These were, nevertheless, exceptions in the wave of constitution-making that begun in the 19th century and continued in the 20th century. Most constitutions adopted a state religion, making the state a confessional state, as had been the case since the Treaty of Westphalia in 1648. Over the 20th century, the constitutional developments have, however, seen a weakening of the role of the state religion. This has partly been supported through international human rights law and regional law, in particular, provisions on equality and nondiscrimination. In Europe, the European Court of Human Rights has, for example, supported the development of a reduced role of the state religion based on individual liberty and autonomy.

The Peace of Westphalia of 1648 is often referred to as the first attempt to establish a European order with a secular political foundation, marking the beginning of modern statehood.[88] But it was with the American and French revolutions that constitutional secularity was translated into binding constitutional norms. In the 18th and 19th centuries, the bond between the "Crown and the Altar" was challenged and this brought more separation between church and state. Political power had to be legitimized by the nation instead of God. A strict separation as prescribed by the French 1905 Act on the Separation between Church and State was, however, quite rare. In Eastern Europe, the Russian Revolution in 1917 brought an abrupt end to the close bond between the Tsar and the Orthodox Church, and "scientifically based" atheism was instructed from kindergarten to university.[89]

87 Martin Loughlin, "What is Constitutionalism?" in Petra Dobner and Martin Louhglin (eds), *The Twilight of Constitutionalism?* (Oxford University Press, 2010) 48; Dieter Grimm, "Types of Constitutions", in Michael Rosenfeld and Andràs Sajó (eds), *Oxford Handbook of Comparative Constitutional Law* (Oxford University Press, 2012) 101.

88 Dag Michalsen, *Rett en Internasjonal Historie* (Pax Forlag, 2011) 239 and 306.

89 Elena Lisovskaya and Vyacheslav Karpov, "Orthodoxy, Islam, and Desecularization of Russia's State Schools", *Politics and Religion* [2010] 3:2 276–302. State-sponsored atheism was

The latter part of the 20th century and the 21st century and the increasing and more dynamic globalization took the constitutional church-state relationship into a new phase. Religion itself was globalizing and challenged the territorially based national religion of the confessional state.

Within the category of confessional constitutions, we find a range of different forms of arrangements.[90] On one end, we find constitutions that establish an official state religion, but without granting it any further role in the legal order. These can be categorized as "symbolic confessional constitutions". Yet, the symbolic reference to religion may in practice have implications on governance. On the other end are constitutions that establish a theocracy. In between the symbolic confessional constitutions and theocratic constitutions, we find a variety of models where the official state religion is given different degrees of influence in the legal system, whether in legislation, education, policy-making, or state institutions. And similarly, the degree of state influence over religious affairs differs.

The notion of a "state church" has historically been a European phenomenon linked with the history of Europe's monarchies.[91] Historically, under the state church arrangement, the state had influence over religious affairs. Today, the monarch's role is more symbolic, even though the state church enjoys certain privileges. Constitutionally recognized state churches include the Roman Catholic Church, the Evangelical Lutheran Church, the Armenian Apostolic Holy Church, the Anglican Church of England, and the Presbyterian Church of Scotland. With the exception of the Constitution of Liechtenstein, which explicitly proclaims the Roman Catholic Church as the state church, Roman Catholicism is normally established as the state religion and not as the state church, because the Holy See is vested with the central government of this church.

England and Scotland have each their national church, whereas in Northern Ireland and Wales, the Anglican Church of Ireland and the Anglican Church in Wales have been disestablished since 1871 and 1920, respectively.[92] There is currently no constitution that declares Christianity as such as a state religion, although some constitutions refer to the "Christian heritage" or "culture" in the constitution.[93] Normally it is a specific Christian denomination that is established as state

not explicitly provided for under the Soviet 1918 Constitution, which only stated the following in Article 13: "For the purpose of securing to the workers real freedom of conscience, the church is to be separated from the state and the school from the church, and the right of religious and anti-religious propaganda is accorded to every citizen".

90 Several studies have analysed state-religion relationships at a global comparative constitutional level. I base this section on the study by Jeroen Temperman, *State-Religion Relationships and Human Rights Law: Towards a Right to Religiously Neutral Governance* (Martinus Nijhoff Publishers, 2010).

91 Ibid. 44.

92 Ibid. 47–48.

93 See, for example, the Constitution of Norway (1814) which following amendments in 2012 transformed the original state-church arrangement, and included the following reference in Article 2: "Our values will remain our Christian and humanist heritage. This Constitution shall ensure democracy, a state based on the rule of law and human rights".

religion or state church. The Roman Catholic State of the Vatican City is the clearest contemporary example of a Christian state, where the Pope is simultaneously Head of the Government of the State of the Vatican City as well as leader of the Roman Catholic Church, and possesses absolute authority over the legislative, executive, and judicial branches.[94,95] Roman Catholicism is established as the state religion in Costa Rica, Malta, and Monaco.[96] According to the Constitution of Malta, for example, the "authorities of the Roman Catholic Apostolic Church have the duty and the right to teach which principles are right and which are wrong".[97]

A number of constitutions proclaim a religious identity for the state. Israel is established as a "Jewish State", under the Declaration of the Establishment of the State of Israel of 1948 and the basic laws of Israel. The polysomic adjective "Jewish" can refer to both the people adhering to Judaism as a religion, but also to Jews as a people. The Declaration of Independence does not give an answer to this question. Some commentators argue that the omission in itself suggests that the drafters had a secular Jewish state in mind, or at least that the intention was not to establish a clear-cut religious state.

Several contemporary constitutions establish an "Islamic state" or "Islamic Republic": Afghanistan, Bahrain, Brunei Darussalaam, Iran, Mauritania, Oman, Pakistan, Saudi Arabia, and Yemen.[98] Such constitutions expressly declare Islam as the state religion. As the last remaining sultanates, Brunei Darussalam and Oman are somewhat unique.[99] The title of the head of state is a "Sultan", an Islamic hereditary title, where the holder of the title is bestowed with both spiritual and political authority. The constitutions of Iran and Brunei are unique in that they establish a specific branch of Islam as the state religion. Iran is the only state establishing the Shi'a branch of Islam as the official religion, and even more specifically the "Twelver" sect of Shi'a Islam.[100] Brunei establishes a particular

94 New Fundamental Law of the State of the Vatican City (2000) and the Lateran Pacts of 1929.

95 Article 1 of the New Fundamental Law of the State of the Vatican City (2000).

96 Constitution of the Republic of Costa Rica (1949), Article 75; Constitution of Malta (1964), Article 2; and Constitution of the Principality of Monaco (1962), Article 9.

97 Constitution of Malta, Article 2(1) and (2).

98 Constitution of the Islamic Republic of Afghanistan (2004), Article 1; Constitution of the Kingdom of Bahrain (2002), Article 1; Constitution of Brunei Darussalam (1959), Preamble and Articles 1–2; Constitution of the Islamic Republic of Iran (1979); Constitution of Mauritania (1991), Article 1; Basic Statute of the State of Oman (1996), Article 1; Constitution of the Islamic Republic of Pakistan (1973), Article 1; Basic Law of Saudi Arabia (1992), Article 1; and Constitution of the Republic of Yemen (1990), Article 1.

99 Constitution of Brunei Darussalam, Article 4 and the Basic Statute of Oman, Articles 1 and 5. A related form of government is found in Malaysia, where the Constitution establishes a sultanate without expressly declaring a religious state. Nonetheless, nine out of the thirteen states that compose the Federation of Malaysia are either sultanates or formed after a sultanate. For these states, the King is the "head of the religion of Islam".

100 Constitution of Iran (1979), Article 12. The Shi'a doctrine holds that the 12th imam since his disappearance at a young age has been hidden and that he will one day resurrect. In the meantime, Ayatollahs are to rule in his place.

Sunni branch as the state religion.[101] In these constitutions, the role of religion is comprehensive, and is involved in the constitutional regulation of legislative, executive, and judicial activities.

In addition to the states declared as "Islamic state" or "Islamic Republic", a number of constitutions establish Islam as the official state religion without declaring the state as such as an "Islamic republic" or "Islamic state". This includes the constitutions of Algeria, Bangladesh, Djibouti, Egypt, Iraq, Jordan, Kuwait, Libya, Malaysia, the Maldives, Qatar, Somalia, Tunisia, and the UAE.

Some constitutions are monotheistic states without defining any particular religion. The Indonesian constitution, for example, proclaims that the "State shall be based upon the belief in the One and Only God".[102] A number of other constitutions make more generic references to God, without explicitly establishing any particular religion.[103]

The role of the state religion in confessional states varies considerably. One feature that is often found in many confessional states is that the official state religion is a criterion for the head of state. A survey from 2014 found that 30 constitutions require the head of state to have a particular religious affiliation.[104] These include both republics and monarchies. Andorra and Lebanon require that the head of state is Christian.[105] Bhutan and Thailand require that the head of state be Buddhist. Afghanistan, Algeria, Brunei, Iran, Jordan, Malaysia, the Maldives, Mauritania, Morocco, Oman, Pakistan, Qatar, Saudi Arabia, Somalia, Syria, Tunisia, and Yemen require the head of state to be Muslim. In addition, another 19 states have religious requirements for ceremonial monarchs who serve as head of state. The UK, Australia, Canada, and New Zealand have Queen Elizabeth II, known as the "Defender of the Faith" as their head of state. Other countries in this category are Denmark, Norway, and Sweden.

The requirement that the head of state belong to the official state religion is a remnant of the historical conception of state sovereignty and its identification with the head of state.[106] By contrast, the US Constitution specifically prohibits

101 Constitution of Brunei Darussalam (1959), Article 3(1) establishing Shafi'i Islam as the official state religion.

102 Constitution of the Republic of Indonesia (1945), Article 29.

103 Examples of such states are Saint Kitts and Nevis; Antigua and Barbuda; Barbados; Belize; Canada; Dominica; Grenada; and Trinidad and Tobago.

104 http://www.pewresearch.org/fact-tank/2014/07/22/in-30-countries-heads-of-state-must-belong-to-a-certain-religion.

105 Constitution of Andorra (1993), Article 43. In Lebanon, the consociational system has historically been based on the unwritten National Pact dating from Lebanon's independence in 1943. Today, the legal basis for the consociational system is the *Ta'if* Accord of 1989.

106 For an account of this development, see Kristoffer Lidén and Henrik Syse, "The Politics of Peace and Law: Realism, Internationalism and the Cosmopolitan Challenge", in Cecilia Bailliet and Kjetil Larsen (eds), *Promoting Peace Through International Law* (Oxford University Press, 2015) 21–42.

any kind of "religious test" as a qualification for holding federal or state public office.[107]

Some commentators draw a distinction between constitutions that declare a state secular or *laïque* on the one hand, and constitutions that declare a separation of religion and state on the other.[108] The secularist/*laïque* arrangement is typically described as an arrangement where the state not only has no official religion but also restricts aspects of the display of religion in the public sphere to preserve neutrality. This model is associated with the French and Turkish constitutions.[109] By contrast, under the separationist arrangement, the state neither gives preference to any particular religion nor does it restrict any aspects of religion in the public sphere.

While the modern state in the vast majority of cases emerged as a confessional state, the development of constitutionalism has contributed to a development towards increased constitutional secularity. This trend is reflected in global constitutional developments. According to one study that looks into 188 countries, 111 had a state religion in the year 1900, while the number went down to 75 in the year 2000.[110]

Constitutional secularity is a matter of degree. It remains fragmented in most systems that identify as secular. In France, for example, *laïcité* does not apply in Alsace-Moselle, and in the country as a whole, church buildings are subsidized, which may also be viewed not as an exception from the principle of *laïcité*, but equally reflecting a protection of cultural heritage. In Turkey, despite secularity enshrined in the constitution, there is mandatory religious instruction in public schools that is based exclusively on Sunni Islam. The government has expanded religious schools to create, in the words of the president "a pious generation".[111] Because of the widely diverse practices of constitutional secularity, the concept remains fuzzy. In addition, many states are *de facto* constitutionally secular, yet do not expressly recognize the concept in the constitution.

Only exceptionally has constitutional secularity been expressly written into the constitution. The American non-establishment model has translated into a fairly strict wall of separation, which requires that the state neither supports

107 US Constitution (1787), Article 6(3).

108 Jonathan Fox, *A World Survey of Religion and the State* (Cambridge University Press, 2008) 385.

109 Ahmet Kuru, *Secularism and State Policies Toward Religion: The United States, France and Turkey* (Cambridge University Press, 2009); Elizabeth Hurd, "The Political Authority of Secularism in International Relations", *European Journal of International Relations* [2004] 10:2 235–262; Jeffrey Haynes, *Democracy and Civil Society in the Third World: Politics and New Political Movements* (Polity Press, 1997).

110 Roger Barro and Rachel McCleary, "Which Countries Have State Religions?" *The Quarterly Journal of Economics* [2005] 120:4 1334–1335.

111 Report by Journalists and Writers Foundation, "Assault on Education in Turkey and Abroad" (2017). Available at: http://jwf.org/jwf/wp-content/uploads/2018/05/ASSAULT-ON-EDUCATION-In-Turkey-And-Abroad-Short-version.pdf.

nor hinders any religion. The German non-establishment clause does not, by contrast, prevent far-reaching forms of interaction and cooperation between state and religion. Sometimes, only specific practices of secularity were written into the constitution, without using the term. In France, the commitment to *laïcité* was constitutionalized as a concept only in 1946.[112] A number of post-communist constitutions have adopted broad non-establishment provisions that proclaim that no ideology may be instituted as official state ideology.[113] These non-establishment provisions go beyond religion, as they also prohibit the establishment of secular ideologies. Some constitutions do not establish or support one specific religion, nor do they position themselves as clear-cut secular or separationist state. The non-identification constitution is characterized by the avoidance of all language that would give evidence of religious preferences on the part of the state. Among non-identification constitutions, we find the constitutions of Bosnia and Herzegovina, Botswana, the Central African Republic, Eritrea, and New Zealand. Within the category of non-confessional constitutions, we find also constitutions that are explicitly secular or that have a non-establishment clause.

3.2.4 Constitutional secularity and international human rights law

Under international human rights law, there is no explicit endorsement or prohibition of specific forms of state-religion identification. This has largely been considered to be a matter that falls within the sovereignty of each state, as long as the state religion does not infringe upon individual rights.

This has led some commentators to draw the conclusion that established religion is not *per se* in conflict with international human rights law.[114] The argument for this position is two-fold. Firstly, it is often held that the intention of the drafter of human rights treaties was not to outlaw established religion. Secondly, that established religion does not *per se* prejudice the religious rights of people who do not adhere to the state religion.

112 Andras Sájo, "Preliminaries to a Concept of Constitutional Secularism", *International Journal of Constitutional Law* [2008] 6:3–4 609. Prior to that, the concept was expressed in ordinary legislation, culminating in the 1905 Act on the separation of church and state, but the laws prior to the constitutionalization in 1946 reflected very different perspectives. Some were anti-clerical, some anti-religious, while others were concerned with the influence of the Catholic Church on political and public life. See Émile Poulat, *Notre Laïcité Public* (Berg International, 2013).

113 See, for example, the constitutions of Belarus, the Czech Republic, Kazakhstan, Moldova, Russia, and Tajikistan.

114 See, for example, Rex Ahdar and Ian Leigh, *Religious Freedom in the Liberal State* (Oxford University Press, 2005); Stephen Neff, "An Evolving International Legal Norm of Religious Freedom: Problems and Prospects", *California Western International Law Journal* [1977] 7:3 543; Malcolm Evans, *Religious Liberty and International Law in Europe* (Cambridge University Press, 1997).

The first argument has limited legal relevance. Human rights law is a constantly evolving body of law, and human rights treaties are considered "living instruments".[115] Moreover, the lack of explicit prohibition of established religions does not necessarily lead us to conclude that it is therefore permissible. In arguing that international human rights law precludes established religion, some commentators have pointed to the *travaux préparatoires*, and their ambiguousness on the issue of religion-state identification.[116]

However, the question remains as to whether a standard for constitutional secularity can be deduced from international human rights law. The UN Human Rights Committee has stated the following regarding established religions:

> The fact that a religion is recognized as a state religion or that it is established as official or traditional or that its followers comprise the majority of the population, shall not result in any impairment of the enjoyment of any of the rights under the Covenant ... nor in any discrimination against adherents to other religions or nonbelievers. In particular, certain measures discriminating against the latter, such as measures restricting eligibility for government service to members of the dominant religion or giving economic privileges to them or imposing special restrictions on the practice of other faiths, are not in accordance with the prohibition of discrimination based on religion or belief and the guarantee of equal protection.[117]

The Human Rights Committee has furthermore held that

> If a set of beliefs is treated as official ideology in constitutions, statutes, proclamations of ruling parties, etc., or in actual practice, this shall not result in any impairment of the freedoms under article 18 or any other rights recognized under the Covenant nor in any discrimination against persons who do not accept the official ideology or who oppose it.[118]

International human rights law does not use or define the word "secular", nor does it explicitly establish secularity as a constitutional requirement. On a substantive level, however, the content of international law and its interpretation is secular, in the sense that none of its provisions draw their validity from

115 Daniel Moeckli and Nigel White, "Treaties as 'Living Instruments'", in Dino Kritsiotis and Michael Bowman (eds), *Conceptual and Contextual Perspectives on the Modern Law of Treaties* (Cambridge University Press, 2016).

116 Jeroen Temperman, *State-Religion Relationships and Human Rights Law: Towards a Right to Religiously Neutral Governance* (Martinus Nijhoff Publishers, 2010) 154–157.

117 Human Rights Committee, General Comment No. 22, para. 9.

118 Human Rights Committee, General Comment No. 22. In the area of public education, the Human Rights Committee has stated that the teaching of religion and ethics in schools should be done in a neutral and objective way.

religious arguments, hence leaving the law and its interpretation independent from religion.[119]

To the extent that constitutions are to give force to international human rights law, they are therefore required to respect the secularity of international human rights law, in the sense that international human rights law is to be interpreted in its own terms. Treaty bodies and special procedures have held that human rights law cannot be limited on the basis of religion and that such provisions must be interpreted on their own terms.[120]

While not explicitly prescribing constitutional secularity, international human rights law thus precludes certain ways that an official state religion can be entrenched, and provides some legal benchmarks for constitutional design with respect to official state religions. In a more direct fashion, the Human Rights Committee and other monitoring bodies have addressed the issue of established religion in their reviews of individual State compliance with the ICCPR. In this regard, they have repeatedly pointed out the difficulty of reconciling the existence of an established religion with states' human rights obligations.[121] For example, in its review of the Dominican Republic, the Committee on the Elimination of All Forms of Discrimination against Women (CEDAW) stressed that "Steps should be taken to ensure the de facto separation of the secular and religious spheres, with a view to ensuring the full implementation of the Convention".[122]

119 In the context of limitations to the right to freedom of religion or belief, the Human Rights Committee has, for example, held that such limitations must be based on principles not deriving exclusively from one tradition, General Comment No. 22.

120 See, for example, CEDAW Article 12(1); Human Rights Committee, General Comment No. 34.

121 For example, A/56/40 Vol.I (2001) 49 para. 77 (25) regarding Venezuela : "The privileged status of the Roman Catholic Church … is of concern"; CCPR/C/SR.1128(1992), para. 38 (Algeria); A/46/40(1991), para. 341 (Sweden); A/36/40(1998), para. 466 (Norway). Other treaty bodies, for example, the Committee on Economic, Social and Cultural Rights, have also addressed this issue; see, for example, E/1999/22 (1998) 43 RPA 236 (Israel): "It is of concern that excessive emphasis upon the State as a 'Jewish State' encourages discrimination and accords a second-class status to its non-Jewish citizens".

122 CEDAW Committee, A/53/38/rev. 1 part 1 (1998) para. 351 (Dominican Republic).

Part III

The past, the present, and the perhaps: constitutional desecularization in context

4 Political change and constitutional change in Afghanistan, Iran, and Iraq

Two major transitions mark the modern constitutional history of Afghanistan, Iran, and Iraq. The first is the transition to modern constitutions, largely unfolding at the turn of the 20th century. This was a transition from feudal systems (Iran and Iraq) and tribal systems (Afghanistan) without unified legislation, subject to absolute rule, yet with multiple competing authorities, including the clergy, and with a concept of rights based on that of religious law and tradition and their justification of a hierarchical distribution. The transition represented by the transition to, and adoption of, modern constitutions introduced constitutional rights in their modern conception, justified and guaranteed by constitutions with a scope that had up to then been unprecedented. While several of the rights would fall short of today's standards, the scope of those able to enjoy these rights was gradually expanded over the course of the 20th century. Moreover, the first transition to modern constitutions involved a centralization of political authority in the state, transferring power previously in the hands of others, including the clergy, to the state and newly established institutions, forming the beginning of modern bureaucracy.

The second major transition is represented by what we can refer to as constitutional desecularization, taking place at the end of the 20th century (Iran) and in the beginning of the 21st century (Afghanistan and Iraq). In all three countries, constitutional desecularization took place following a regime change, either through revolution (Iran) or war (Afghanistan). While the first transition had involved a considerable weakening of the role of religion in the exercise of political authority, the second transition involves a general strengthening of religious language in a historically unprecedented ways, again largely affecting the conception of rights and the scope of such rights, including equal liberty, in ways that are a reminder of the conception of rights that ruled prior to the first transition, only this time, the scope of rights was reversed.

Common to the processes of constitutional desecularization as they unfolded in Afghanistan, Iran, and Iraq is that they did not take place through constitutional amendments, nor did they take place within the framework of the existing constitution. Instead, they were the result of a complete regime change and a transition brought about through revolution or war. Thus, we are speaking of a context that consists of more than a mere shift in political power; it consists of an entire shift of the political system through an overthrow of the preceding one. In such a context, the constitutional drafting processes in the three countries found itself largely in the shadow of the political turmoil and instability that followed the regime changes. Despite efforts to give the constitutional drafting process an appearance of legitimacy through the inclusion of formal procedures such as the holding of constitutional referenda and seemingly consultative processes, the constitutional drafting processes in the three countries fall significantly short of late 20th- and early 21st-century standards for constitution-making. In the case of Afghanistan and Iraq, the processes could be characterized as involving "too many cooks", with few meaningful deliberative and consultative processes, which in any event would have been extremely challenging in a war-torn society, and these processes were furthermore administered by the occupying powers, international actors, and experts. In the case of Iran, the initial drafting process that had involved a broader segment of the actors of the revolution was soon taken over by the Islamic faction with the support of the main communist party that, after placing the majority of the drafting committee with members of the clergy, turned the initial Republican draft into a constitution that reflected the ideological project of Khomeini and which set the framework for a contemporary theocracy. The Constitution was reported to receive 99.5% approval in the constitutional referendum in December 1979, with a turnout of approximately 71%, despite calls for a boycott by several political groups, both religious and secular. The main communist party, by contrast, urged people to vote yes to the theocratic constitution.

Despite the distinctive character of constitutional desecularization in Afghanistan, Iran, and Iraq, some general features can be observed. First, religion is stated as a justification for political authority, and, in the case of Afghanistan and Iran, also as an aim of governance. Secondly, religion is established as a justificatory ground for the scope and limitation of rights. Thirdly, the clergy is established as a central actor in existing institutions or in newly created institutions, including in the judiciary. Fourthly, affiliation to the state religion is established as a criterion to hold certain positions, including in the executive, legislative, and judicial branch. Fifthly, the conceptualization of rights is changed to one where rights are understood within a religious framework and limited through religious language.

4.1 The constitutional past

Leaving aside the differences between Afghanistan, Iran, and Iraq, the three countries share some central similarities in their constitutional developments in the 20th century. The legal orders of the three countries underwent significant change in the late 19th and early 20th century, with the first half of the 20th century seeing state-building and rapid modernization. As a result, many functions that had previously been held by the clergy or that had been in the hands of private actors were moved first by law and, increasingly, in practice to a centralized state. The formal role of religion in the legal sphere was correspondingly reduced. At the same time, gaining strength in the second half of the 20th century, particularly in Afghanistan and Iran, Islamic political movements sought to push forward an agenda with an increased role for Islam, not just in the political sphere, but also in the legal order. In Iran, this culminated with the Islamic Revolution in 1979, resulting in an Islamic ideological constitution. In Afghanistan, the Taliban, that had been supported and trained with extensive support by external actors as a force against Soviet influence, held power in the period 1996–2001, and ruled without a constitution, enforcing strict fundamentalist interpretations of Islamic law. In Iraq, a country with a largely secular constitutional past, Islamization at the constitutional level took place for the first time under the current Constitution of 2005. In all three countries, the contemporary interaction between politicized religion and law is not only justified by the legal order but has been constitutionally prescribed as a mandatory interaction through legal requirements.

The modern constitutional history of Afghanistan, Iran, and Iraq dates back to the first half of the 20th century, with the arrival and emergence of the idea of constitutionalism in the region. The first constitutions were adopted in 1906–1907 (Iran),[1] in 1923 (Afghanistan), and in 1925 (Iraq), replacing a form of governance characterized by absolute and arbitrary rule. A central feature of the new constitutions was precisely the regulation and conditioning of the exercise of political authority, the introduction of rights, and the reduction of the power of religious actors and institutions, instead moving these powers to a centralized state in the making.

Although the first constitutions were confessional, in the sense that they established an official state religion, there were different origins for the high degree of constitutional secularity in the first constitutions of the three countries. In Iran, this high degree of constitutional secularity came as a result of the processes that were part of the Constitutional Revolution.[2] Led by an elite, the Constitutional Revolution included large segments of society, including women. In Afghanistan, constitutional secularity was a policy led by the monarch in an attempt to modernize the state internally and strengthen it externally. In Iraq, constitutional secularity in the second half of the 20th century was largely enforced by the Ba'ath party as part of its secular and socialist political identity. Despite the three different origins for constitutional secularity in the three countries, the arguments in support of the necessity for a secular constitution were to a large extent similar.

1 The first Iranian Constitution was adopted in 1906, with a supplement adopted in 1907. In the following, I will refer to the first constitution as the Constitution of 1906–1907.

2 H.E. Chehabi and Vanessa Martin, *Iran's Constitutional Revolution: Popular Politics, Cultural Transformations and Transnational Connections* (Bloomsbury Academic, 2010); Stephen Poulson, *Social Movements in Twentieth Century Iran: Culture, Ideology and Mobilizing Frameworks* (Lexington Books, 2006) 103ff; Mansour Bonakdarian, *Britain and the Iranian Constitutional Revolution of 1906–1911: Foreign Policy, Imperialism and Dissent* (Syracuse University Press, 2006).

A central argument was resistance from foreign influence, at the time represented by Great Britain, Russia, and France, a resistance which was perceived to require a strong state and state-building.

The transition to modern constitutional governments in the three countries involves three distinct types of constitutional births. In Iran, the first modern constitution came following a longer process starting in the mid-1800s and culminating in what has become known as the Constitutional Revolution. In Afghanistan, the first constitution was created by the monarch as a tool for restoration, modernization, and state-building.[3] The first Iraqi constitution was a product of British colonial power.[4] What the three constitutions have in common is that they were monarchical constitutions adopted in a context in part characterized by internal crisis and in part as a response to the external power struggle between the great powers.

By the 19th century, Afghanistan, Iran, and Iraq could be placed into two geo-political narratives. Iraq was part of the Ottoman Empire, while Afghanistan and Iran found themselves caught in the strategic rivalry between Great Britain and Russia. The AngloRussian conflict about influence in the strategically important Central Asia began with the Russian-Iranian Treaty of 1813, and its first chapter ended formally with the AngloRussian Convention of 1907. During this period, state borders were changed, monarchs were inserted and removed, alliances were established and later broken, and wars were initiated and brought to an end. Even if Afghanistan and Iran to a large extent were buffer states, at times they also benefited from the rivalry between the great powers. In Iran, the population grew increasingly dissatisfied with the Qajar dynasty's significant concessions to foreign powers in a time of internal crisis. The dissatisfaction facilitated, if not prompted, the emergence of the constitutional movement.

An additional external factor that we can point to was the increasing gap between Europe and North America on the one hand and the rest of the world on the other in terms of advancements of technology and industrial progress at the time of the emergence of the new constitutions. By the end of the 19th century, the industrial revolution was accelerating at great speed in Europe and North America, but had yet to move eastwards. These technological advances were looked upon with admiration by Afghan, Iranian, and Iraqi constitutionalists who were familiar with them and who presented the technological developments as an argument in their urge for the introduction of constitutions. As one constitutionalist put it: "we can only reach the level of technology in Europe if we also adopt their form of government".[5]

3 Mohammad Kamali, *Law in Afghanistan: A Study of the Constitutions; Matrimonial Law and the Judiciary* (Brill, 1985) 110.

4 Helen Chapin Metz, "Iraq, A Country Study", in Leon Jeffries (ed), *Iraq: Issues, Historical Background, Bibliography* (Nova Science Publishers, 2003) 141ff.

5 Fereydoon Adamiyat, *Eide-ology Nahzate Mashroutiyate Iran* (in Farsi) (Gostareh Publications, 2009); Ahmad Kasravi, *Tarikh-e Mashrute-ye Iran* (in Farsi) (Sepehr, 1991).

Among the internal factors, the most significant can be found in the precarious economic, social, and political situation, leading to increasing social unrest. By the mid-19th century, Afghanistan, Iran, and Iraq were societies where the basis for political authority was taken to be the divinely ordained system of aristocracy, monarchy, land-ownership, and ecclesiastical authority. Absolutism did not, however, overlap with a unity of power. As in most early feudal societies, political and judicial power were obtained through private transaction and held as a private good, largely by four main groups: the monarch and the royal family; the higher clergy; merchants; and landowners and tribes. Through this system emerged what one commentator has described as "private islands" of judicial independence that proliferated outside vertical power relations.[6] In Afghanistan, Iran, and Iraq, these "private islands" were further intensified because of the system of Islamic law, whereby the law was administered by individual jurists who operated independently of one another.[7] Power was thus in the hands of many, and while the system of governance was absolutist, it was therefore also decentralized, rather than unitary. The de-centralized power was, moreover, increasingly arbitrarily, unevenly, and often violently executed.[8]

In the region, the clergy had in the last 300 years before the 20th century acquired significant power and wealth. In the absence of a strong central state, the clergy increasingly gained an influential role as arbiters in judicial, social, and commercial matters. Particularly in Iran, the clergy's ownership of religious foundations, "*waqfs*", which were exempted from taxation, reinforced their power.[9] Moreover, the wealthier class of the clergy also engaged in trade and accumulated considerable wealth that reinforced their traditionally close relationship with the merchant class. By the mid-19th century, the lack of security, lack of predictability, and harsh punishments in the legal system, combined with an economic crisis blamed on financial mismanagement created social unrest and an increasingly weak state. While people articulated their cry for change through general demands for "justice", a term familiar also from the religious tradition, some members of society began articulating more specific demands for a system that could limit and condition the exercise of power and the establishment of institutions that could execute power in a more consistent and organized way. The introduction of modern constitutions, under the influence of constitutionalism, came to be seen as necessary, both as a means to repair the state from within, to be able to compete with foreign states in terms of industrial and technological development, and to be able to resist the great foreign powers and their influence. To this end, one needed a centralized and strong state and a professionalized

6 Chris Thornhill, *A Sociology of Constitutions: Constitutions and State Legitimacy in Historical-Sociological Perspective* (Cambridge University Press, 2011) 21.

7 Knut Vikør, *Mellom Gud og stat: Ei historie om islamsk lov og rettsvesen* (Spartacus Forlag, 2003).

8 Vanessa Martin, *Islam and Modernism: The Iranian Revolution of 1906* (Syracuse University Press, 1989) 48–51.

9 Ibid.

bureaucracy whereby power would be transferred from multiple power-holders, including from the merchants and the clergy, to a centralized state.

4.1.1 The 20th-century constitutional developments

Afghanistan

The legal landscape in Afghanistan over the 20th century has consisted of three competing sources of law: local customary practice, Islamic law, and centralized state law. Prior to the latest Constitution of 2004, Afghanistan had six constitutions: adopted in 1923, 1931, 1964, 1976, 1987, and 1990, respectively.

At the turn of the century and prior to the adoption of the first constitution, Afghanistan was a hereditary monarchy without a written constitution. The society was largely tribal, comprised of different tribes on the basis of ethnicity and was regulated through Islamic law and customary law, including the Pashtunwali, which was the tribal code of Pashtun peoples. Tribal councils (*Jirga* or *majlis*) adjudicated disputes within a tribe according to local traditions. The *de facto* state power was shared between the monarch and the tribes, and the clergy performed an adjudicatory role. The clergy was granted large allowances and privileges for the administration of justice in accordance with their interpretation of Islamic principles.[10]

Until the formation of the modern Afghan state in the late 19th century, the clergy and religious legal scholars, "*ulama*", were largely independent in their administration of justice.[11] They both provided a body of laws and were the judges interpreting it. Unified state legal codes were first introduced in Afghanistan in the early 20th century, after the adoption of the first constitution. Under the reign of King Amanullah Khan (1919–1929), Afghanistan for the first time introduced state law codes designed to supersede the system of religious law, although religious law was to remain in force in the absence of any state regulation. The king also began appointing non-clerics as judges to staff the courts using the new national codes.

Afghanistan, like neighboring Iran, was subject to significant foreign influence due to the strategic rivalry in the region between Russia and Great Britain at the turn of the 20th century. Britain viewed Afghanistan as a buffer state that would guard India against Russian expansion. As a result, a number of wars were initiated, known as the Anglo-Afghan Wars. It was in the aftermath of one of these wars that King Amanullah Khan acceded to the Afghan throne in 1919, defeating the British. Familiar with and informed of the modernization efforts undertaken in the Ottoman Empire, Amanullah Khan began adopting a series

10 Mohammad Kamali, *Law in Afghanistan: A Study of the Constitutions, Matrimonial Law and the Judiciary* (Brill Academic Publishers, 1985).

11 Thomas Barfield, *Afghanistan: A Cultural and Political History* (Princeton University Press, 2010).

of ambitious legal reforms.[12] Among the reforms was the adoption of the first Afghan Constitution in 1923, transforming the country from absolute monarchy to a constitutional monarchy. The 1923 Constitution was based on the 1906 Iranian Constitution and the 1921 Constitution of Atatürk in Turkey.[13] It contained a bill of rights that guaranteed that all Afghan subjects would "have equal rights and duties to the country in accordance with *Shari'a* and the laws of the state".[14] The Constitution moreover abolished torture, slavery, and forced labor, and, rather boldly for its time, provided that followers of religions other than Islam were entitled to the protection of the state. Elementary education was made compulsory for boys and girls, and freedom of the press, freedom of association, and property rights were guaranteed explicitly by the Constitution. The judiciary, moreover, was made independent. One particularly controversial reform was that Hindu and Jewish Afghans were no longer required to wear distinctive dress marking their status, as had been the norm up until then. In addition to the new Constitution, the King also introduced legislative reforms, including laws that outlawed child marriage, marriages between close relatives, polygamy, excessive dowries, and the exchange of women as "blood money" in interfamilial disputes, as well as establishing programs for women students to travel abroad for higher education.[15]

With regard to the role of religion, the 1923 Constitution contained a number of references to Islam. Islam was established as the religion of the state and the King was the "servant and the protector of the true religion of Islam".[16] Article 72 provided that legislators had to give "careful" consideration to the requirements of the laws of the *Shari'a*. However, in more moderate terms, this provision also stated that in the process of legislation, actual living conditions of the people and the requirements of the time would be given serious consideration *in addition* to the rules of the *Shari'a*. The constitution provided that "all disputes and cases will be decided in accordance with the principles of *Shari'a* and of general civil and criminal laws".[17] But unlike the Iranian Constitution that had established a clerical review body to ensure legislation's compatibility with Islam, the Afghan Constitution of 1923 had no Islamic supremacy clause, and no institutionalized process for review, rendering the state religion's role in legislation more symbolic.[18]

12 Leon Pullada, *Reform and Rebellion in Afghanistan, 1919–1929: King Amanullah's Failure to Modernize a Tribal Society* (Cornell University Press, 1973) 66.

13 Nighat Chisti, *Constitutional Development in Afghanistan* (Royal Book Co., 1998).

14 Constitution of Afghanistan (1923), Article 16.

15 Ahmad Dawood and Tom Ginsburg, "Constitutional Islamization and Human Rights: The Surprising Origin and Spread of Islamic Supremacy in Constitutions", *University of Chicago Public Law & Legal Theory Working Paper* [2014] No. 477 49.

16 Constitution of Afghanistan (1923), Article 5.

17 Constitution of Afghanistan (1923), Article 72.

18 Ahmad Dawood and Tom Ginsburg, "Constitutional Islamization and Human Rights: The Surprising Origin and Spread of Islamic Supremacy in Constitutions", *University of Chicago*

The Constitution was considerably liberal in the Afghan and regional context of its time.[19] While it was written absent a consultative process on the part of those outside of government, it established the foundation for political participation and brought significant social and political changes to the country.

Despite the King invoking Islamic principles in support for his reforms, the Constitution was perceived as too progressive by conservative segments and groups in society. The religious elite and the tribes saw the constitutional provisions on individual rights as an attack on what they perceived to be traditional values, culture, and religion. Conservatives objected to the provisions on compulsory education for girls, the abolition of the requirement for Hindus and Jews to wear distinct clothing, the free press, restrictions on polygamy and child marriage, and to what they saw as a failure of the Constitution to identify the Hanafi School of Islamic jurisprudence as the leading school of law.[20] A revolt broke out in 1924, with the clergy at the forefront of the opposition. The clergy saw the efforts of King Amanullah Khan to codify Islamic law as a means to "secularize" the law that would dilute the social force of Islam and encroaching upon their previously held prerogatives. The rebellion was, however, also partially caused by the introduction of universal conscription and tax reforms, efforts at centralization, and state-building, which all significantly affected tribal autonomy.[21]

In the midst of the rebellion and facing regime collapse, King Amanullah called the *Loya Jirga* to review and possibly reconsider certain provisions of the Constitution and of legislation.[22] In addition to the repeal of some of the laws, the clerics of the *Loya Jirga* urged that Article 2 of the Constitution be amended to declare the Hanafi School of Islam as the official school of religious jurisprudence. They also demanded that restrictions on nonMuslims be reinstated. Rights granted to women were diluted, the prohibition of torture was removed, the prior abolition of child marriage and polygamy rescinded, and Hindu and Jewish Afghans were again to pay a special tax and wear distinctive signs as a marker of their identity. Furthermore, similar to the Iranian Constitution, an Islamic supremacy clause was inserted and a Council of Islamic Scholars was provided with the authority to review the compatibility of new legislation with

Public Law & Legal Theory Working Paper [2014] No. 477 47. The authors argue that unlike the first constitution of Iran, the Afghan Constitution of 1923 failed to balance constitutional rights with Islam, leading to its demise.

19 Ramin Moschtaghi, "Structure and Principles of the State", in Tilmann Röder (ed), *Max Planck Manual on Afghan Constitutional Law*, vol. 1 (Max Planck Institute for Comparative Public Law and International Law, 2009) 15.

20 Leon Pullada, *Reform and Rebellion in Afghanistan, 1919–1929: King Amanullah's Failure to Modernize a Tribal Society* (Cornell University Press, 1973) 85; Mohammad Kamali, *Law in Afghanistan: A Study of the Constitutions, Matrimonial Law and the Judiciary* (Brill Academic Publishers, 1985) 28.

21 Ahmad Dawood and Tom Ginsburg, "Constitutional Islamization and Human Rights: The Surprising Origin and Spread of Islamic Supremacy in Constitutions", *University of Chicago Public Law & Legal Theory Working Paper* [2014] No. 477 51.

22 Leon Pullada, *Reform and Rebellion in Afghanistan, 1919–1929: King Amanullah's Failure to Modernize a Tribal Society* (Cornell University Press, 1973) 94.

Islamic law.[23] Article 9 was amended to read that "Afghan subjects are bound by the religious rites and political institutions of Afghanistan". And, the clergy demanded a redefinition of the word "freedom" used in Article 9. In return for these changes, the *Loya Jirga* unanimously approved the Constitution.

During the reigns of succeeding monarchs, the clergy again dominated the judiciary until the end of the 1940s. It was not until 1964 and the Constitution under King Zahir Shah that an explicit provision was adopted stating that state law would override *Shari'a* law where the two were in conflict, but only after asserting in another clause that all laws must comply with the *Shari'a*. Conservative clerics who opposed the social and legal reforms in the 1970s had little influence within the religious establishment.[24] The 1964 Constitution, which was Afghanistan's most stable constitution, introduced a greater degree of democratic participation and was drafted over an 18-month period in a process that for the first time included consultations from society at large.[25] The 1964 Constitution provided, for the first time, for a popularly elected parliament, elected city council, provisional advisory councils, and an independent legislature, starting the period known as "the new democracy" in Afghanistan.

The monarchy came to an end in 1973, following a coup staged by Muhammad Daud.[26] He subsequently proclaimed a republic and a one-party government that adopted a Constitution in 1977 that introduced land reforms, established cooperatives, and declared that women were to enjoy equal rights, and that every citizen above 18 years old had the right to vote. The 1977 Constitution furthermore centralized the judicial order. In 1978, Daoud was overthrown by his Marxist followers. The People's Democratic Party of Afghanistan (PDPA) declared Afghanistan a secular socialist state in 1978, and removed religious figures and religious symbolism from government. The Parliament was replaced with a National Council, while the Revolutionary Council became the highest authority in the state. Revolutionary and extraordinary courts were set up for political offenses, but religious courts were not abolished. There was, however, resistance to the PDPA's policies. In order to win broader support, the new government reverted to the old formula of conformity with Islam, employed by previous governments. It also reintroduced public displays of religiosity. Resistance to the Marxist regime turned into a war after Soviet forces entered Afghanistan in 1978. The fall of the PDPA in 1992 brought the Mujahedeen to power, followed by a civil war ending with the rise of the Taliban. During the Taliban's rule of Afghanistan in the years 1996–2001, state law codes were largely superseded by the Taliban version of the *Shari'a*. Taking advantage of Pashtun nationalism, the

23 Ibid. 122.

24 Thomas Barfield, *Afghanistan: A Cultural and Political History* (Princeton University Press, 2010) 47.

25 Mohammad Kamali, *Law in Afghanistan: A Study of the Constitutions, Matrimonial Law and the Judiciary* (Brill Academic Publishers, 1985).

26 Nighat Chisti, *Constitutional Development in Afghanistan* (Royal Book Co., 1998).

yearning for stability, and not least, considerable assistance from the Pakistan side of the border, the Taliban were able to consolidate their control of the Pashtun areas. Mulla Omar adopted the title "Commander of the faithful" and most ministerial and administrative positions were held by members of the clergy. Hence, the Islamic Emirate of Afghanistan began to implement its version of the Islamic state, in which the *Shari'a* replaced the constitution and all manifestations of what was perceived as so-called "Westernization" were abolished. Women were no longer permitted to work, they were forced to wear a veil covering the whole body, schools for girls were closed, radio and television were permitted only to broadcast religious programs, and music, photography, and games were forbidden. Attendance at prayers became obligatory, and Islamic punishments long discontinued since 1747 were reinstated.

The politicization of religion in Afghanistan gained its paramount implementation under the Taliban. But in the absence of a constitution, this politicization of religion did not take a constitutional form. Instead, the process of constitution making after the 2001 war took place against the international legal framework for the rebuilding of Afghanistan, known as the "Bonn process". The Bonn Agreement set the roadmap for what was stated to be "Afghanistan's transition from a collapsed state to a democratic one".[27] Under the mandate of the Bonn Agreement and the Afghanistan Compact, the United Nations supported the implementation of the roadmap for the establishment of the interim administration and the introduction of constitutional and legislative reforms necessary for the functioning of a democratic state.[28] While considerable international attention was placed on ensuring a democratic constitution, the Constitution that was finally adopted suffered from insufficient legal considerations.[29] As observed by some commentators, the focus was more on meeting the deadlines of the Bonn Agreement rather than developing a legally consistent document. The Afghan Constitution was first drafted by a Constitution Commission, established by the Bonn Agreement in December 2001.[30] Two months after the beginning of the war against the Taliban, the main leaders of the Afghan opposition met in Bonn under the auspices of the UN. The Bonn Agreement provided for the transfer of powers and of Afghan sovereignty to a provisional governmental structure for the state, called the Afghan Interim Authority (AIA). This was made up of an interim

27 Agreement on Provisional Arrangements in Afghanistan Pending the Re-Establishment of Permanent Government Institutions, Bonn, F.R.G (5 December 2001), endorsed by the Security Council in Resolution 1383, UN Doc. S/RES/1383 (6 December 2001).

28 For a critical analysis of the legal status of the Bonn Agreement, see Michael Schoiswohl, "Linking the International Legal Framework to Building the Formal Foundations of a "State at Risk": Constitution-Making and International Law in Post-Conflict Afghanistan", *Vanderbilt Journal of Transnational Law* [2006] 39.

29 Ibid. 844–845.

30 Agreement on Provisional Arrangements in Afghanistan Pending the Re-Establishment of Permanent Government Institutions, Bonn, F.R.G (5 December 2001), endorsed by the Security Council in Resolution 1383, UN Doc. S/RES/1383 (6 December 2001).

administration governed by a President; a Special Independent Commission envisaging the summoning of an emergency *Loya Jirga* (Grand Assembly) within six months; and a Supreme Court. Hamid Karzai, a known political figure who had formerly been active in gathering support for the Mujahedeen in the 1980s, was appointed as the President of the Afghan Interim Authority on 22 December 2001. The text of the draft constitution was agreed through the 2003 Constitutional *Loya Jirga* (CLJ). The US held a veto over the final constitution. There were disagreements over which languages would dominate in the new political order and whether delegates had been given sufficient information and input into the process to be able to give informed consent to the draft. Ultimately, the new Constitution was approved by the CLJ on 4 January 2004, to provide the legal framework for a new state to be known as "The Islamic Republic of Afghanistan".[31]

Iran

Iran has had two constitutions, both adopted in the aftermath of revolutions, with significantly different aims. The first of these, known as "The Constitutional Revolution" resulted in the Constitution of 1906–1907 which remained in force under two different dynasties. It transformed the Qajar dynasty which had been in power since 1789 from an absolutist monarchy into a constitutional monarchy, and remained in force under the succeeding Pahlavi dynasty (1925–1979). The second Constitution was adopted after the Islamic revolution of 1979, and remains in force.

What came to be known as the Constitutional Revolution in Iran at the turn of the 20th century and culminating in the Constitution of 1906–1907, covers a broad spectrum of ideas and objectives.[32] Some commentators ascribe the Constitutional Revolution to the leadership of the clergy and the notion of justice in Shi'a theology, while other commentators focus on the influence of modern ideas, economic factors, and foreign policy. Interestingly, both Islamic doctrine and secular ideas were invoked as arguments in favor of the introduction of constitutionalism in support of a legal order that would control political authority through a constitution and through a Parliament that would ensure popular representation.[33]

The central demand of the diverse group of individuals and groups in the Constitutional Revolution at the turn of the previous century was a demand for rule of law and establishment of representative government. The system up until then, as one commentator notes, with an absence of written law, meant that

31 Matthew Gray, "Islam in the Iraqi and Afghan Constitutions: A Comparative Perspective", *Global Peace, Change and Security* [2007] 19:1 26–27.

32 Homa Katouzian, *State and Society in Iran* (I.B. Tauris, 2000).

33 Mateo Mohammad Farzaneh, *The Iranian Constitutional Revolution and the Clerical Leadership of Khurasani* (Syracuse University Press, 2015).

political authority was often "arbitrary and unsystematic. Many of the complaints of the merchants ... related to arbitrary taxation and to maladministration of the revenues .... One of the themes of the Constitutional Revolution was that government be regulated by law".[34] Moreover, since around 1860, there had been a recurring demand for a House of Justice – "*Adalat Khane*" –that would dispense justice, differently to the arbitrary justice of the time.

The situation in the latter part of the 1800s contributes to explaining why such a change was made possible and deemed necessary. The administrative, military, educational, and economic reforms that were put into action already in the first half of the 19th century under Prime Minister Amir Kabir, continued to expose Iran to new ideas and institutions.[35] The foreign relations of Iran were also a significant contributing factor to the force of the idea of constitutionalism in society. The protest over the Tobacco Agreement in 1891–92, signed between the King Nasir al-Din Shah and Great Britain, granted British control over growth, sale, and export of tobacco, and was among the first signs of popular opposition against the existing order. From the early 19th century, demands for justice had already become widespread in a number of newspapers and pamphlets, aided by the growth in press media. The period prior to the Constitutional Revolution had seen a flourishing of newspapers with reform ideas and debates on the role of law, reflecting a variety of voices, some of which were expressed in ways that would less than a century later become criminalized.[36] The voices participating in these debates included religious, non-religious, orthodox, atheist, socialist, and nationalist. Part of these demands justified the demand for justice in religious terms. Others were inspired by the French Revolution and the Turkish Young Ottoman movement and sought to establish a society with social justice and equal rights for the citizens.

Among the external factors contributing to the Constitutional Revolution that would ultimately lead up to the introduction of a constitution under the idea of constitutionalism was Iran's role in the foreign relations between Russia and Great Britain. During the course of the 19th century, Iran had become economically and militarily weak. Together with a growing rate of unemployment and arbitrary, and often violent, rule, the situation prompted debates about the need for modernization, as well as debates about how to curb the impact of the great foreign powers on the country's financial situation.[37] Iran was increasingly dependent on Russia and Great Britain, with the reigning Qajar dynasty making Iran

34 Vanessa Martin, *Islam and Modernism: The Iranian Revolution of 1906* (Syracuse University Press, 1989) 10.

35 Abbas Amanat, *Pivot of the Universe: Nasir al-Din Shah Qajar and the Iranian Monarchy (1831–1896)* (Tauris, 1997).

36 Edward Browne, *Press and Poetry in Modern Persia* (Cambridge University Press, 1914); Ali Asghar Seyed-Gohrab (ed), *Literature of the Early Twentieth Century: From the Early Constitutional Period to Reza Shah* (I.B. Tauris, 2015) 411–445.

37 Janet Afary, *The Iranian Constitutional Revolution 1906–1911: Grassroots Democracy, Social Democracy and the Origins of Feminism* (Columbia University Press, 1996) 17. Afary details

into what one commentator has described as "a prisoner of imperial interests".[38] During this time, economic concessions were made to the great powers through a number of commercial agreements.[39] When King Nasir Al-Din Shah made public the news of a concession granted to the British tobacco industry in 1891, an alliance of secular reformers and religious dissidents, merchants, and Shi'a clerics, opposed the concession. In the next decade, the resentment against the government intensified. The Russian Revolution and the Russo-Japanese war played a role in catalyzing the opposition. The Russian revolution demonstrated that it was possible to have "another and better form of government", and the Japanese victory symbolized the victory of a "non-western nation armed with a constitution over a major European power without a constitution".[40]

On 5 August 1906, the monarch finally issued a proclamation for the formation of a Parliament, the first of its kind in the country, and the drafting of a constitution. Subsequently, elections were held and members of the newly established Parliament were elected. These members drafted a constitution which was ratified on 30 December 1906. Influenced by the French 1791 Constitution and the Belgian 1831 Constitution, the Iranian Constitution of 1906 significantly reduced the monarch's absolute powers and made him duty-bound to uphold the constitution, turning the form of government into a constitutional monarchy.[41] Government ministers were now responsible to the elected Parliament. Equality before the law and personal freedoms were guaranteed in unprecedented ways, although subject to stated limitations. Press freedom was established in the Constitution, together with public education, a significant step in a country where the vast majority of the population was illiterate. The Constitution marked the transition from absolutist monarchic government to a constitutional monarchy and a parliamentary government. However, soon after the 1906 Constitution was adopted, the alliance of the Constitutional Revolution that had led to the adoption of the Constitution split. Some segments of society were alarmed by the progressive direction of the new Parliament. The landowning class was unsympathetic to the social and economic reform programs. The constitutional rights provisions began to cause anguish, especially among the clerics and conservatives.[42] Parliament's power and sovereignty to enact all kinds of laws were troubling,

the origin of the Constitutional Revolution of 1906 and the structural and ideological transformations at the turn of the century.

38 Ali Gheissari, "Constitutional Rights and the Development of Civil Law in Iran, 1907–41", in Houchang Chehabi and Vanessa Martin (eds), *Iran's Constitutional Revolution: Popular Politics, Cultural Transformations and Transnational Connections* (I.B. Tauris, 2010) 71.

39 Nikki Keddi, "Iranian Revolutions in Comparative Perspective", *American Historical Review* [1983] 88 579.

40 Ibid. 586.

41 Ibid. 593.

42 Vanessa Martin, *Islam and Modernism: The Iranian Revolution of 1906* (Syracuse University Press, 1989) 79 and 115; Sarah Ansari and Vanessa Martin (eds), *Women, Religion and Culture in Iran* (Routledge, 2002).

and the previously constitutionalist clerics believed that the Parliament should incorporate the rules of Islamic law in all its work. One prominent cleric, Sheikh Fazlullah Nouri, who had previously supported the constitutionalist movement, emerged as a strong opponent of both the Parliament and of the Constitution.[43] He argued that constitutionalism was an innovation against Islam.[44] Among the provisions pointed to in this opposition was the provision on equal rights given to Jews, Muslims, and Zoroastrians, as well as the provision on freedom of the press. Other clerics joined his position and began invoking religious rhetoric as a means to undermine the Constitution. They now argued that the Constitution violated Islam and that only a legal code based on the *Shari'a* would be acceptable. The new clerical opposition furthermore attacked the Parliament, arguing that it was an institution that had no legitimate basis in Islamic law and was introducing European law that had no place in Islam. The Constitution was, in their view, an instrument of cultural imperialism that would weaken Islam. The clerical class was, nonetheless, not united in its position towards the Constitution. While Nouri and his followers declared the Constitution to be un-Islamic, other clerics invoked Islamic arguments in support of the Constitution and led protests against Nouri's opposition to the Constitution and to constitutionalism.[45]

As opposition to the new-born Constitution was building up, the idea of constitutionalism itself met new challenges as the financial situation of the country deteriorated further. King Nasir Al-Din Shah who had signed the 1906 Constitution had meanwhile died, and his son Muhammad Ali Shah was intent on dismantling that constitution. The most effective way to do so was to assert, as part of the clerical opposition had done, that the Constitution was incompatible with Islamic law.[46] Thus began work on a supplementary Constitution with a view to modifying the 1906 Constitution. The deliberations on this supplement became polarized between those who wanted to advance the goals of the Constitutional Revolution through including a bill of rights in the Supplementary Constitution, and those who wanted to reduce the relevance of the Constitution. That the drafting committee was constituted by constitutionalists raised concern among the clerics who thought the initial Constitution had been too un-Islamic. Hoping to placate clerical opposition, the Parliament agreed to the formation of an additional committee, composed of ranking clerics and headed by Sheikh

43 Janet Afary, *The Iranian Constitutional Revolution 1906–1911: Grassroots Democracy, Social Democracy and the Origins of Feminism* (Columbia University Press, 1996) 71.

44 Masoud Kamali, *Revolutionary Iran: Civil Society and State in the Modernization Process* (Ashgate Publishers, 1998) 119. More general, see Ali-Asghar Seyed-Gohrab (ed), *Literature of the Early Twentieth Century: From the Constitutional Period to Reza Shah* (I.B. Tauris, 2015); Abdul-Hadi Hariri, "Shaykh Fazl Allah Nuri's Refutation of the Idea of Constitutionalism", *Middle Eastern Studies* [1977] 13:3 327–335.

45 Said Amir Arjomand, "The Ulama's Traditionalist Opposition to Parliamentarianism: 1907–1909", *Middle Eastern Studies* [1981] 17:2 174–190.

46 Janet Afary, *The Iranian Constitutional Revolution 1906–1911: Grassroots Democracy, Social Democracy and the Origins of Feminism* (Columbia University Press, 1996) 115.

Fazlollah Nouri. Their role would be to review amendments so as to decide what was, and what was not, compatible with the *Shari'a*. During these meetings, discussions were held on the place of the Quran in the Constitution, where some were of the opinion that it should be the foundation of the Constitution itself, while others were arguing that it was only the foundation of religion and not of the Constitution.[47] Conservative clerics and deputies initially rejected many of the proposed civil liberties in the Supplementary Constitution on the grounds that they were incompatible with Islam. Opposed to compulsory public education, freedom of the press, and the equal treatment of Muslims and non-Muslims, they asserted that equal rights and mandatory education were imported European ideas, views that continued to be persuasive in the coming century.[48] They were furthermore of the view that the very doctrine behind constitutional equality represented a disregard of the rules of Islam.[49] Similarly, many clerics opposed the notion of freedom. Freedom was, in their view, equated with non-religiosity and immorality, and with regard to gender, such freedom represented a doubly negative connotation.[50]

Ultimately, to guard against non-Islamic rights and legislation, the anti-constitutionalist clerics called for the creation of a Council of Clerics that would have power of review and veto over all laws of parliament.[51] As a result, a compromise was made and this Council was introduced in the 1907 Supplementary Constitution. A comparison between the first draft of the 1907 Supplement and the final version highlights that major concessions were made to the anti-constitutionalist faction. As a result, a duality emerges in which the goals of the 1906 Constitution are sought to be furthered through the inclusion of individual rights, while the Supplement at the same time qualifies a number of these rights by conditioning them through religious rhetoric.[52]

The 1907 Supplementary Constitution as finally adopted contained an extensive bill of rights, including provisions on life, property, privacy of letters and telegrams, domicile, and the right to trial. The State, rather than the clergy, was placed at the head of the public educational system. Yet, many rights were limited to reference to Islamic law. Freedom of the press in Article 20 of the Supplementary Constitution was, for example, provided with the exception of "heretical books and matters hurtful to the perspicuous religion". Freedom of association was

47 Masoud Kamali, *Revolutionary Iran: Civil Society and State in the Modernization Process* (Ashgate Publishers, 1998) 113.

48 Vanessa Martin, *Islam and Modernism: The Iranian Revolution of 1906* (Syracuse University Press, 1989) 129.

49 Amirhassan Boozari, *Shi'I Jurisprudence and Constitution: Revolution in Iran* (Palgrave, 2011) 119.

50 Janet Afary, *The Iranian Constitutional Revolution 1906–1911: Grassroots Democracy, Social Democracy and the Origins of Feminism* (Columbia University Press, 1996) 89.

51 Ibid. 27.

52 Vanessa Martin, *Islam and Modernism: The Iranian Revolution of 1906* (Syracuse University Press, 1989).

granted in Article 21, providing that associations were "not productive of mischief to religion or the state". Alarmed by constitutional secularity, the clerical establishment also sought a concept of constitutionalism compatible with their understanding of Shi'a Islam. Most importantly, the 1907 Supplement, unlike the Constitution of 1906, contained a strong form of Islamic supremacy clause. Article 2 of the Supplement called for the establishment of a Council of Clerics to review legislation and the provision also included a restraining principle, stating that legislation could not be at variance with the *Shari'a*. As a compromise to this Islamic supremacy clause, the most controversial article of the Constitution was retained – that of constitutional equality for all. Article 8 of the Supplementary Constitution provided that citizens would enjoy equal rights before the law, regardless of religion. The provision was included despite the prevailing view at the time that such a clause was in clear contradiction of what Islamic law permitted. The 1907 Supplementary Constitution thus became a document through which the anti-constitutionalists safeguarded their concerns in return for acceding to some progressive provisions in the constitution.[53] The Constitution remained unchanged under the next monarch, Reza Shah, but would see changes under his son. Following the accession to the throne in 1941, King Mohammad Reza Pahlavi convened a Constituent Assembly in 1949 that amended the Constitution to grant the king the power to dissolve Parliament's lower and upper house, while requiring him to arrange elections for a new Parliament within three months. In 1963, a constitutional referendum was held to approve reforms known as the "White Revolution", that would be launched the same year and go on for the next 15 years. Among the reforms was the extension of the right to vote to women, land reforms, educational reforms, and programs against illiteracy, rural modernization, social security, and economic reforms.

Following the Islamic revolution in 1979, the 1906–1907 Constitution was jettisoned in favor of a new Constitution that established Iran for the first time as an "Islamic Republic". Following the revolution, the Revolutionary Council presented a draft Constitution that replaced the monarchical form of government with a strong presidential system but built otherwise on the 1906–1907 Constitution. However, several leftist groups demanded the draft to be submitted for a full review, following which a constituent assembly named "Assembly of Experts for Constitution" was established to consider the initial draft. The assembly, dominated by clerics, spent the next three months re-drafting the first draft and institutionalized a theocratic state based on the concept of "The Guardianship of the Jurist" – "*velayat-e faqih*". The 1979 Constitution contains a lengthy preamble, laying out the historical events according to the drafters and establishing the political ideology of the new state. The preamble states, amongst other things, that the "anti-despotic movement for constitutional government (1906–1911), and anti-colonialist movement for the nationalization of petroleum" failed because of the lack of a religious basis, and that the

53 Asghar Shirazi, *The Constitution of Iran: Politics and State in the Islamic Republic* (I.B. Tauris, 1997).

century to come will "witness the establishment of a universal holy government and the downfall of all others".

Iraq

The 20th-century constitutional history of Iraq is dominated by a series of *coup d'états* and interim constitutions.[54] Since the founding of the state of Iraq in 1921 up until 2003, successive Iraqi governments and the constitutions relegated religion mostly to the private domain.

Iraq had been under the Ottoman Empire, which by the 19th century saw its power declining throughout.[55] Concerns about the growing independence of provincial rulers within the Empire prompted reformers to propose changes based on European models of law and administration, known as *tanzimat* (adjustments), which faced considerable opposition from conservative groups. The reforms, established through the Noble Edict of the Rose Chamber of 1839, regulated taxation and administration and established secular schools.[56] A key provision guaranteed the equality of all subjects, regardless of religion, in taxation, military service, eligibility for civil service jobs, and entrance to institutions of higher education.[57] Representative assemblies were set up to provide civil rule, independent of control by religious authorities. For the first time, legal limits were established on the absolute power of the Ottoman monarch. A number of laws were introduced in the following years, including the Penal Code in 1858, the Land Law of 1858, the Vilayet Law of 1864, and the Civil Code of 1876. From 1869, the new governor of Iraq worked to implement the *tanzimat* reform program from Baghdad, but was recalled to Istanbul in 1872 before completing the program throughout Iraq.[58] The reforms had, however, led to change, and at the beginning of the 20th century, constitutionalism and secularism became topics of discussion in Baghdad.

Iraq's first constitution was adopted in 1925, at a time when the country was under British military occupation, Britain having gained Iraq under the Sykes–Picot Agreement concluded during the First World War.[59,60] Prior to this, the British abolished some of the institutions established during the Ottoman reform

54 On the entry "Iraq" in Gerhard Robbers and Cole Durham (eds), *Encyclopedia of Law and Religion* (Brill, 2015).

55 William Spencer, *Iraq: Old Land, New Nation in Conflict* (Twenty-First Century Books, 2000).

56 Patrick Kinross, *The Ottoman Centuries: The Rise and Fall of the Turkish Empire* (Morrow Quill, 1977).

57 William Spencer, *Iraq: Old Land, New Nation in Conflict* (Twenty-First Century Books, 2000) 53.

58 Charles Tripp, *A History of Iraq* (Cambridge University Press, 2000) 16–18.

59 Adeed Dawisha, *Iraq: A Political History From Independence to Occupation* (Princeton University Press, 2009); Thomas Hall, *The British Occupation of Iraq, 1915–1948* (University of Vermont Press, 2008).

60 Ian Rutledge, *Enemy on the Euphrates: The British Occupation of Iraq and the Great Arab Revolt, 1914–1921* (Saqi Books, 2014).

period, including the elected municipal councils. The governing elite of state officials established by the British was almost in its entirety Sunni Arab Iraqis, leading to societal divisions that would remain in the coming century. A government was formed in 1920, modeled on that of Great Britain, with a constitutional monarchy and a parliament.[61] In the Cairo Conference in March 1921, the British chose Prince Faisal bin Hussein to be the first monarch.[62] The 1925 Constitution was written by a committee of British political officers who submitted their draft to an Iraqi committee that approved the draft in 1925.[63] The Constitution, composed of 123 articles, established a constitutional monarchy. An amendment in 1943 increased the power of the monarch towards the parliament.[64] While the Constitution established Islam as the official religion, the role of religion was limited and the Constitution laid the foundation for a largely secular form of governance.[65] After the overthrow of the monarchy following a coup in 1958, a series of interim or provisional constitutions followed that were based on: the National Revolutionary Command Council Law no. 25 of 1963 and 1964; the National Revolutionary Command Council Laws no. 61 of 1964; no. 173 of 1964; no. 137 of 1965; the Revolutionary Command Council Law of 1968; and the Revolutionary Command Council Resolution no. 792 of 1970.[66] In 1990–1991, constitutions were drafted but not promulgated. The 1970 Interim Constitution was never expressly repealed or set aside and was thus in force until the Coalition Provisional Authority (CPA) Order 100 of 28 June 2004.

With the 1958 coup, the 1925 Constitution was replaced that same year with a new provisional Constitution, containing only 30 articles, and establishing a republic. The provisional Constitution of 1958 was Iraq's first Constitution adopted as an independent state. However, its most significant feature was the creation of a body with absolute authority – the Revolutionary Command Council. The provisional Constitution of 1958 emphasized the Kurd and Arab

61 Ronen Zeidel, Amatzia Baram and Achim Rohde, *Iraq Between Occupations: Perspectives from 1920 to the Present* (Palgrave Macmillan, 2010).

62 Charles Tripp, *A History of Iraq* (Cambridge University Press, 2000) 47–48; William Spencer, *Iraq: Old Land, New Nation in Conflict* (Twenty-First Century Books, 2000) 59. In addition to the Constitution, the Anglo-Iraqi Protectorate Treaty of 1922 confirmed that for the next 20 years, Iraq would follow British advice in matters related to British interests, including fiscal policy. This meant that Parliament could not enact legislation on financial matters, as the British retained control over this area See Bernard Lewis, *The Shaping of the Modern Middle East* (Oxford University Press, 1994) 36.

63 Saad Jawad, *The Iraqi Constitution: Structural Flaws and Political Implications*, LSE Middle Eastern Centre Paper Series [2013] 6.

64 Adeed Dawisha, *Iraq: A Political History from Independence to Occupation* (Princeton University Press, 2009) 161.

65 Constitution of Iraq (1925), Article 13. Under Article 69, the Constitution established a three-part court system made up of religious courts, civil courts and special courts, each with distinct areas of jurisdiction.

66 Amended by RCC Resolutions 567 of 1973; 247 of 1974; 928 of 1979; 385 of 1980; 836 of 1982; 196 of 1985; 1130 of 1985; 700 of 1987; 630 of 1988; 83 of 1991; 336 of 1991; 398 of 1991; 15 of 1993; 460 of 1992; and 112 of 2000.

identity of the country, emphasized the sovereignty of the people, and guaranteed a number of rights, including freedom of the press and equality before the law.[67] Between 1968 and 2003, the Iraqi political and constitutional landscape was dominated by the Ba'ath party ideology, and governed by the Arab Socialist Ba'ath Party. The period was characterized by a number of internal political conflicts resulting in frequent *coup d'états* and elimination of opposition. Originally established in Syria, the Ba'ath ideology advocated the formation of a single Arab socialist nation.[68] The one-party system formed an authoritarian form of governance, while the socialist aspect downplayed the role of religion and pursued a largely secular program.[69]

The 1970 interim Constitution stayed in force until the invasion of Iraq in 2003. The only reference to Islam in the 1970 interim Constitution was a symbolic reference, declaring Islam as the religion of the state.[70] The Constitution furthermore confirmed the Revolutionary Command Council as the highest authority, including the power to ratify and issue legislation. Religion had no further role in the constitution, except for the handling of personal status matters, such as marriage, divorce, and inheritance, and followed the various schools of Islamic jurisprudence. Separate courts would handle similar issues for the Christian and Jewish communities.[71] The rise in oil prices in the late 1970s helped the initiation of a number of economic reform programs, including wider distribution of wealth, redistribution of land, and increased access to services like health care and education.[72] In 1979, Saddam Hussein succeeded President Bakr. Between 1979 and 2003, Iraq went through several military conflicts, a policy of destruction of the Kurdish population, and United Nations sanctions with severe economic and social impact. In 1990, an Interim Constitution was re-issued, but not formally ratified.

The constitutional process following the invasion in 2003 took place in two steps. Soon after the invasion, the Coalition Provisional Authority (CPA), created and funded as a division of the US Department of Defense, was established as a transitional government with executive, legislative, and judicial authority.[73] Furthermore, the CPA was given the authority to appoint a Constituent

67 Juan Romero, *The Iraqi Revolution of 1958: A Revolutionary Quest for Unity and Security* (UPA, 2010) 139.

68 Samir Al-Khalil, *The Republic of Fear: The Politics of Modern Iraq* (University of California Press, 1989); Adeed Dawisha, *Iraq: A Political History From Independence to Occupation* (Princeton University Press, 2009).

69 Eric Davis, *Memories of State: Politics, History, and Collective Identity in Modern Iraq* (University of California Press, 2005).

70 Interim Constitution of Iraq (1970), Article 4.

71 Bernard Lewis, *The Shaping of the Modern Middle East* (Oxford University Press, 1994) 184.

72 Ibid. 62.

73 On 20 January 2003, two months prior to the invasion of Iraq, the US Government established the Office for Reconstruction and Humanitarian Assistance (ORHR) to act as a caretaker administration in Iraq until the creation of the government. Upon the dissolution of ORHA, its powers were transferred to the CPA.

Assembly. On 22 July 2003, the CPA formed the Iraqi Governing Council (IGC). In opposition to this, Iraq's leading Shi'a Cleric, Grand Ayatollah Sistani, issued a religious opinion in 2003 declaring that the Constituent Assembly should be elected, not appointed.[74] The CPA thus released an alternative process, envisaging the constitutional drafting in two stages. The constitution was eventually to be written by an elected Constituent Assembly. In the interim, however, the country would be governed by a Transitional National Assembly to be selected by caucuses, rather than through direct elections.[75] A temporary fundamental law known as the Transitional Administrative Law (TAL) would be drafted by the IGC and serve as the governing document until a permanent constitution was promulgated.[76]

Article 7 of the TAL, for the first time in Iraqi constitutional history, entrenched two types of Islamic supremacy clauses, stating that

> Islam ... is to be considered a source of legislation (and) no law that contradicts the universally agreed tenets of Islam, the principles of democracy, or the rights cited in Chapter Two of this Law may be enacted during the transitional period.[77]

Never before had the constitutional order of Iraq granted religion a similarly fundamental role in legislation.

The permanent Constitution of 2005 retained the Islamic supremacy clause, though formulated in different terms to that of the TAL, and represented a strengthening of the clause. Some commentators explain the reason for the strengthening of the Islamic supremacy clause in the fact that religious groups were more organized compared to secular groups in the process leading up to the election of the Constituent Assembly. Ayatollah Sistani managed to organize the Shi'a population into a single electoral list, the United Iraqi Alliance (UIA) that won about 48% of the vote and secured 140 seats in the National Constitutional Assembly. The Kurds, acting through the Democratic Patriotic Alliance of Kurdistan came second, securing 25% of the vote and 75 seats. The secular group, the Iraqi List, obtained 13% and only 40 seats. Further, the Sunni boycott had led to Sunni Iraqis being significantly under-represented and left without influence in the drafting of the new constitution.

In terms of the compromises during the drafting of the Constitution of 2005, two main issues of disagreement were the role of religion and regional autonomy, which somehow become interlinked in the ensuing debates. On these

74 Noah Feldman, "The Democratic Fatwa: Islam and Democracy in the Realm of Constitutional Politics", *Oklahoma Law Review* [2005] 58 6.

75 Ibid. 7.

76 Andrew Arato, *Constitution-Making Under Occupation: The Politics of Imposed Revolution in Iraq* (Columbia University Press, 2009) 110.

77 Law of the Administration for the State of Iraqi for the Transitional Period, 8 March 2004, Article 7.

two issues, the debates on the Constitution were divided along ethno-religious lines. The relatively secular Kurdish faction was willing to make concessions on religious issues in return for federalism and regional autonomy. On the other hand, the Shi'a Islamic faction wanted to entrench the role of Islam further. The Constitution also become a battleground over women's rights, and many women's rights advocates signaled the dangerous direction towards which the country was heading, in particular through the increasingly expanding role of religion.[78]

4.2 The constitutional present: the scope of equal liberty

What is the scope of equal liberty under the de-secularized constitution? In this section, I highlight two of the features that shape and define the scope of equal liberty and constitutional rights under the de-secularized constitutions of Afghanistan, Iran, and Iraq. These features establish a conception of rights that is different from that found under the standard of constitutionalism and international human rights law. First, rights are limited through the system of government prescribed by the constitution. At this level, the primary barrier to equal rights is represented by the establishment of a system of government which is neither based on, nor facilitates, equal liberty. Under constitutionalism, equal liberty is the foundation for political authority, and political authority is thus accountable to each and every person. By contrast, under the de-secularized constitution, the constitution entrenches inequality and allows for broad limitations to liberty. As a result, while every person is subject to political authority, they are not granted equal rights, nor are the rights themselves sufficiently broad to make political authority accountable to each and every person.

Secondly, rights are limited through the constitutional provisions themselves. Of these, the restraining principle and non-discrimination provisions will have a direct impact on how rights are construed and limited. The restraining principles establish the state religion as not only a criterion for legislation, but also for the interpretation of rights. The nondiscrimination provision establishes the constitutional standard for *who* can be considered as a rights-holder. In addition, the specific rights provisions, through their wording, construe the right in question Unlike the broadly stated wording of rights that characterizes rights under a modern constitutional system, the de-secularized constitution formulates rights

78 Isobel Coleman, "Women, Islam, and the New Iraq", *Foreign Affairs* [2006] 85:1 28–29. Although the Constitution guarantees gender equality under Article 14, Article 2(a) of the restraining principle has been cited as being in conflict with rights that Iraqi women held in family and inheritance law under the 1959 Personal Status Law which removed personal legal issues from the jurisdiction of religious courts and instead created a unified, codified law on personal status. The Governing Council attempted in December 2003 to annul the 1959 Personal Status Code by passing Resolution 137 which sought to replace the 1959 Law with the *Shari'a*. Once this move proved to be controversial, the Coalition Provisional Authority reversed the resolution.

more narrowly and establishes a constitutionally entrenched hierarchy based on religious affiliation.

The structure of constitutional rights is thus subject to a larger degree of influence by the state. The state religion becomes a condition for the scope of the right and for access to rights. Limitations to rights are based on one particular religion, or rather, on the state's version of that religion.

4.2.1 Form of government

Because rights establish a relationship between the individual and political authority, a duality arises in the relationship between constitutional rights and the constitutional regulation of political authority. On the one hand, the way in which rights are construed says something about the form of government. Under constitutionalism, rights create a sphere of autonomy in which the government cannot interfere, and they also establish the conditions upon which the government exists. On the other hand, the form of government defines the outer boundaries of rights. The more democratic a system of government is, the more will it reflect the idea of equal rights, as this is a prerequisite for democracy. The less democratic a system of government is, the narrower is the sphere of autonomy established by rights. Moreover, the form of government would also tell us something about the level of accountability for state institutions and about implications for violations of rights.

The constitutions of Afghanistan, Iran, and Iraq, while all de-secularized, establish different forms of government. Afghanistan is established as an "Islamic Republic" with a strong presidential system. Iran is established as an "Islamic Republic" and as a theocracy. Iraq is established as a federal republic with a relatively weak central government.

Afghanistan

The Afghan Constitution of 2004 establishes an "Islamic Republic" with a presidential system in which the elected president has broad powers. Under Article 1, "Afghanistan shall be an Islamic Republic, independent, unitary and indivisible state".

The president serves a five-year term with a two-term limit.[79] The broad powers of the president are stated in Article 64 and include the power to appoint all "high ranking officials", which includes cabinet ministers, members of the Supreme Court, judges, provincial and district governors, local security chiefs, and members of the independent commissions, including the Afghan Independent Human Rights Commission (AIHRC). The appointments are subject to confirmation by the National Assembly. The legislative branch consists of the National Assembly, composed of a 259-seat all-elected lower house (*Wholesi Jirga* – House of the

79 Constitution of Afghanistan (2004), Article 62.

People), and a selected 102-seat upper house (*Meshrano Jirga* – House of the Elders). One-third of the upper house is selected by the president for a five-year term, and half of them must be women. One-third is appointed by the elected provincial councils for a four-year term, and one-third is appointed by elected district councils for a three-year term. The powers of the National Assembly are set out in Chapter 5 of the Constitution.

The Constitution provides for an independent judiciary, led by a nine-member Supreme Court. All Supreme Court members are appointed by the president, subject to confirmation by the lower house of the National Assembly.

On matters involving constitutional interpretation, in addition to the Supreme Court, the Constitution establishes the Independent Commission for the Supervision of the Implementation of the Constitution (ICSIC), consisting of seven commissioners appointed by the president and subject to confirmation by the lower house. According to available data, 80% of cases are decided in the informal justice system, particularly on issues such as local property, family disputes, and personal status. The informal justice sector consists of local consultative mechanisms that often meet at the village level. The justice sector is heavily dominated by males, partly because of tradition, but more importantly because the legal criteria established by the Constitution.

At the national level, the traditional decision-making mechanism of *Loya Jirga* has been entrenched in the Constitution, regulated in Chapter 6, and established as "the highest manifestation of the will of the people of Afghanistan".[80] The *Loya Jirga* consists of around 1,500 delegates, including all members of the National Assembly, as well as presidents of the provincial and district assemblies.[81] The AIHRC was set up under Article 58 of the Constitution to refer cases of human rights violations to "the legal authorities".

Iran

The Iranian version of "Islamic Republic" differs radically from the Afghan version. The Iranian Constitution establishes a form of government where the clergy inhabits the executive, legislative, and judicial branches. The form of government under the Constitution is known as "*Velayat-e faqih*", the "Guardianship of the Islamic Jurist", and was developed by Ayatollah Khomeini who set out the idea in the book *Islamic Government*, published in 1970.[82] The exercise of the highest political position is reserved to a "*faqih*", a high-ranking Islamic jurist. The notion of "guardian" indicates that individuals are neither free nor equal, but are in need of a substitute decision-maker to guide their actions. This concept marks the starting point for understanding the Iranian Constitution's notion of

80 Constitution of Afghanistan (2004), Article 110(1).

81 Ibid.

82 Khomeini, "Islamic Government" translated to English, in Hamid Algar (ed), *Khomeini: Islam and Revolution* (Mizan Press, 1981) 27.

the relationship between political authority and individuals. Moreover, in *Islamic Government*, Islam is described as a necessary tool to fight imperialism, and the government is created to that end.[83] Constitutionalism is presented as an imperialistic tool, and the previous Constitution of 1906–1907 is described as an imperialist and anti-Islamic document which "violates the system of government and the laws of Islam".[84] This view echoes that of the anti-constitutionalist movement that opposed the introduction of a constitution in the early 20th century.

In *Islamic Government*, Khomeini explicitly rejects a separation of religion and government: "This slogan of the separation of religion and politics and the demand that Islamic scholars not intervene in social and political affairs have been formulated and propagated by the imperialists: it is only the irreligious who repeat them".[85] He also explicitly rejects democracy:

> Islamic government does not correspond to any of the existing forms of government … It is not constitutional in the current sense of the word, i.e. based on the approval of laws in accordance with the opinion of the majority. It is constitutional in the sense that the rulers are subject to a certain set of conditions in governing and administering the country, conditions that are set forth in the Noble Quran and the Sunna of the Most Noble Messenger. It is the laws and ordinances of Islam comprising this set of conditions that must be observed and practiced, Islamic government may therefore be defined as the rule of divine law over men.[86]

The head of state and holding the supreme executive, legislative and judicial authority, is the "*Vali-e faqih*", the Supreme Leader. The concept entails that in the absence of the divinely inspired imam, political leadership is to be held by a *faqih*, a jurist in Islamic law, male, whose characteristics best qualify him to lead the community as set out in Articles 5 and 109 of the Constitution. The position is a life tenure, and entails supreme authority over the legislative, executive, and judicial branch, as set out in Article 57 of the Constitution. The Supreme Leader is not a popularly elected position. The Assembly of Experts (*Majlese Khobregan*), established by the Constitution and composed of 88 members of the clergy, chooses the leader from among qualified Shi'ite clergy on the basis of his expertise in Islamic law, personal piety, and political acumen. The powers of the Supreme Leader are extensive: he appoints the senior officers of the military and Revolutionary Guards, the clerical members of the Council of Guardians, and members of the judiciary. Most importantly, he sets out the general direction of the nation's policy.[87] The Supreme Leader also appoints members of a particular

83 Ibid. 28–29.
84 Ibid. 30–31.
85 Ibid. 48.
86 Ibid. 55–56.
87 Constitution of Iran (1979), Article 220.

body called The Expediency Discernment Council, established by Article 112 of the Constitution following an amendment in 1988, to resolve conflicts between the Consultative Assembly and the Guardian Council.

The president answers to the Supreme Leader on executive matters, and is elected by popular ballot, overseen by the Guardian Council. The qualifications for the President are established in Chapter 9 of the Constitution and require, amongst others, that a candidate be an Iranian-born Shi'a Muslim. A constitutional amendment in 1989 abolished the post of prime minister, leading to some power being transferred to the President, who until then had held a ceremonial post. The President selects the Council of Ministers for approval by the legislature, appoints a portion of the members of the Committee to Determine the Expediency of the Islamic Order (the Expedience Discernment Council), and serves as chairman of the Supreme Council for National Security.

The Islamic Consultative Assembly is a 290-member unicameral body and is regulated in Articles 62–90. Deputies are elected for four years by universal suffrage, but must fulfill a number of criteria in order to be approved as candidates. The role of the legislative power is limited under the constitutional framework, and follows largely the idea set out in *Islamic Government:*

> The fundamental difference between Islamic government, on the one hand, and constitutional monarchies and republics, on the other, is this: whereas the representatives of the people or the monarch in such regimes engage in legislation, in Islam the legislative power and competence to establish laws belongs exclusively to God Almighty ... No-one has the right to legislate and no law may be executed except the law of the Divine Legislator. It is for this reason that in Islamic government, a simple planning body takes the place of the legislative assembly that is one of the three branches of government.[88]

The more significant body in the area of legislation is the Guardian Council, which is tasked with reviewing the compatibility of legislation with the state religion and with the Constitution. The Guardian Council has twelve members, of which half must be Islamic scholars, chosen by the Supreme Leader, while the other six are jurists elected by the Islamic Consultative Assembly from among Muslim jurists that have been nominated by the Chief Justice, who himself is selected by the Supreme Leader.

With the revolution, the judiciary was partially dismantled, and judges who had been trained in law were replaced with judges who had been educated in religious seminaries. Women judges were initially also removed and were only allowed to return in 1997, but even then only as secondary judges in civil cases. In the first years of the revolution, Revolutionary Courts were established to rule on "Islamic law", but were often presided over by people with neither legal nor religious

88 Khomeini, "Islamic Government" translated to English, in Hamid Algar (ed), *Khomeini: Islam and Revolution* (Mizan Press, 1981) 55–56.

training, on the basis of which a large number of executions and convictions took place. The processes often consisted of trials lasting a few minutes, without defense lawyers, as this was dismissed as a "western absurdity". Common charges included "sowing corruption on earth", "insulting Islam", "insulting the clergy", "opposing the Islamic Revolution", or supporting the previous monarch. In the period 1979–89, the Revolutionary Courts ordered the execution of at least 10,000 individuals belonging to opposition groups, and others were sentenced for crimes including adultery, sodomy, kidnapping, disruption of public order, and terrorism. In 1982, the Revolutionary Courts became part of the court system, ruling on cases concerning "national security", "drug crimes", and political and "anti-revolutionary" crimes. The legal system, moreover, underwent significant change as religious laws were introduced into state law, including in criminal law where the Public Punishment Law of 1924 was replaced with the Retribution Law of 1982. The Head of the Judiciary is to be a "*mujtahed*", a clergy member of a particular rank, and is appointed by the Supreme Leader. Similarly, the Head of the Supreme Court and the Prosecutor-General are to be "*mujtaheds*", nominated by the Head of the Judiciary in consultation with the Supreme Court. In addition to the ordinary court system, including the Revolutionary Courts, the Constitution establishes a Special Clerical Court, which is accountable only to the Supreme Leader, and tries crimes allegedly committed by clerics, and which has been used to discipline and prosecute dissident clerics.[89]

The Constitution also grants religion an extensive role in the creation of an ideological army, as set out in the Preamble, who are responsible for

> fulfilling the ideological mission of jihad in God's way; that is, extending the sovereignty of God's law throughout the world (this is in accordance with the Qur'anic verse 'Prepare against them whatever force you are able to muster, and strings of horses, striking fear into the enemy of God and your enemy, and others besides them' 1979 Constitution of Iran, preamble[8:60]).

Moreover, Article 144 stresses that the Army must be "an Islamic Army, i.e., committed to Islamic ideology and the people, and must recruit into its service individuals who have faith in the objectives of the Islamic Revolution and are devoted to the cause of realizing its goals". In addition to the Army of the Islamic Republic, the Constitution establishes the Islamic Revolutionary Guard Corps to "continue in its role in guarding the Revolution and its achievements".[90]

In his 2004 report, the UN Special Rapporteur on the right to freedom of opinion and expression observed in relation to Iran, that the state of the right in the country was closely linked to the overall system of government: "a major impediment to reform consists of various institutional lacks on governmental,

89 Mirjam Künkler, "The Special Courts of the Clergy and the Repression of Dissident Clergy in Iran", in Said Arjomand and Nathan Brown (eds), *The Rule of Law, Islam and Constitutional Politics in Egypt and Iran* (SUNY Press, 2013).

90 Constitution of Iran (1979), Article 150.

parliamentary and judicial processes resulting from the control exercised thereon by unelected institutions and bodies that are not accountable to the people".[91]

Iraq

Unlike Afghanistan and Iran, the Constitution of Iraq does not establish an Islamic Republic. The 2005 Constitution establishes Iraq for the first time as a federal republic. The federal system is largely established along ethno-religious lines, with a Kurdish region (mostly Sunni Iraqi Kurds); a Sunni region (mostly Arab Iraqis) and a Shi'a region (mostly Shi'a Iraqi). The constitution defines the system of government in the following way: "The Republic of Iraq is a single, independent federal State with full sovereignty. Its system of government is republican, representative, parliamentary and democratic. This Constitution is the guarantor of its unity".[92]

The President is the head of state; the Prime Minister heads the government, and the constitution provides for a Council of Representatives and the Council of Union. The judiciary is independent of the executive and the legislature. Members of the Supreme Court are required to be experts in civil law and Islamic law.

4.2.2 The restraining principle and the source of law provision

The strength of the state religion is partly determined by its role in legislation. Under the desecularized constitution, this comes into play in two related ways. One is through the restraining principle – sometimes referred to as the "*repugnancy clause*" – which requires that legislation be compatible with the state religion, and the other is through the source of law provision, which establishes that the state religion is either "*a*" or "*the*" source of legislation.

The historical origin of the restraining principle can be traced to the Iranian Constitution of 1906–07, more precisely in the supplement of 1907, and has since migrated to other countries.[93] Article 2 of the 1907 Supplement to the Constitution held that laws "repugnant to Islam" would be void and that a council of clergy would review laws to control their compatibility. This latter part that institutionalized the review in a council of clergy was, however, not implemented

91 Report of the UN Special Rapporteur on the protection and promotion of the right to freedom of opinion and expression, E/CN.4/2004/62/Add.2.

92 Constitution of Iraq (2005), Article 1.

93 Some commentators argue that the idea of the Islamic restraining principles comes from colonial India where the British had implemented a similar repugnancy doctrine to constrain the application of domestic and customary laws which were deemed repugnant to British law or moral sentiment. See, for example, Noah Feldman, *The Fall and Rise of the Islamic State* (Princeton University Press, 2008) 83; and Ahmad Dawood and Tom Ginsburg, "Constitutional Islamization and Human Rights: The Surprising Origin and Spread of Islamic Supremacy in Constitutions", *University of Chicago Public Law & Legal Theory Working Paper*, No. 477 [2014]. There are, however, no indications from in the constitutional debates in Iran that suggests that the inspiration for the restraining principle came from India.

beyond one term.[94] As a result, the restraining principle's interpretation was therefore left to the parliament, strengthening parliamentary sovereignty over the institutional role of the clergy.

In contemporary constitutions, the restraining principle is formulated in a variety of ways. In some constitutions, it has a negative formulation, requiring that legislation does not contravene Islamic law or principles. In others, the formulation requires legislation to be in accordance with Islamic law or principles.

While the restraining principle is new in the Iraqi Constitution, it is not so in the Afghan and Iranian constitutions. What is different, however, is that the de-secularized constitutions have further strengthened the restraining principle by provisions that strengthen the enforcement of the restraining principle as a rights-limiting tool.

The restraining principle and source of law provisions are thus provisions that make the state religion binding on legislation and on the legislature. While such provisions are in themselves a limitation to legislation, the extent of the limitation depends on the framework that the constitution establishes for the enforcement of such provisions. This includes the question of whether the provisions are left for the legislature to interpret, in which case the provisions are political, and would depend on the majority view in parliament. Alternatively, the principle is sought to be upheld through institutions or organs separate from the legislature, such as the courts.

The inclusion of the restraining principle and source of law provision was subject to disagreement during the drafting processes of the de-secularized constitutions. The disagreements concerned both the question of *whether* such provisions should be included in the first place, and what the wording and criteria of the provisions should be.

The restraining principle and source of law provisions represent a particular challenge with respect to the justification of modern constitutional law. The constitution as a higher law entails that all other sources of law and legal authority are placed lower than the constitution in the legal hierarchy. That means that laws and policies must not violate the constitution. By establishing an external source – religion – as superior to the norms of the constitution, the restraining principle and the source of law provisions thus run counter to this particular feature of constitutionalism as an idea and to modern constitutional law as practice.

Afghanistan

In the Afghan Constitution, the restraining principle is found in Article 3 which states that "No law shall contravene the tenets and provisions of the holy religion of Islam in Afghanistan".[95] The draft that had been submitted earlier by the

94 Amirhassan Boozari, *Shi'I Jurisprudence and Constitution: Revolution in Iran* (Palgrave, 2011) 159.
95 Hannibal Travis, "Freedom or Theocracy: Constitutionalism in Afghanistan and Iraq", *Northwestern University Journal of International Human Rights* [2005] 4:3 1–52.

Constitutional Commission to the *Loya Jirga* that was summoned in December 2003 proposed a substantially secular state, with symbolic references to religion, largely inspired by the 1964 Constitution, and did not contain a restraining principle. However, the final version goes farther than did the 1964 Constitution toward enshrining the state religion's role in legislation.[96]

The wording of the Afghan restraining principle is vague, since there is no agreement as to what constitutes "the tenets and provisions" of Islam, and whether this differs from the tenets and provisions of Islamic *law*, as opposed to Islam as a religion. None of the drafts submitted during the drafting process contain further guidelines as to how to interpret the restraining principle or as to how it relates to other constitutional provisions. The ultimate content of the provision is decided by the Supreme Court, which is empowered to interpret the provision.

Compared to previous constitutions, the current version of the restraining principle is the strictest, even if the wording is vague. The first Afghan Constitution of 1923 while referring to religion in the legislative area was not absolute in its wording. Instead, it provided that legislators had to give "careful consideration" to the "requirements of the laws of *Shari'a*".[97] The provision was further moderated since the rather liberal Article 72 stated that in the process of legislation, the actual living conditions of the people and the requirements of the time would be given serious consideration, ***in addition to*** the rules of the *Shari'a*. Following the clergy's opposition to the Constitution of 1923, in particular to the constitutional rights it provided, the Constitution of 1931 was adopted. The 1931 Constitution contained more references to Islam, including in the area of legislation.[98] Under Article 5, "measures passed by the National Council should not contravene the canons of the religion of Islam or the policy of the country".[99] In stating that the state religion and the policy of the country stand on an equal footing, the restraining principle of the Constitution of 1931 is still more moderate than the version of the principle found in the current constitution.

Iran

Under the current Iranian Constitution of 1979, the restraining principle articulated in the preamble as well as in several articles, of which Article 4 is the main one.[100] It requires that:

> All civil, penal, financial, economic, administrative, cultural, military, political, and other laws and regulations must be based on Islamic criteria. This principle applies absolutely and generally to all articles of the Constitution

96 Constitution of Afghanistan (1964), Article 64.
97 Constitution of Afghanistan (1923), Article 72.
98 Constitution of Afghanistan (1931), Articles 11, 21, 22, and 65. The Constitution, moreover, contained a general provision in Article 10, requiring all Afghans to strictly respect the law of the land as well as the state religion.
99 Constitution of Afghanistan (1931), Article 5.
100 Constitution of Iran (1979), Preamble and Articles 2, 3, 4, 91, and 94.

as well as to all other laws and regulations, and the fuqaha of the Guardian Council are the judges in this matter.

Moreover, Article 2 which lays out the system of belief of the Islamic Republic, establishes amongst others the "divine inspiration and its foundational role in the articulation of the laws; resurrection and its constructive role in explanation of laws; the justice of God in creation and legislation".

Compared to the restraining principle under the current Afghan and Iraqi constitutions, as well as the Iranian Constitution of 1906–1907, the restraining principle in Article 4 of the 1979 Constitution has a far more comprehensive reach. The requirements under this restraining principle, which speaks of "Islamic criteria" are vaguer than the criteria under the Afghan and Iraqi principles which speak of "the tenets and provisions" and "the established provisions" of Islam, respectively. There is no general agreement as to what constitutes "Islamic criteria", and the terminology was not discussed during the drafting process. As a result of the vagueness, wide discretion is given to the Guardian Council, which is empowered to control the compatibility of legislation with "Islamic criteria".

Iraq

With the Constitution of 2005, the restraining principle is, for the first time in Iraq's constitutional memory, introduced in the legal system. None of the past Iraqi constitutions established the state religion as a limitation to legislation. The principle is found in Article 2(1)A: "No law may be enacted that contradicts the established provisions of Islam".[101] During the drafting of the constitution, this was one of the main points of dispute.[102] Some commentators have pointed out that the Iraqi restraining principle, in limiting the scope of "established provisions" as opposed to all provisions provide for a weaker restraining principle.[103]

During the drafting process, there was some consensus that Islam should play a role in the constitutional framework. However, the language and scope of this role were subject to disagreement, largely polarized along ethno-religious lines. The Shia parties wanted to entrench the strongest language possible for Islam, while some of the more secular groups and the Kurdish parties wanted it to have a limited role.

101 Constitution of Iraq (2005), contains three restraining principles in Article 2(1). The first is a restraining principle based on the state religion. The second is a restraining principle based on "the principles of democracy", while the third is based on "the rights and basic freedoms" of the Constitution itself. I will return to the relationship between these three principles.

102 Ashley Deeks and Matthew Burton, "Iraq's Constitution: A Drafting History", *Cornell International Law Journal* [2007] 40.

103 Noah Feldman and Roman Martinez, "Constitutional Politics and Text in the New Iraq: An Experiment in Islamic Democracy", *Fordham Law Review* [2006] 883–920.

The background for the introduction of the restraining principle in the 2005 Constitution can be found in the Interim Constitution. Article 7 of the Transitional Administrative Law (TAL), which served as the governing document from the beginning of the occupation until the promulgation of the permanent constitution, contained both a source of law provision and a restraining principle stating that

> Islam … is to be considered a source of legislation and no law that contradicts the universally agreed tenets of Islam, the principles of democracy, or the rights cited in Chapter Two of this Law may be enacted during the transitional period.

There was considerable pressure on the Coalition Provisional Authority to avoid the inclusion of Islam in the TAL and in the later permanent constitution. At the same time, the Shia Islamist parties proposed that the TAL declare Islam as "the basis of all law".[104] Later drafts referred to Islam as "a principal source". The Kurdish faction agreed to this language, while the Sunni Arab faction demanded that a reference to "democratic values" be added to the restraining principle in Article 7.[105]

During the drafting, one member on the drafting committee made a counterproposal that Article 7 be drafted to forbid laws that "contradicts the universally agreed tenets of Islam, the principles of democracy or the rights cited in Chapter 2 of the law".[106] As a result, the restraining principle in the TAL turned multifaceted in an effort to reach a compromise on the role of Islam.[107] From the seeds sawn in the TAL, the restraining principle found its way into the permanent Constitution 2005, albeit with different wording, leading to the adoption of a stronger restraining principle in the permanent constitution. The reasons behind this strengthening are unclear. Some commentators have sought to explain this by pointing to the lack of experience. Deeks and Burton comment that "if Iraq's brief democratic experience is any guide, we only once saw or heard legislators refer to Islam as a source of law during the year in which the TNA produced legislation".[108] Another reason can be found in the result of the elections for the National Constitutional Assembly. These elections took place in January 2005, with the Shi'a Iraqis succeeding in organizing a single electoral list. The Shia

104 Ahmad Dawood and Tom Ginsburg, "Constitutional Islamization and Human Rights: The Surprising Origin and Spread of Islamic Supremacy in Constitutions", *University of Chicago Public Law & Legal Theory Working Paper*, No. 477 [2014] 70.

105 Paul Bremer, referenced in Dawood and Ginsburg (2014) ibid. 70.

106 Ibid. 71.

107 Noah Feldman and Roman Martinez, "Constitutional Politics and Text in the New Iraq: An Experiment in Islamic Democracy", *Fordham Law Review* [2006] 904.

108 Ashley Deeks and Matthew Burton, "Iraq's Constitution: A Drafting History", *Cornell International Law Journal* [2007] 40 7.

victory made them the most significant political force in Iraq.[109] The secular group obtained only 13% of the vote. The Sunni boycott of the process had, moreover, left Sunni Iraqis without much influence in the drafting. The Kurdish faction was, despite being otherwise secular, willing to make concessions on religious issues in return for a demand of federalism and regional autonomy.[110] Feldman argues that the "Shi'i-Kurd understanding on federalism allowed a larger role for Islam at the national level than might otherwise have been possible".[111]

In addition to the debates about whether Islam should be "*a*" or "*the*" source of legislation, there was also debate around whether the word "principal" or "fundamental" should be used. Secular groups wanted to use the word "principal" to guarantee against Islam being used as *the* primary source. The Shia Islamist faction insisted on "the principal source of law" terminology. Ultimately, the wording was changed to "foundation". Haider Ala Hamoudi argues that the Iraqi constitutional drafters were aware that Egypt had been operating under an Islamic restraining principle for nearly two decades, and that a similar principle had appeared in the constitution of Afghanistan. As a result, Islamists within Iraq, both Shia and Sunni, wanted to ensure a similar provision in the Iraqi constitution.[112] While the Shia faction initially had agreed not to have a restraining principle in the TAL, they changed their position upon learning that the Afghan Constitution would include one.[113]

Why did the inclusion of Islam become such a central point in the political power struggle during the drafting of the 2005 Constitution? For the Kurdish and Sunni faction, entrenching Islam strongly would signify a risk that their political interests might be subjugated to Shia interpretations. The restraining principle and source of law provisions were therefore not only assertions of identity, but as Dawood and Ginsburg point out, they reflected and were "symptomatic of competing strategic political visions".[114]

4.2.3 The interpretation of the restraining principle

There is no general agreement about what constitutes "Islamic criteria", "tenets and provisions of Islam", or "established provisions" of Islam. Ultimately it is the

109 Andrew Arato, *Constitution-Making Under Occupation: The Politics of Imposed Revolution in Iraq* (Columbia University Press, 2009) 2 and 7.

110 Noah Feldman and Roman Martinez, "Constitutional Politics and Text in the New Iraq: An Experiment in Islamic Democracy", *Fordham Law Review* [2006] 75 898.

111 Ibid. 915.

112 Haider Hamoudi, "Repugnancy in the Arab World", *Willamette Law Review* (2012) 48 439.

113 Noah Feldman and Roman Martinez, "Constitutional Politics and Text in the New Iraq: An Experiment in Islamic Democracy", *Fordham Law Review* [2006] 75 903.

114 Ahmad Dawood and Tom Ginsburg, "Constitutional Islamization and Human Rights: The Surprising Origin and Spread of Islamic Supremacy in Constitutions", *University of Chicago Public Law & Legal Theory Working Paper*, No. 477 [2014] 80.

State, through the organ empowered to interpret the constitution that will decide on how the restraining principle is to be interpreted, and thus to what extent legislation is to be restricted. In practice, legislation could therefore be enacted that according to some is contrary to established religious doctrine, yet be deemed to be in accordance with it, since the power to decide so rests with the State. Similarly, legislation that traditionally would be seen as compatible with religious doctrine may be rejected if the interpreting authority deems it so. The ultimate content of the restraining principle and the source of law principle thus depends on the interpreting authority, whether it is the Supreme Court as in Afghanistan and Iraq, or the Guardian Council as in Iran. In systems where the interpreting authority is appointed by the executive power, this would mean that the executive will have increased power in legislative matters.

The primary problem of the restraining principle is therefore not the issue of interpretation or the type of content one gives it. The primary problem is the additional basis that the restraining principles gives for limiting legislation in the first place, including legislation that limits constitutional rights. The restraining principle may not materialize in practice, or it may be interpreted in a way that is consistent with international human rights law. However, the mere existence of the potential is in itself problematic. The existence of such restraining principles may weaken the role of the legislative branch and thus also renders weak the principle of popular sovereignty. In the past constitutions, the enforcement of the restraining principle was in the hands of the legislative branch itself – making the parliament sovereign when it came to how to interpret the principle. The content of the restraining principle and its impact would therefore largely depend on the composition of the parliament. However, the de-secularized constitutions move the power of implementation of the principle out of the legislative branch and to judicial organs that are increasingly de-secularized themselves and composed of members with religious training but not necessarily trained in law. In Iran, the control rests with the six Islamic jurists in the Guardian Council who perform a priori review of all legislation and its compatibility with Article 4. In Afghanistan and Iraq, the control is with the Supreme Court, but such review takes place only if the constitutionality of legislation is challenged before the court.

The extent to which the restraining principle in practice limits constitutional rights depends in part on how the principle is interpreted against other constitutional provisions. In the Afghan and Iraqi Constitution, there is in addition to the restraining principle also provisions that require legislation to comply with democracy and human rights. As such these constitutions have three restraining principles – one based on religion, the second based on human rights and the third based on democracy. Some commentators have argued that there is not necessarily any inherent contradiction between the different principles if one interprets the content of religion in accordance with international human rights law and democratic principles. The drafting processes of the Afghan and Iraqi Constitution, however, clearly show that the inclusion of the Islamic restraining principle resulted from a process attempting to include the interests of the non-secular factions while at the same time seeking to prevent wider references to religion.[115]

In the Iraqi Constitution, all the restraining principles are contained in the same provision, suggesting their equal standing. Article 2(1) holds:

Islam is the official religion of the State and is a foundation source of legislation:

A. No law may be enacted that contradicts the established provisions of Islam.
B. No law may be enacted that contradicts the principles of democracy.
C. No law may be enacted that contradicts the rights and basic freedoms stipulated in this Constitution.

The judiciary has the power to review legislation for compatibility with religion, but has no similar review power to review compatibility with democracy and basic rights.[116] While some courts may balance the restraining principle in favor of democratic rights, the constitutional structure offers no guarantee.[117] The restraining principle would, furthermore, preclude the application of the principle of proportionality as a principle for considering limitations to constitutional rights under constitutionalism. When rights are limited to what follows from Islamic principles or criteria, an examination of proportionality becomes irrelevant. What distinguishes the consideration of limitations to rights under the de-secularized constitutions with those under that of modern constitutionalism is not primarily the limitation of the right through legislation, but that the constitutional right is already limited in scope through the constitutional provision itself. The de-secularized constitution limits the scope of the right itself firstly through limiting the scope of the right, and next by precluding the application of the principle of proportionality.

4.2.4 Non-discrimination and equality provisions

The constitution of the three states contain provisions on non-discrimination and equal treatment, yet the scope of these provisions differ with respect to the grounds upon which discrimination is prohibited and with respect to the scope of those who are considered as rights-holders.

115 Ashley Deeks and Matthew Burton, "Iraq's Constitution: A Drafting History", *Cornell International Law Journal* [2007] 40; Noah Feldman and Roman Martinez, "Constitutional Politics and Text in the New Iraq: An Experiment in Islamic Democracy", *Fordham Law Review* [2006] 75.

116 For the opposite view, see Ran Hirschl, *Constitutional Theocracy* (Harvard University Press, 2010). Hirschl presents the argument that courts in these systems operate as secularizing agents.

117 See, for example, UN Special Rapporteur on the protection and promotion of the right to freedom of opinion and expression, 2E/CN.4/2004/62/Add.2 (2004); Human Rights Committee, A/48/40/Vol. 1 (1993) 44, at para. 262 (Iran).

Afghanistan

In the Afghan Constitution, the general non-discrimination and equality provision is found in Article 22: "Any kind of discrimination and distinction between citizens of Afghanistan shall be forbidden. The citizens of Afghanistan, man and woman, have equal rights and duties before the law". The provision is limited to "citizens" of Afghanistan. The limitation of constitutional rights to the citizens of the country is, with some exceptions, a general feature of the Afghan Constitution, where most of the rights are limited to either "citizens" or "Afghans". Exceptions to this are the rights to freedom of religion (Article 2), right to life (Article 23), the general liberty provision in Article 24, due process rights (Articles 25–27, 30–32), prohibition against torture and persecution (Article 29), privacy and property rights (Articles 37–38, 40), and compensation provisions (Article 51), which are articulated as rights for "everyone" or "each individual".

The Constitution's distinction between constitutional rights reserved for citizens and constitutional rights that apply to everyone is supported by Article 57 which states that

> The state shall guarantee the rights and liberties of foreign citizens in Afghanistan in accordance with the law. These people shall be obliged to respect the laws of the state of Afghanistan within the limits of the provisions of international law.

With the exception of those constitutional rights listed previously that apply equally to non-citizens, the constitution thus allows for limitation of the rights of non-Afghans through ordinary law. This would, for example, be the case with freedom of expression, which in Article 34 is articulated as a citizenship right.

Iran

The non-discrimination principles in the Iranian Constitution are found in Articles 19 and 20. Article 19 states that "All people of Iran, whatever ethnic group or tribe to which they belong, enjoy equal rights; and color, race, language, and the like, do not bestow any privilege". The provision is geared towards ethnic equality. Although the list of grounds upon which discrimination is prohibited is articulated as being non-exhaustive, it is particularly noticeable that grounds such as religion and gender are not explicitly mentioned in the provision, particularly considering that the Constitution is from 1979. There is thus no positive provision explicitly prohibiting discrimination based on religion or belief.

Article 20, directed towards equal protection under the law states that "All citizens of the country, both men and women, equally enjoy the protection of the law and enjoy all human, political, economic, social and cultural rights, in conformity with Islamic criteria". This provision limits equality and non-discrimination in two ways. Firstly, the provision is limited to "citizens". Secondly, the content and interpretation of equality and non-discrimination are to be interpreted according to "Islamic criteria". The reference to "human" rights in the provision could at first glance suggest a reference to international human rights. However, in Farsi, the provision applies the term "*ensani*" which literally means "human", but which is not the expression used for the legal term "human rights". In Farsi, "human rights" would be translated to "*hooghoogh-e bashar*". The same expression is found in Article 14 which concerns the treatment of non-Muslims. In the French translation of the provision, the expression is translated as "*droits en tant qu'êtres humains*", which is different from "*droits humains*", which would be the usual way of referring to human rights.[118] The expression in Article 14 and 21 thus speaks of a concept different from that of *human rights*, and refers to the Islamic legal notion of not harming non-Muslims, which is a concept very different from that of enjoying human rights. It is a prime example of the rhetoric of modern constitutional law merging with that of Islamic law, which does not necessarily reflect the same content. The discussions during the constitutional drafting confirm that the expression is viewed in its Islamic sense, and not as a reference to human rights and the concepts of individual rights and equality.[119] Furthermore, during the drafting process, there was no discussion about gender equality, understood as equal rights between men and women. By contrast, a number of the members of the drafting assembly argued for the removal of Article 21, based on the argument that there was no such thing as gender equality in Islamic law.[120]

Iraq

The right to non-discrimination and equality is expressed in three articles in the Iraqi Constitution. Article 14 concerns equality before the law. As with the Afghan provision, the Iraqi provision is limited to citizens, but unlike the Afghan provision which is formulated in general terms, the Iraqi provision lists the grounds upon which discrimination is prohibited: "Iraqis are equal before the law without discrimination based on gender, race, ethnicity, origin, color, religion, creed, belief or opinion, economic and social status".

The provision is limited to "citizens". The express inclusion of "religion, creed, belief or opinion" represents a strengthening of the rights to freedom of opinion, expression, and religion in a society where religious sectarianism is a serious challenge. However, the list of grounds appears exhaustive in the absence of the words "such as". In addition to Article 14, two other provisions are concerned with equality and non-discrimination. Article 16 guarantees equal opportunities for "all Iraqis", while Article 20 is directed towards political rights and

118 Although the expression "*hooghoogh-e ensani*" is used in both Article 14 and Article 21, the French translation of the Constitution uses "*droits humains*" in the latter, and "*leur droits en tant qu'êtres humains*" in the former.

119 Discussions in the Assembly for Revision of the Constitutional Draft, Vol. 3, 1781–1784.

120 Discussions in the Assembly for Revisions of the Constitutional Draft, Vol. 4, 319–320.

participation in public affairs, and particularly guarantees gender equality in this area. These two articles are also limited to Iraqi citizens.

Here, a contradiction appears between Article 14 and Article 41. Article 41 states that "Iraqis are free in their commitment to their personal status according to their religions, sects, beliefs, or choices, and this shall be regulated by law". In its review of Iraq, the Committee on the Elimination of Discrimination against Women (CEDAW Committee) has highlighted that a number of discriminatory provisions against women remain in the Penal Code, the Code of Criminal Procedure, and the Personal Status Act, and recommends that Article 41 of the Constitution be repealed with the aim of guaranteeing equality between women and men in line with Article 14 of the constitution.[121]

4.2.5 *Institutional aspects of the adjudication of rights*

Ultimately, the content of constitutional rights is determined by the authority empowered to interpret the constitution, and on whether individuals who believe that their constitutional rights have been infringed upon can try their claim before an independent judiciary. Of particular interest in this regard are the competencies and composition of the institutions tasked with interpreting constitutional rights, and the role of the state religion in this regard.

Judicial review has not been part of the constitutional culture of the three States, and it is not expressly guaranteed in the new constitutions. Under the past constitutions of the three countries, legislation was assumed to be in accordance with the Constitution, a presumption that reflects a version of parliamentary sovereignty.[122] Moreover, the tradition of constitutional review as such has been weak. The new constitutions, while falling short of express guarantee for judicial review, do contain mechanisms for review of constitutionality of legislation, both with respect to whether legislation is in accordance with the restraining principle and with respect to the constitutionality of legislation in general. Since it is the judiciary, either ordinary courts or special judicial bodies, that are tasked with the power of judicial review, the composition of these organs would be significant.

Under the Afghan Constitution, the interpretation of the Constitution rests with the Supreme Court, composed of nine members appointed by the President and endorsed by the Lower House of the National Assembly.[123] Article 121 states that the Supreme Court, being the highest judicial organ, has the power to review the constitutionality of legislation and international treaties "at the request of the Government or courts". The Constitution expressly mandates the use of religious

121 CEDAW/C/IRQ/CO/4-6, 10 March 2014, para. 17 and 18.

122 The Iranian Constitution of 1906–1907 contained a provision establishing a council composed of religious scholars to perform a priori review of legislation to ensure its compatibility with Islam. However, the provisions was not implemented. See Vanessa Martin, *Islam and Modernism: The Iranian Revolution of 1906* (Syracuse University Press, 1989).

123 Constitution of Afghanistan (2004), Articles 116, 117, and 121.

law in two situations. Firstly, in cases where there is no provision in law or in the Constitution itself, the court is to use the law of the Hanafi branch of Sunni Islam, with the limits set by the Constitution.[124] Secondly, in personal status cases relating to Shi'a Muslims, the courts are to apply Shi'a jurisprudence.[125]

The composition and qualifications set for the Supreme Court give the state religion a further influence on the scope of constitutional rights. Article 118, establishing the qualifications for the judges of the Supreme Court, requires that they must have higher education in either legal studies or in Islamic jurisprudence. As a result, qualifications in law and religious studies are set as equal. In principle, this means that one may have a Supreme Court entirely made up of judges without legal education. In the first years of the new Constitution, the Supreme Court was indeed dominated by conservative religiously trained judges, rendering judgments that reflected a highly orthodox interpretation of the restraining principle. Among the judgments rendered were a ban on cable TV, a ban on women singing on television, affirmation of the death penalty for blasphemy, affirmation of the death penalty for homosexuality – despite the fact that the Afghan Penal Code stipulates imprisonment – and a judgment ruling that a 13-year-old girl could not get a divorce from her husband, despite the law setting the legal age for marriage to 16 years for girls.[126] These rulings were all based on the use of the restraining principle, stating an interpretation of the official state religion was the basis for the decisions.

In Iran, the interpretation of the constitutional rights rests with the Guardian Council and ordinary courts.[127] Contrary to the Afghan and Iraqi Constitutions where the Supreme Court is granted the power to interpret the Constitution and the restraining principle, the Iranian Constitution gives this power to a special organ outside the ordinary judiciary. The Guardian Council is a twelve-member body composed of six religious scholars (*faqih*), chosen by the Supreme Leader, and six jurists specialized in different areas of law, selected by the Parliament after nomination by the Head of the Judiciary.[128] All members of the Guardian Council must be Muslim.[129] In addition to overseeing the elections, the Guardian Council reviews and determines the compatibility of legislation with the restraining principle and reviews the general constitutionality of legislation. The review of compatibility with the restraining principle is reserved to the six religiously trained members, while the general review of constitutionality is decided by all

124 Constitution of Afghanistan (2004), Article 130.

125 Constitution of Afghanistan (2004), Article 131.

126 Report of the UN High Commissioner for Human Rights on the situation of human rights in Afghanistan and on the achievement of technical assistance in the field of human rights. A/HRC/13/62.

127 Iranian Constitution (1979), Articles 91, 94, 95, 96, and 98.

128 Constitution of Iran (1979), Article 91. The Head of the Judiciary is elected by the Supreme Leader, in accordance with Article 157.

129 Constitution of Iran (1979), Article 91. So far, all members of the Guardian Council have been male.

members.[130] Because the deliberations of the Guardian Council are not public, and the published decisions only consist of a short conclusion without providing the reasoning leading up to it, it is difficult to determine the considerations and deliberations behind the reviews.

The review of the Guardian Council is *a priori*, meaning that all legislation passed by Parliament must be sent to the Guardian Council for review before it can enter into force.[131] If the Guardian Council decides that a law is incompatible with either the restraining principle or with the Constitution, it returns the bill to Parliament.[132] In cases of continued conflict, the bill will be put before a different organ, the Expediency Discernment Council.[133]

The regular adjudication of constitutional rights rests with the courts.[134] The Constitution requires that the Chief of the Supreme Court and the Prosecutor General be religious scholars.[135] The qualifications of ordinary judges are set in ordinary law, but the Constitution requires that these qualifications must be in accordance with the criteria of Islamic law.[136]

The Islamization of the judiciary that took place with the 1979 Constitution, the purge of judges trained in modern law under the previous Constitution, and a change in the curriculum of law faculties have, moreover, contributed to a significant change in the composition of judges and of the legal sphere in general.

The Iraqi Constitution empowers the Federal Supreme Court, as the highest judicial organ, with "overseeing the constitutionality of laws and regulations in effect" and with "interpreting the provisions of the Constitution".[137] The wording "in effect" suggests that the control is exercised *a posteriori*, and could, in principle, grant the Supreme Court the power to perform judicial review. Unlike the Afghan and Iranian Constitution, the Iraqi Constitution does not require the use of religious law in constitutional interpretation.

However, the state religion enters the adjudication of constitutional rights through the constitutional requirements for the qualifications of the judges. The Constitution establishes that the Federal Supreme Court is to be composed of judges who are experts in Islamic jurisprudence and judges who are experts in law.[138] Unlike the Afghan Constitution which states that judges must be trained in either Islamic jurisprudence or in law, the Iraqi Constitution requires that the Federal Supreme Court consists of both.[139] The wording thus prevents the court

130 Constitution of Iran (1979), Articles 96 and 98.
131 Constitution of Iran (1979), Article 94.
132 Ibid.
133 Constitution of Iran (1979), Article 112. The members of the Expediency Discernment Council are chosen by the Supreme Leader.
134 Constitution of Iran (1979), Article 156.
135 Constitution of Iran (1979), Article 162.
136 Constitution of Iran (1979), Article 163.
137 Constitution of Iraq (2005), Article 93.
138 Constitution of Iraq (2005), Article 92(2).
139 Ibid.

being composed of judges who solely have religious training and are without a background in law. However, the inclusion of members with a background only in religious law is unprecedented in Iraqi constitutional history and represents a further institutionalization of the official state religion.

Although there is no specific provision on the use of religious law in adjudication, the question remains whether the restraining principle has any bearing on the interpretation of constitutional rights. In the first years following the adoption of the Constitution, the Federal Supreme Court was reluctant to apply the restraining principle and refrained from raising questions on constitutional interpretation. Between the entering into force of the Constitution in 2005 and 2010, the question of compatibility with the restraining principle came up in only one case. The case, which dealt with the issue of contract law, was in itself fairly uncontroversial. However, the court rendered a principled decision on the use of the restraining principle, holding that Islamic jurists had been wrong in their interpretation of Islamic law as it concerns contracts.[140]

In 2010 and 2011, however, two decisions were rendered that dealt explicitly with the restraining principle and the role of Islam in the Constitution. Both cases dealt with questions that have traditionally been considered at the center of Islamic law.[141] The decisions concerned the role of the court itself, and the extent to which it should play a role in ensuring that legislation is compatible with the restraining principle. In both decisions, the court showed a high level of deference to the legislative branch. The first case, concerning the concept "divorce by agency", was brought before the court by a Shi'a woman. Generally, under both Sunni and Shia Islamic law, the only party who unilaterally has the right to divorce is the husband. However, since Islamic law regards marriage as a contract, the woman can negotiate to include in her marriage contract the right for her to divorce. Within Sunni Islam, this right is generally referred to as a right to "divorce by delegation", while Shia Islam refers to the right as "divorce by agency" or *wakala*. The 1959 Personal Status Code of Iraq, in force also under the new Constitution, largely defers to religious law in areas of personal status, and recognized both methods as valid.[142]

However, a 1980 amendment to the Personal Status Code, which intended to ban the ability of the husband to give a third party the power of agency to issue a divorce ended up appearing to ban all divorces by agency, though not by delegation, although the content of the two are the same. As a result, the right was abolished for Shi'a women, while permitted for Sunni women. Article 34(1) indicates that a divorce may be issued by a wife through agency or delegation, while Article 34(2) bans the use of agency in divorce, creating two provisions that contradict

140 Decision 60, 2010, Federal Supreme Court of Iraq.

141 I have based the account of these two cases on the English commentary to the case by Haider Hamoudi, *Judicial Review of Islamic Law under Iraq's Constitution*, JURIST-Forum, 26 April 2011.

142 Personal Status Code of Iraq (1969), Article 34.

each other. The plaintiff had issued her divorce through agency in accordance with Shia Islamic law, which was also reflected in Article 34(1) of the Personal Status Code, and she demanded that such rules be recognized under Article 14 of the Iraqi Constitution which gives "each Iraqi the right to live by the rules of their religion or sect in areas of personal status, hereunder family law". In its decision, the Federal Supreme Court decided to immunize the Personal Status Code from judicial review, at least with respect to applying the restraining principle. While it did not suggest that the provision under the Personal Status Code was in accordance with Islamic law, the court concluded that it was not the institution to effect the necessary changes to the law. The restraining principle in Article 2 of the Constitution, which was not raised by the plaintiff, would have enabled the court to strike down the legislation by arguing that to deny a wife the right to divorce violates Islam's "established provisions". That the court decided not to apply Article 2 is in this regard significant. In abstaining from applying the restraining principle, the Federal Supreme Court placed the interpretation of the restraining principle into the domain of the legislature.

The second case concerned *waqfs*, a common form of trust under Islamic law which usually holds significant financial resources.[143] The litigant challenged a law that permitted the state administrative agency responsible for the administration of *waqfs* that were set up by private parties, to appropriate 10% of the value of the *waqfs* to itself as an administrative fee. The litigant claimed that this was a violation of the restraining principle in Article 2 of the Constitution since Shi'a Islamic law did not permit the assessment of an administrative fee against a *waqf*. The court's approach was similar to the previous case. It refused to alter or amend the law, but invited the legislature to do so in a "specialized review" manner that would ensure conformity with Islam. The court held that it could not apply Article 2, since the legislation in question was a matter relying heavily on Islamic law. According to the court, the proper amendments to such legislation required a detailed and specialized review that only the legislature could undertake. In both the 2010 and 2011 case, the Federal Supreme Court avoided applying the restraining principle in Article 2, stating that because the law in question relied on Islamic sources, the legislature would be better able to address it.

In the three countries, the de-secularized constitution involves a desecularization of the judiciary as well, both through the change in the qualification of judges and in the mandatory use of the official state religion in adjudication. The constitutions introduce a requirement that all or some of the judges are Islamic scholars. This will arguably have an impact on the way in which constitutional provisions, including constitutional rights, are interpreted and applied. Although this, in theory, does not necessarily lead to a more restrictive interpretation of constitutional rights, it will, however, limit the judiciary in its decisions.

143 Decision 61, 2011, Federal Supreme Court of Iraq.

4.2.6 Constitutional amendments

Another limitation on constitutional rights under the de-secularized constitutions is through the role of the state religion as a restriction on permissible future constitutional amendments.

The Constitution of Afghanistan prohibits amendments to "the principles of adherence to the tenets of the Holy religion of Islam as well as Islamic Republicanism".[144] The provision continues with the contradictory criteria for amendments, holding that "Amending fundamental rights of the people shall be permitted only to make them more effective".

Under the Iraqi Constitution, there are no substantive criteria that limit constitutional amendments. The procedural criteria differ depending on the type of constitutional provisions, distinguishing between, on the one hand, amendments to the fundamental principles and fundamental rights in Section One and Section Two of the Constitution, and, on the other hand, amendments to the other constitutional provisions. The Constitution establishes stricter rules for amendments to the former, which would entail that it would be more difficult to repeal or amend the restraining principle.[145]

The Iranian Constitution's amendment provisions contain, in addition to procedural criteria, wide-ranging substantive limits to the types of amendments. Article 177 establishes that:

> The content of the Articles of the Constitution related to the Islamic character of the political system; the basis of all the rules and regulations according to Islamic criteria, the religious footing; the objectives of the Islamic Republic of Iran; the democratic character of the government; the *wailayat al-amr*; the Imamate of Ummah; and the administration of the affairs of the country based on national referenda; official religion of Iran (Islam and the school (Twelver *Ja'fari*) are unalterable.

The provision's wide substantive limitations make it near-impossible to amend any of the existing constitutional provisions, including the constitutional rights provisions. In addition, all of the features that fall under external qualifiers would be covered by the provision and cannot be subject to amendments.

4.2.7 Constitutional rights provisions

The de-secularized constitution commonly articulates constitutional rights by stating the right, and require its exercise "in accordance with Islamic criteria",

144 Constitution of Afghanistan (2004), Article 149.

145 Constitution of Iraq (2005), Article 126(2). Amendments to the constitutional rights provisions in chapter 2 of the Constitution requires in two successive electoral terms, the approval of two-thirds of the members of the federal parliament; the approval of the people in a referendum; and ratification by the President within seven days.

or similar phrases. In some instances, the formulation of the right is limited both through the official state religion and, in addition, through the formulation of the right itself in a way that is fundamentally different from the formulation found under international human rights law.[146]

In the Iranian Constitution, the large majority of the constitutional rights state that the right is to be interpreted in conformity with Islamic criteria.[147] The state religion thus functions as a limitation on two levels. Firstly, through the form of government, the restraining principle and the narrow scope of the non-discrimination and equality provisions. Secondly, through the wording of the constitutional rights in themselves. A similar use of the official state religion is not found in the Iraqi Constitution. The Afghan Constitution, however, has included the state religion as a condition with respect to two of the rights provisions.[148]

The conditioning of constitutional rights by reference to the state religion grants the State broader discretion to limit rights, and reduces its responsibility to respect, protect, and promote rights. Such conditioning also gives broad powers to the state institution vested with the power to interpret constitutional rights. The second point to note about the conditioning of constitutional rights through the state religion is that this form of articulating constitutional rights limits the application of the proportionality principle in the interpretation and adjudication of rights.

The three constitutions reserve several rights to "citizens". Moreover, in the Afghan and Iranian constitutions, a number of constitutional rights are explicitly conditioned by the religion of an individual.[149] The "right to hold rights" thus depend in some areas on the religious affiliation of a person, where affiliation with the state religion grants privileges that would not apply to those of a different religion. Among the three constitutions, the Iranian Constitution goes the furthest in establishing an affiliation with the state religion as a criterion for being able to have rights.

146 The constitutional protection of freedom of expression under the Iranian 1979 Constitution is, for example, limited to press and publications, and differs widely from the general and broad right to freedom of expression that exists under international human rights law, including Article 19 of the ICCPR.

147 Constitution of Iran (1979), see, for example, Articles 20, 21, 24, 26, 27, and 28.

148 Constitution of Afghanistan (2004) – these are the rights to association and political parties, and the right to education in Articles 35(1) and 45. In addition, Article 54 concerning the state's obligation to adopt measures to protect the family, provides that the state is under the obligation to eliminate "traditions contrary to the principles of the sacred religion of Islam".

149 Constitution of Iraq (2005) does not explicitly condition the right to hold rights to the religion of a person.

5 The formal regulation of freedom of thought, expression, and political participation in the Afghan, Iranian, and Iraqi constitutions

This chapter examines to what extent the use of the state religion in the de-secularized constitutions of Afghanistan, Iran, and Iraq limits the rights to freedom of thought, expression, and political participation. Freedom of thought and opinion include the right to choose, maintain, or change one's thought. Thought is thus unrestricted. Yet, the way in which a constitution limits other rights may impact the ability of an individual to form a free opinion. Freedom of thought captures both religious and non-religious beliefs, and as interpreted by the UN Human Rights Committee, freedom of thought and freedom of conscience are protected equally with the freedom of religion or belief.[1] In the context of constitutional desecularization, one of the questions that arises is to what extent the state religion interferes with beliefs other than that of the state. Historically, freedom of religion has had a particular privileged status compared to that of freedom of conscience in general, sometimes in strong contrast and opposition to freedom of thought.[2] International human rights law and domestic systems are increasingly equating freedom of religion with other forms of non-religious thought.[3] According to some commentators, the notion of "freedom of religion" has become superfluous, since the type of manifestations it covers are already protected by other rights.[4] The emergence of constitutionalism

1 The Human Rights Committee, General Comment 22. Article 18 of the ICCPR protects theistic, non-theistic, and atheistic beliefs, as well as the right not to profess any religion or belief.

2 A critical philosophical approach to this is found in Spinoza, whose philosophy of thought is partly a critique of religion. See Vicente Serrano,"Freedom of Thought as Radical Freedom in Spinoza's Critique of Religion", *Reformation and Renaissance Review* [2012] 14:1 23–39.

3 International human rights law increasingly applies the notion "freedom of thought, conscience and religion", and this formulation is indeed what is found in the main international human rights documents. See UDHR, Article 18; ICCPR, Article 18; CERD, Article 1; CRC, Article 14; CRMW, Article 12.

4 See, for example, Henrik Palmer Olsen, "The Right to Freedom of Religion: A Critical Review", *Scandinavian Studies in Law* [2007] 52 227–254. Olsen argues that freedom of religion can be incorporated into other rights, such as freedom of expression, freedom of association and assembly, and prohibition against discrimination. As such, there is therefore no principled reason why religious activities should have a privileged status compared to other activities, such as, for example, sport, music, literature, and science.

began in most countries with the establishment of a confessional state, with an official state religion in combination with freedom of religion for a selected and limited number of other religions.[5] With the confessional state, religion and religious authorities became, one may say, nationalized, subject to state control instead of having transnational, cross-border authority. As observed by one commentator in the European context, "confessionalization strengthened political centralization when the early modern state used religion to consolidate territorial boundary, to incorporate the Church into the state bureaucracy and impose social control on its subjects".[6] Therefore, religious conformity became more of a "political necessity rather than a religious one".[7] The confessional state and the limited freedom of religion and thought in the early stages of constitutionalism are therefore better understood under the paradigm of state sovereignty and consolidation. Under that paradigm, freedom of religion was more a matter of strengthening the state rather than the individual. Under modern constitutionalism, the justification for freedom of religion and thought is based on the principle of equality. Rawls, developing this in his first principle of the theory of justice, argues that it is not possible to support freedom religion and opinion without also supporting the same right for others.[8] In international human rights law, in addition to being guaranteed in the United Nations Charter and the Universal Declaration of Human Rights (UDHR), the rights of freedom of thought and religion are guaranteed in a multitude of conventions, including the ICCPR, ICESCR, CERD, CRC, CEDAW, CMW, and the Refugee Convention.[9] Under Article 18 of the ICCPR, which builds on Article 18 of the UDHR, the right has a broad scope, and pertains to "everyone" as opposed to only to citizens. While the aspect of the right pertaining to the belief part of the right cannot be restricted, the right to manifestation may be limited under certain conditions, listed in sub-paragraph 3 of the Article. The pre-conditions for limitations to

5 Benjamin de Carvalho, "The Confessional State in International Politics: Tudor England, Religion and the Eclipse of Dynasticism", *Diplomacy & Statecraft* [2014] 25:3 407431.

6 Ronnie Po-Chia, *Social Discipline in the Reformation: Central Europe 1550–1750* (Routledge, 1992) 3.

7 Michael C. Questier, *Conversion, Politics and Religion in England, 1580–1625* (Cambridge University Press, 1996) 166.

8 John Rawls, *A Theory of Justice* (Harvard University Press, 1999).

9 UN General Assembly, International Covenant on Civil and Political Rights, 16 December 1966, United Nations, Treaty Series, vol. 999, p. 171; N General Assembly, International Covenant on Economic, Social and Cultural Rights, 16 December 1966, United Nations, Treaty Series, vol. 993, p. 3; UN General Assembly, International Convention on the Elimination of All Forms of Racial Discrimination, 21 December 1965, United Nations, Treaty Series, vol. 660, p. 195; UN General Assembly, Convention on the Rights of the Child, 20 November 1989, United Nations, Treaty Series, vol. 1577, p. 3; UN General Assembly, Convention on the Elimination of All Forms of Discrimination Against Women, 18 December 1979, United Nations, Treaty Series, vol. 1249, p. 13; UN General Assembly, International Convention on the Protection of the Rights of All Migrant Workers and Members of their Families, 18 December 1990, A/RES/45/158; UN General Assembly, Convention Relating to the Status of Refugees, 28 July 1951, United Nations, Treaty Series, vol. 189, p. 137.

the right are that such limitations must be "prescribed by law", and be necessary and proportionate for one of the listed grounds for limitation ("public safety", "order", "health", "morals", or the "fundamental rights and freedoms of others"). Article 18 bars coercion, including policies and practices having the same intention or effect. The particular concern with respect to confessional states and their degree of coercion, have been addressed by the UN Human Rights Committee, which has held that the state religion "shall not result in any impairment of the enjoyment of any of the rights under the Covenant, including articles 18 and 27, nor in any discrimination against adherents to other religions or non-believers".[10]

It is worth noting that freedom of thought is granted expressly only by the Constitution of Iraq, which grants the right to *everyone*. By contrast, the Afghan and Iranian constitutions do not guarantee freedom of *thought*, but do address freedom of religion, limited to being construed as a citizen-right. However, even this regulation is subject to significant limitations.

In terms of freedom of expression, this is a right that only in the modern period has become defined as a right.[11] Even in countries with extensive legal protection afforded to speech, there is a continuous debate about its interpretation. Jonathan Israel notes the 17th-century dispute about whether the publication and general discussion of fundamental philosophical, religious, moral, and political issues was beneficial or harmful to the general good.[12] Spinoza's argument for freedom of expression, and especially for the press, was under attack by a number of Enlightenment thinkers who feared that making the public and each individual the arbiter of everything would lead to a destruction of ecclesiastical authority. Under international human rights law, freedom of expression is recognized as a prerequisite for the exercise of all other rights.[13] Freedom of expression is closely related to freedom of thought and belief, and the right to political participation. Article 19 of the ICCPR, building on Article 19 of UDHR, protects in absolute terms the right to freedom of opinion, and provides a broad definition of expression, which includes "the right to seek, receive and impart information and ideas

10 General Comment 22, para. 9. The same applies to official ideologies, whether religious or non-religious. See para. 10.

11 Liam Gearon, *Freedom of Expression and Human Rights: Historical, Literary and Political Context* (Sussex Academic Press, 2006). Gearon identifies the Nobel Prize in Literature as central to our considerations of freedom of expression. While in prior centuries, religions and states often had been responsible for the repression of writing, the Nobel Prize in Literature, Gearon argues, makes a constructive positive link between the ideal of literary output and the making of a better world.

12 Jonathan Israel, "Libertas Philosophand in the Eighteenth Century: Radical Enlightenment versus Moderate Enlightenment (1775–1776)", in Elizabeth Powers (ed), *Freedom of Speech: The History of an Idea* (Bucknell University Press, 2011) 3–13 and 159–174.

13 The Human Rights Committee affirms that freedom of opinion and expression are "indispensable conditions for the full development of the person", "essential for any society", and "constitute the foundation stone for every free and democratic society". General Comment 34, para. 2.

of all kinds, regardless of frontiers, either orally, in writing or in print, in the form of art, or through any other media of his choice". As with restrictions to freedom of religion or belief, the right to freedom of expression can only be limited if the limitation is provided by law, and necessary and proportionate for the protection of either "the rights or reputations of others", or "national security or of public order (*ordre public*) or of public health or morals". Such restrictions must "not put into jeopardy the right itself", and it must "never be invoked as a justification for the muzzling of any advocacy of multi-party democracy, democratic tenets and human rights".[14] In terms of the use of religion to limit freedom of expression, the Human Rights Committee has underlined that

> prohibitions of displays of lack of respect for a religion or other belief systems, including blasphemy laws, are incompatible with the Covenant, except in the specific circumstances envisaged in article 20, paragraph 2, of the Covenant. Such prohibitions must also comply with the strict requirements of article 19, paragraph 3, as well as such articles as 2, 5, 17, 18 and 26. Thus for instance, it would be impermissible for any such laws to discriminate in favor of or against one or certain religions or belief systems, or their adherents over another, or religious believers over non-believers. Nor would it be permissible for such prohibitions to be used to prevent or punish criticism of religious leaders or commentary on religious doctrine and tenets of faith.[15]

Moreover, the Committee has precluded the use of religion to limit expression, as it is not compatible with Article 19 of the ICCPR "for a restriction to be enshrined in traditional, religious or other such customary law".[16] While Article 19(3) permit limitations based on "morals", the Human Rights Committee notes that "the concept of morals derives from many social, philosophical and religious traditions; consequently limitations ... for the purpose of protecting morals must be based on principles not deriving exclusively from one single tradition", and they must be understood in light of the universality of human rights and the principle of non-discrimination.[17] The Special Rapporteur on the promotion and protection of the right to freedom of opinion and expression, furthermore, has held that criminal defamation laws may not be used to protect abstract or subjective notions or concepts, such as the State, national symbols, national identity, cultures, schools of thought, religions, ideologies, or political doctrines.[18]

14 Human Rights Committee, General Comment 34, para. 2 and 23.
15 General Comment 34, para. 48.
16 Ibid. para. 24.
17 Ibid. para. 26, 32, and General Comment 22.
18 A/HRC/14/23, para. 82. The Special Rapporteur lists explicit areas where restrictions on freedom of expression are not permissible, including in discussion of government policies and political debate, reporting on human rights, government activities, and corruption in government, expression of opinion and dissent, religion or belief, including by persons belonging to minorities or vulnerable groups, the banning or closing of publications, and

The right to freedom of expression cannot be limited to precluding political speech, as it constitutes a prerequisite for a meaningful exercise of political participation.[19] The notion of political participation encompasses a number of elements. Traditionally, political participation has been associated primarily with the right to vote and the right to stand for election. In a broad sense, it also includes freedom of expression, association, and assembly, and socio-economic rights that can enable individuals to exercise their political rights.[20] While the next sections will fall short of examining all aspects of political participation, they will instead highlight three elements of the right: form of government, the right to vote, and the right to stand for election. Form of government, the right to vote, and the right to stand for election are intertwined, in the sense that the scope and content of each has an impact on the scope and content of the other.[21] Neither political participation nor equality began as rights. Political participation has historically been a privilege linked to status, and subject to a largely uneven and unequal distribution. Political participation has traditionally been an exclusive right for a portion of the male population. The idea of constitutionalism and the democratization of political authority have represented a significant normative shift to the acknowledgment of the formal, equal right to political participation, even though the idea of who, and what, count as free and equal has been changing and expanding. The limitations established under the desecularization constitutions establish a new divide between women and men in terms of their right to political participation, but these limitations also go beyond gender. However, the re-introduction of the link between gender and political participation represents a particular feature of the desecularized constitutions.

The right to political participation has full meaning only if it is understood in the context of the form of political authority or system of governance that is based on equal liberty. A oneparty system will, for example, fall outside the framework, because it conditions political participation to adherence to a particular set of ideas. Under such a system, freedom and equality are limited to those adhering to that particular idea. A meritocracy falls outside the framework because it conditions political participation to the possession of certain merits. A theocracy falls outside the framework because it conditions political participation

access to, or use of, information and communication technologies, including radio, television, and the internet.

19 Ibid.

20 See also Human Rights Committee, General Comment 25, para. 25. The link between political participation and all other human rights was also highlighted in the 2014 Report of the Office for the United Nations High Commissioner for Human Rights, *The Factors that impede equal political participation and on steps to overcome those challenges*: "The right to participate on a basis of equality in public and political life is a central feature of the concept of inclusive democracy. The effective participation of all individuals and groups in political and public affairs underpins the realization of human rights and forms a central component of rightsbased strategies aimed at eradicating discrimination and inequalities". A/HRC/27/29, para. 6.

21 Dag Michalsen, *Rett en Internasjonal Historie* (Pax Forlag, 2011).

to a particular thought and religion, and to religious education. So, while people may have a general right to vote under these systems, such a right will arguably not qualify as a right to political participation because the right fulfills only half the equation. One may have the right to vote, but there is no equal right to exercise political authority, and to have an impact on decisions that will have an impact on them. Political authority is, in other words, not accountable to each and every person. Under such systems, individuals are receivers of the decisions of political authority, but unable to contribute to its content and exercise. In international human rights law, the right to political participation can be found in a number of instruments, including the UDHR, ICCPR, and CEDAW. The latter places a particular emphasis on the state's active duty to ensure women's right to political participation.[22] Article 25 of the ICCPR, building on Article 21 of the UDHR, provides that "every citizen", without any of the distinctions mentioned in Article 2, and without unreasonable restrictions, shall have the right to participate in the conduct of public affairs, to vote, and to be elected at genuine periodic elections by universal and equal suffrage, and to have access on general terms of equality to public service. Article 2 prohibits restrictions that discriminate on the basis of "race, color, sex, language, gender, religion, political or other opinion, national or social origin, property, birth or other status".

In terms of the form of government, there is no explicit provision prescribing an international human right to democracy as a form of governance.[23] Prior to the fall of the Berlin Wall, it was widely accepted that international law does not address this issue.[24] However, the argument and interpretation that the international human rights framework presumes that human rights are exercised within a system of constitutional democracy has gained strength. The UN Human Rights Council has adopted a number of resolutions highlighting the interdependent and mutually reinforcing relationship between democracy and human rights.[25] Nonetheless, that such a right exists is still rejected by many. Part of the opposition is based on the concern that such a right may give rise to military interventions and use of force.[26] On the other hand, others maintain that there has

22 CEDAW, Article 7.

23 By contrast, at the regional level, the 1948 Charter of the Organization of American States declares that "representative democracy is an indispensable condition for the stability, peace and development of the region". The 1950 European Convention for the Protection of Human Rights and Fundamental Freedoms states in its Preamble that "an effective political democracy is essential to the protection of fundamental freedoms".

24 For a discussion on the scholarship on democracy and international law, see Gregory Fox and Brad Roth (eds), *Democratic Governance and International Law* (Cambridge University Press, 2000).

25 See, for example, HRC/RES/19/36. Prior to this, the former Commission on Human Rights adopted several resolutions on democracy, including Resolutions 2000/47a and 2002/46.

26 A well-known example is, for example, the US declaring that one of its principle aims in invading Iraq was to turn it into a democracy.

emerged an enforceable right to democratic governance in international law.[27] A distinction can in any case be made between the existence of the right on the one hand and its enforceability through military use of force on the other.[28]

As originally drafted, Article 25 did not prohibit one-party states *per se*, based on the theoretical presumption that a single party of homogenous views in some occasions could reflect the free expression of the will of the people. The Human Rights Committee has, however, consistently showed skepticism towards whether one-party elections are possible. In 1993, the Committee found that one-party systems impose inherent limitations on genuine electoral choice. Three years later, General Comment 25 noted the centrality of the electoral processes outlined in Article 25 to an effective democratic system.[29] While the Committee acknowledged that Article 25 does not envision any particular form of electoral system, it noted that "any system operation in a State party must ... guarantee and give effect to the free expression of the will of the electors".[30] Establishing broad electoral choice as a principle animating Article 25, the Committee addresses restrictions on party activities from three different perspectives. Firstly, addressing the right of voters, the Committee notes that "party membership should not be a condition of eligibility to vote, nor a ground of disqualification".[31] Secondly, regarding candidates, "the rights of persons to stand for election should not be limited unreasonably by requiring candidates to be members of parties or of specific parties".[32] Thirdly, in setting out other political rights necessary for meaningful political participation, the Committee states that "the right to freedom of association concerned with political and public affairs, is an essential adjunct to the rights protected by article 25".[33] The Human Rights Committee has interpreted the obligations of States under this provision as requiring an active duty that positive measures are to be taken to ensure the full, effective, and equal enjoyment of electoral rights. The equal rights of women in this regard are protected by Article 25, and are more specifically addressed by the CEDAW Committee in General Recommendation 23, which interprets Articles 7 and 8 of the CEDAW. The CEDAW Committee observes that traditional cultural values and religious beliefs

27 See for example, Thomas Franck, "The Emerging Right to Democratic Governance", *American Journal of International Law* [1992] 86:1 46–91.

28 In her analysis, Alyssa Bernstein presumes such a distinction between the right itself and its enforceability. Her argument is that political rights of procedural democracy are not enforceable because they are not basic. The aim of establishing procedurally democratic regimes is different and distinct from the aim of stopping grave violations of basic human rights, and therefore cannot justify military actions. Alyssa Bernstein, "A Human Right to Intervention? Legitimacy and Intervention", in Rex Martina and David Reidy (eds), *Rawls's Law of Peoples: A Realistic Utopia?* (Blackwell Publishing Ltd, 2006) 278–298.

29 General Comment 25, para. 1

30 Ibid. para. 21.

31 General Comment 25, para. 10.

32 Ibid. para. 17.

33 Ibid. para. 26.

are amongst the issues that offer a narrow vision of women's political concerns and the systematic exclusion of women from public life.[34]

In the context of Afghanistan, Iran and Iraq, the concept of political participation was introduced in the first constitutions as a revolutionary break with the absolutist system of the 19th century. In Iran and Iraq, the concept was introduced through the establishment of a parliament that, together with the monarch, would constitute the law-making body. In Afghanistan, the first Parliament under the first Constitution had an advisory, rather than legislative, role, and it was not until the Constitution of 1964 that its powers were expanded to law-making. The introduction of a parliament in the three countries marked a significant change towards including popular participation in governance. Prior to this, law-making had been fragmented. The creation of new norms had been largely a judicial enterprise, in the hands of religious judges who based their reasoning on religious sources.

Although the right to political participation under the first constitutions was a right that could be enjoyed only by a limited part of the adult male population, it introduced for the first time a right that enabled part of the population to take part in governance. The idea of popular governance is reflected in Article 2 of the Iranian Constitution of 1906: "The National Consultative Assembly represents the whole of the people of Persia, who thus participate in the economic and political affairs of the country". Over the 20th century, the right to political participation gradually expanded in the three countries to include all men and women. Women were allowed to vote and to be elected following constitutional amendments and legislative changes in Iran in 1964, in Afghanistan in 1965, and in Iraq in 1980. At the same time, with respect to political pluralism, the constitutions had limited meaning in practice. In Iraq, in particular, political participation in the second half of the 20th century was largely dominated by the Ba'ath ideology.

The situation *from which* desecularization is a transition was thus characterized by what can be described as a development towards increased popular participation in governance, yet with a number of *de facto* limitations. However, the changes in the area of political participation introduced through the first constitutions and developed over the decades to follow were themselves a significant step towards expanding equal liberty.

5.1 Afghanistan

Afghanistan is declared an "Islamic Republic" under Article 1 of the Constitution of 2004. Article 2 states that: "The sacred religion of Islam is the religion of the Islamic Republic of Afghanistan. Followers of other faiths shall be free within the bounds of law in the exercise and performance of their religious rituals".

The wording "faith" and "religious rituals" suggests that the right is primarily a right that protects *religious* thought, rather than thought or opinion in general.

34 CEDAW Committee, General Recommendation 23.

The provision, moreover, establishes the state religion on a superior level and does not offer a general protection to other faiths. The wording of Article 2, "within the bounds of law", allows for unconditional limitations by ordinary legislation to the manifestation of other faiths. Similar limitations do not apply to the state religion, which thereby is granted superior protection. Another aspect of the formulation of the right in Article 2 is that although the provision protects Islam as the state religion, it emphasizes the state and is not in fact articulated as an individual right. The provision does not expressly guarantee freedom of religion for *individuals* affiliated with the state religion.

Article 2 must, moreover, be interpreted in light of the restraining principle under Article 3, which may limit freedom of thought considerably, since it prohibits legislation that contravenes the state religion. This presents several contradictions within the Afghan constitution. Since Articles 2 and 3 do not protect freedom of thought in general and since they limit freedom of religion in ways that go further than the standards of international human rights law, they contravene the Constitution's Articles 6 and 7 which oblige the state to uphold international human rights law. Furthermore, Article 2 limits the interpretation of Article 22 which prohibits "any kind of discrimination and distinction between citizens of Afghanistan". The restrictions on freedom of thought and religion are, furthermore, inconsistent with the general liberty clause in Article 24. Under Article 24, liberty can be limited only if it affects other freedoms and public interest, and it can only be regulated through law. Another constitutional contradiction with Article 2 is Article 35 which holds that the charter of political parties cannot contravene the state religion, thus limiting freedom of thought and its expression in the political context. In the absence of any definition of what the state religion entails, this limitation becomes a vague and potentially extensively broad limitation to freedom of thought. Finally, freedom of thought and the development of opinion is limited through the provisions on education found in Articles 17 and 45 which establish that the content of education has to be based on Islam.

Freedom of thought and religion is, furthermore, limited through a number of provisions that condition the exercise of other constitutional rights to affiliation with the state religion. In other words, some constitutional rights are reserved to those belonging to the state religion, while those who do not have such affiliation are excluded from enjoying the same right. This includes the right to stand as a candidate for the presidency and the right to assembly.[35] Courts are moreover obliged to apply religious law in cases where there is no applicable law, and Shi'a jurisprudence in cases involving personal matters of followers of the Shi'a sect.[36] The constitutional provision on constitutional amendments prohibits amendments to provisions that involve Islam and the Islamic Republicanism.[37]

35 Constitution of Afghanistan (2004), Articles 35 and 62.
36 Constitution of Afghanistan (2004), Articles 130 and 131.
37 Constitution of Afghanistan (2004), Article 149.

The main provision on freedom of expression in the Afghan constitution is found in Article 34:

> Freedom of expression shall be inviolable. Every Afghan shall have the right to express thoughts through speech, writing, illustrations, as well as other means in accordance with the provisions of this constitution. Every Afghan shall have the right, according to provisions of law, to print and publish on subjects without prior submission to state authorities. Directives related to the press, radio and television as well as publications and other mass media shall be regulated by law.

Despite the broad and unconditional statement of the right in the first sentence, the rest of the provision contains several limitations. The scope of the right is determined by three forms of limitations. First, the right is limited to "Afghans", as opposed to "everyone". The right therefore has a character of a citizen-right as opposed to a general right that applies to everyone.[38] By contrast, freedom of expression under international human rights law is a right that applies to "everyone", regardless of nationality or citizenship.[39]

Freedom of expression shall be interpreted "in accordance with the provisions of this constitution". A question that arises in this regard is how the restraining principle in Article 3 and the other state religion provisions impact the interpretation of the scope of freedom of expression. An area where the relationship between the broad statement of freedom of expression in Article 34 and the role of the state religion arises is the question of blasphemy. Part of the answer to this can be found in legislation. A new Mass Media Law came into force in 2009, elaborating on the content of Article 34 of the Constitution. Under Article 45 of the Mass Media Law, the production, reproduction, printing, and publishing of works and material contrary to the principles of Islam are prohibited. The same is the case for works and materials that are offensive to other religions or sects, or to real or legal persons, and that are contrary to the constitution or the penal code. The Mass Media Law furthermore prohibits the publicizing and promotion of religions other than Islam.

The interpretation of the freedom of expression provision of the Constitution and its relationship with the restraining principle was brought up in the *Kambakhsh*

38 A reason for this particular wording may be that the provision is largely based on the 1964 Constitution, Article 31, which used the word *"Afghan"* in relation to the right to freedom of expression. However, that provision made a distinction between "Afghan" in the first part of the provision which dealt with the right to freedom of expression, and "Afghan citizen" in the second part of the provision which regulated ownership of publishing houses. This could suggest that "Afghan" in the first part was a broader notion which included more than those holding Afghan citizenship. By contrast, the freedom of expression provision in the Constitution of 2004 does not make a similar distinction, and the drafting process does not give any indication as to why the right is limited in its wording to citizens.

39 Article 19 of the UDHR and ICCPR provide that the right applies to "everyone".

case of 2007.[40] In 2007, a student, Sayed Parwiz Kambakhsh was arrested and charged with blasphemy after he had downloaded and distributed articles on women's rights in Islam. The court of first instance sentenced him to death for blasphemy, and upon appeal, the Court of Appeal changed the sentence to 20 years imprisonment, which was upheld by the Supreme Court.[41]

The concept of political participation as a right was introduced in Article 27 of the first Constitution of Afghanistan of 1923, as a break with the past absolutist system of government. Under this provision, Parliament was established, but it held a more advisory role, rather than a role as legislator, and it was not until the Constitution of 1964 that its powers were expanded.

Under the current Constitution, the Afghan form of "Islamic Republic" consists of a strong presidential system, a relatively weak Parliament, a hierarchical court system, and an expressed openness to international law, which is nonetheless restricted by some of the constitutional provisions. The president is elected directly for four years and has extensive powers. The National Assembly is bicameral and shall "manifest the will of its people as well as represent the entire nation".[42] The House of the People (the Lower House) is directly elected,[43] while the elections for the House of Elders (the Upper House) are indirect, following a three-tier system.[44]In addition to the National Assembly, the Constitution retains the traditional body of representation of "*Loya Jirga*", which is convened in three situations, and which the Constitution recognizes as "the highest manifestation of the will of the people of Afghanistan".[45] In addition to the executive and legislative bodies, the Constitution establishes a hierarchical system of courts, headed by the Supreme Court, consisting of judges appointed by the president and approved by the House of the People.[46]

Within this system of government, the right to political participation is established in Article 33 of the Constitution, which holds that "the citizens of Afghanistan shall have the right to elect and be elected". Nonetheless, this provision has to be read in light of Article 62(1), which limits the initial broad scope of the right by establishing a criterion of religious affiliation to the state religion, stating that only Muslim citizens qualify as presidential candidates. The presidential oath, perhaps more symbolically, but nonetheless explicitly, requires the

40 The case is referenced in John Witte and Christian Green, *Religion and Human Rights: An Introduction* (Oxford University Press, 2011) 3.

41 After two years in detention, the President signed the pardon, following which Kambakhsh left the country.

42 Constitution of Afghanistan (2004), Article 81.

43 Constitution of Afghanistan (2004), Article 83.

44 Constitution of Afghanistan (2004), Article 84 (one-third of the members of the House of Elders are elected by provincial councils, one-third by district councils, and one-third by the president).

45 Constitution of Afghanistan (2004), Articles 110 and 111. For an account on the historical roots of the *Loya Jirga*, see Thomas Barfield, *Afghanistan: A Cultural and Political History* (Princeton University Press, 2010).

46 Constitution of Afghanistan (2004), Articles 116 and 117.

President to swear to "obey and protect the holy religion of Islam".[47] The provision limits the scope of the constitutional protection against discrimination in Article 22 of the Constitution which prohibits discrimination on grounds of religion. Article 62(1) similarly weakens the constitutional commitment to human rights and other treaties, as stated in Articles 6 and 7.

The guarantee for pluralism is higher for the legislative branch which does not operate with belief criteria. The provision on the National Assembly stipulates that the elections shall ensure "general and fair representation for all the people of the country", and that a minimum of two females are elected to the House of the People from each province. The constitution also requires that 50% of the House of Elders consist of women.

The 1964 Constitution was the first Constitution in which Afghan women were granted the right to vote and to stand for election in parliamentary elections. Three women were elected into parliament in 1965, and Kubra Nurzai became the first female minister when she was appointed Minister of Health the same year.

5.2 Iran

The main feature of the Iranian Constitution of 1979 is its ideological character, whereby Islamic ideology is explicitly constitutionally entrenched, and is also referenced in the large majority of the provisions.[48] In the area of the right to freedom of thought, the most significant feature of the 1979 Constitution is that Islam and Islamic ideology is stated as a prerequisite for the exercise of most constitutional rights, as well as being established as a criterion for the content of those rights. By establishing Islamic ideology as a component of most constitutional rights, there is neither *de jure* nor *de facto* any freedom of thought and religion under the Constitution of 1979. The absence of freedom of thought and religion is not limited to non-Muslims. The Constitution leaves little room for religious freedom for those adhering to what is established as the official state religion, since the state's definition and interpretation of Islamic ideology is ideological, and thus overrides each individual's freedom to interpret Islam. The equal rights provision in Article 19 is limited to prohibiting discrimination based on ethnic group, tribe, color, race, and language, and does not mention religion, thought, or opinion in the list of grounds upon which discrimination is prohibited.

Thought or religious affiliation is also a condition that limits the exercise of other rights. Under the Constitution, all public and political offices are reserved to persons who not only belong to the official state religion, but who also accept the state ideology as extensively defined under Articles 2 and 3.

47 Constitution of Afghanistan (2004), Article 63.

48 The belief system and goals of the state, hereunder the meaning of "Islamic ideology" used in several of the provisions of the Constitution, are defined under Articles 2 and 3 of the Constitution.

There is no express constitutional provision in the 1979 Constitution that guarantees freedom of thought or freedom of religion in general. Instead, the Constitution through Articles 12, 13, and 14 establishes a hierarchical system of individuals based on their religious affiliation, exclusively listed in the Constitution, each with a different degree of freedom. The constitutional provision explicitly dealing with freedom of religion is found in Article 12:

> The official religion of Iran is Islam and the Twelver *Ja'fari* school (in *usul al-din* and *fiqh*), and this principle will remain eternally immutable. Other Islamic schools, including the Hanafi, Shafi'i, Maliki, Hanbali and Zaydi, are to be accorded full respect, and their followers are free to act in accordance with their own jurisprudence in performing their religious rites. These schools enjoy official status in matters pertaining to religious education, affairs of personal status (marriage, divorce, inheritance, and wills) and related litigation in courts of law. In regions of the country where Muslims following any one of these schools of *fiqh* constitute the majority, local regulations, within the bounds of the jurisdiction of local councils, are to be in accordance with the respective school of *fiqh*, without infringing upon the rights of the followers of other schools.

The provision applies only to "citizens", and not to "everyone". The provision has to be read in connection with Articles 13 and 14. Article 13 provides an exclusive list of recognized religious minorities:

> Zoroastrian, Jewish, and Christian Iranians are the only recognized religious minorities, who, within the limits of the law, are free to perform their religious rites and ceremonies, and to act according to their own canon in matters of personal affairs and religious education.

Article 14 regulates the non-recognized religious minorities:

> In accordance with the sacred verse ('God does not forbid you to deal kindly and justly with those who have not fought against you because of your religion and who have not expelled you from your homes' (60:8), the government of the Islamic Republic of Iran and all Muslims are duty-bound to treat non-Muslims in conformity with ethical norms and the principles of Islamic justice and equity, and to respect their human rights. This principle applies to all who refrain from engaging in conspiracy or activity against Islam and the Islamic Republic of Iran.

The Constitution, through Articles 12, 13, and 14 establishes a system of hierarchy by dividing citizens into four categories. The first category, established by Article 12, consists of the official state religion. It is worth noting that the wording of Article 12 of the Iranian Constitution, like its counterpart in the Afghan Constitution, does not protect individuals, but rather expresses what the official state religion is. That the provision guarantees freedom of religion of citizens who adhere to the official state religion can only be read implicitly. The second category, established by Article 12, regulates followers of other Islamic schools of faith, both Sunni and Shi'a. This group is given a comparatively high status, and the extent of its religious freedom is listed. The third category, established in Article 13, covers acknowledged non-Islamic religions, exhaustively listed as Zoroastrianism, Judaism, and Christianity. Members of these three groups have fewer rights than the two previous groups. The fourth category consists of religious minorities referred to as "non-Muslims". Unlike Articles 12 and 13, Article 14 does not treat individuals in this group as the *subject* of rights, nor does the provision establish any obligations on the part of the State to protect the religious freedom of individuals falling in this groups. Instead, the provision regulates the status of persons falling under this group by providing that Muslims should treat them in conformity with ethical norms. The individuals belonging to the group of non-recognized religious minorities are thus not themselves recognized as right-holders.

The hierarchical system of regulating citizens based on their thoughts and religion has a number of legal implications reflecting the constitutionally entrenched discrimination based on religion that the Constitution allows for. The Constitution does not provide for the rights of Muslim citizens to choose, change, or renounce their religious belief. Non-Muslim citizens may not engage in public religious expression, persuasion, or conversion. The publishing of religious material of religions other than the state religion is restricted. Non-Muslim citizens may not be elected to government bodies or hold senior military positions, with the exception of 5 of the 290 seats Parliament reserved for particular religious minorities. Members of religious minority groups, except Sunni Muslims, may not serve in the judiciary, in security services, or as public school officials. Penal laws and criminal procedure establish a formal basis for different treatment of Muslims and non-Muslims. Government-controlled broadcast and print media continue negative campaigns against religious minorities. The UN Special Rapporteur on human rights in Iran has highlighted the problematic aspect of the lack of formal religious rights: "members of recognized religions alike, including members of Bahai, Christian, Sunni Muslim, Yarsam and other religious communities are increasingly subjected to various forms of legal discrimination, including in employment and education, and often face arbitrary detention, torture and ill-treatment".[49]

The state religion is, furthermore, significant in the field of education, with respect to the content of education as well as with access to education. In a 1991 memorandum on Bahai students and children, the Supreme Council for the Cultural Revolution clarified the centrality of the ideological character of education, holding that Bahais "must be expelled from universities", and Bahai

49 Report of the Special Rapporteur on the situation of human rights in the Islamic Republic of Iran (2014), A/69/356.

children "should be enrolled in schools which have a strong and imposing (Shi'a Islamic) religious ideology". University applicants are, moreover, required to pass examinations in Islamic, Christian, or Jewish theology. In 2018, the Education Ministry banned the English language from being taught in primary schools, calling the subject a "cultural invasion". Prior to this, in 2012, women were banned from 77 university degree courses, including biology and English literature. The ban was justified on the basis that some fields were not suitable for "women's nature":

The hierarchical system of recognized thoughts and beliefs is used to justify state policy towards the limitation of freedom of thought. The constitutional provisions not only prevent the State from taking action with regard to discrimination against religious and thought minorities, they enable and justify an active policy of discrimination.

As was the case under the Constitution of 1906–1907, the Constitution of 1979 does not contain a general provision on freedom of expression.

Instead, some of the constituent elements of expression are recognized, all subject to Islamic criteria, such as freedom of expression for publications and the press (Article 24); freedom of association (Article 26), freedom of assembly and the right to hold public gatherings (Article 27); and freedom of speech and expression of ideas on radio and television (Article 175). However, unlike the 1906–1907 Constitution, the current Constitution contains broader limitations on these aspects of the right to freedom of expression.

Article 24 holds that: "Publications and the press have freedom of expression when it is not detrimental to the fundamental principles of Islam or the rights of the public. The details of this exception will be specified by law".

The provision allows for limitations through ordinary legislation justified under one of two criteria: "principles of Islam" or "the rights of the public". Both of these grounds for limitation are vague and leave much room for interpretation, establishing a very weak protection of press and media freedom. There is no definition in the Constitution nor in legislation as to what these notions entail. The UN Special Rapporteur on the situation of human rights in Iran has pointed out the problematic aspect of the vague criteria in limitations on freedom of expression, including the use of charges of "national security crimes", "propaganda against the system", "assembly and collusion against the system", "insulting the Supreme Leader", and "spreading falsehoods with intent to agitate the public consciousness" for the legitimate exercise of the right to freedom of expression.[50,51] Other grounds used to limit press freedom are "insulting the holy figures of Islam", "showing a degrading image of Shi'ism", and "working illegally for satellite TV stations based in the United States and Great Britain".[52]

50 Report of the Special Rapporteur on the situation of human rights in the Islamic Republic of Iran, A/HRC/28/70.

51 Ibid.

52 Ibid.

In 2014, the Supreme Court upheld the death sentence of a blogger convicted of "insulting Government officials", "insulting the Supreme Leader", and "propaganda against the system".[53]

The Press Law contains provisions that further restrict the press freedom right established under Article 24 of the Constitution. In particular, Article 12 of the Press Law requires the Press Supervisory Board to ban a publication that violates Articles 6, 24–29, and 32 of the Law, which includes "publishing atheistic articles or issues which are prejudicial to Islamic codes", or which promote "subjects which might damage the foundation of the Islamic Republic", "national security", "dignity and interests", "insulting Islam or offending the leader and religious authorities", and publishing libel against officials or institutions or insulting legal or real persons who are "lawfully respected", publishing writings "containing apostasy and matters against Islamic standards", and quoting articles from "the deviant press, parties and groups which oppose Islam (inside or outside the country)". The Law gives the Revolutionary Courts the competence to adjudicate in cases regarding the publication of classified documents or instigation to commit crimes against the country's foreign policy. The Revolutionary Courts, created by edict of the Supreme Leader to try high-level officials of the former regime, were confirmed by the law on Public and Revolutionary Courts of 1992, but have no basis in the Constitution itself. Yet, Revolutionary Courts have in practice been granted jurisdiction over serious security-related crimes. The Press Law also bars "members of anti-revolutionary forces ... those who have been convicted by a Revolutionary Court and all persons (who) indulged in anti-establishment activities" from pursuing press-related activities and/or holding posts in any press institution.

In addition to Article 24 of the Constitution, a number of other provisions directly limit freedom of expression. Under Article 20, the media is required to "strictly refrain" from the "diffusion and propagation of destructive and anti-Islamic practices". Article 40 prohibits the exercise of constitutional rights in a manner that is injurious to others or detrimental to public interests. Furthermore, the restraining principles under Article 4 justify limitations on all constitutional rights by ordinary legislation.

The Penal Code contains a number of provisions penalizing certain forms of expression. These can be categorized into three categories. Firstly, criminalization of expression on the basis of national security, articulated through largely overbroad and vague criteria that allow for a large extent of discretion in the application of the provisions. Articles 498 and 499 provide for prison sentences ranging from two to ten years for anyone "forming or joining a group or association outside or inside the country which seeks to disturb the security of the country". Article 500 provides for the imprisonment of "anyone who undertakes any form of propaganda against the State". Secondly, criminal defamation continues to be applied against the exercise of freedom of expression. Article 513 punishes

53 Ibid.

by death or by prison terms between one and five years, "insult" against Islam. Article 697 punishes defamation by a prison term of between one month and one year, and Article 609 punishes criticism of State officials in connection with carrying out their duties with a fine, 74 lashes, or a prison sentence of between three and six months.

In contrast to the form of "Islamic Republic" in Afghanistan, which retains the main features of a presidential system, the Iranian form of "Islamic Republic" consists of a theocratic form of government, established around the notion and institution of "*velayat-e faqih*", often translated into "the guardianship of the Islamic jurist". The system is mainly based upon the doctrine of the founder of the Islamic Republic of Iran, Ayatollah Khomeini, who theorized the form of government in a book from 1970, called "*Velayat-e faqih*" or "*Hokumat-e Eslami*" (Islamic government).[54] Under this theory, government should be run according to the traditional *Shari'a* and an Islamic jurist, "*faqih*", must provide political and legal guardianship ("*velayat*") over the people, who thus are deemed not to be in a position to understand their own interests. The Iranian Constitution of 1979 incorporates this part of the theory through establishing the office of the Supreme Leader, which is granted extensive powers and has the final word in executive, legislative, and judicial matters. By contrast, the powers of the president and the cabinet are limited.[55] Legislative power is divided between the Parliament ("the Islamic Consultative Assembly") and the Guardian Council. Neither the Guardian Council nor the Council of Exigency is open to women.

In addition to the power to perform constitutional review of legislation, Article 99 of the Constitution grants the Guardian Council a supervisory role in elections. In 1992, offering a new interpretation of Article 99, the Guardian Council gave itself approbatory supervision ("*nezarat-e esteswabi*") with the power to reject applications of candidates despite candidates' fulfillment of the criteria for candidacy under the Electoral Law for Parliamentary Elections, if the Guardian Council deem them undesirable. The Electoral Law for Parliamentary Elections was amended in 1995, establishing this interpretation in law and creating a legal basis for the exclusionary power of the Guardian Council. There are no formal, objective criteria for the grounds upon which exclusions can be made. The reasons for exclusions are, moreover, not transparent, since the Guardian Council is not required to provide reasons for its exclusions. Exclusions are typically defended on religious grounds, and the exclusionary jurisprudence of the Guardian Council to include in its exclusions persons who are known as religious persons, but who do not share certain political views, suggests that the main reason for exclusion is political rather than religious. In response to a question by the Human Rights Committee about the practice of

54 Khomeini, "Islamic Government" translated to English, in Hamid Algar (ed), *Khomeini: Islam and Revolution* (Mizan Press, 1981) 89.

55 Constitution of Iran (1979), Articles 113–142.

excluding candidates with opposing political views, the government has maintained that "no irrational and illegal discrimination has been made in relation to election candidates".[56]

The theocratic system of government created by the Constitution constitutes a first obstacle to political participation in line with the standards of constitutionalism. The system of government, in addition to being a theocracy, amounts to a one-party state, since belief in the ideology of the Islamic Republic is established as a criterion for all government offices.[57] The form of government is therefore not just characterized by members of the clergy holding certain positions, but by members of the clergy who in addition hold a particular political belief.

The 1979 Constitution represents also a nominal change in the name of the legislative body, which went from being named the National Consultative Assembly under the 1906–1907 Constitution to being named the Islamic Consultative Assembly under the 1979 Constitution. The change is, however, more than just nominal. The criteria for parliamentary elections are set out in the Electoral Law for Parliamentary Elections, which in Article 28 sets out the following:

Candidates must meet the following criteria when they register:

1. Belief in and practical obligation to Islam and the holy system of the Islamic Republic of Iran.
2. Citizenship in the Islamic Republic of Iran.
3. Expressed loyalty to the Constitution and progressive principles of the Absolute Guardianship of the Jurisprudent (*Velayat-e Motlaq-e Faqih*).
4. A document proving possession of at least an Associate's degree or equivalent.
5. Not having bad reputation in the electoral district.
6. Physical health such as they at least enjoy the blessings of vision, hearing, and speaking.
7. At least thirty years of age and at most seventy-five.

   Clause 1. As stated in the Constitution, religious minority candidates are exempted from the requirement of 'a practical obligation to Islam' mentioned in the first line. Instead they must prove belief in their professed religion.

   Clause 2. People who have previously served as representatives in the Parliament in the past are exempt from obligation 4.

With the exception of the limitations on citizenship, none of the criteria are compatible with international human rights law. Three of the seven criteria – numbers 1, 3, and 5 – are in direct violation of the prohibited grounds for limitations under the criteria for political participation stated in Article 25 of the ICCPR. Criteria 4, 5 and 6 are based on grounds that the Human Rights Committee has

56 State report to the Human Rights Committee (Iran), CCPR/C/IRN/Q/3/Add.1, para. 5.
57 Constitution of Iran (1979), Articles 2, 3, and 144.

found to be "unreasonable" and hence impermissible under Article 25 of the ICCPR. In particular, the requirement of adherence to the official state ideology precludes political pluralism.

In addition to being in conflict with the standards of international human rights law, this provision is also in conflict with the Constitution. The requirement in the provision of proving personal belief in either Islam or in one of the three recognized religions stands in contradiction to the constitutional prohibition against the investigation of private belief found in Article 23. In addition to the criteria for eligibility found in Article 28 of the Electoral Law, the law contains provisions that concern specific criteria for preclusion of candidates. Article 29 precludes persons from running as candidates if they hold other offices, which can be said to be a "reasonable" ground for preclusion. Article 30 of the Electoral Law, on the other hand, represents significant limitations to political participation and highlights the ideological character of the government and the constitution:

The following are deprived of the right to candidacy for the Parliament:

1. Individuals who played a significant role in strengthening the foundation of the previous regime.
2. Large land owners who have registered unoccupied lands under their own names.
3. Organizational affiliates and supporters of political parties, organizations, and groups that have been declared illegal by the relevant authorities.
4. Individuals that have been convicted of efforts against the Islamic Republic of Iran.
5. Those convicted of apostasy by a qualified judicial court.
6. Those reputed for corruption and debauchery.
7. Those convicted of breaking the *Shari'a* law unless there is proof of their repentance.
8. Drug traffickers and addicts.
9. Those restricted by law from property/wealth ownership and those who are subject to Principle of the Constitution as determined by the courts.
10. Those related to the previous regime such as members of city and town council, affiliates of Freemason organizations, board of directors of branches of the *Rastakhiz* and *Iran-e Novin* political parties and their active members, representatives of the Senate Parliament, members of the National Assembly, and Savak officials.

Together with Article 28, Article 30 precludes political pluralism and considerably renders the right to political participation meaningless.

The interpretation of these provisions by the Guardian Council confirms the law's intent to limit political diversity. In a response to a question of whether Marxists could qualify as candidates for parliament, the Guardian Council issued a binding interpretative statement holding that Article 64 and 67 of the Constitution, which regulate the number of members to Parliament should be interpreted as requiring that only those who are Muslim, or from the recognized religious minorities under Article 64, can be elected to parliament. Therefore, the Guardian Council concluded, Marxists were among the groups that were to be excluded from running as candidates.[58] The significance of this interpretation is not merely that Marxists are excluded, but that the Guardian Council through this binding decision establishes that the provisions on political participation are to be construed narrowly.

The legislative branch includes, moreover, a consociational arrangement whereby the Islamic Consultative Assembly has quota representation for the recognized religious minorities: Zoroastrians, Jews, Assyrians, Chaldean Christians, and Armenian Christians.[59] Similar provisions were found in the 1906–1907 Constitution. However, the consociational system envisioned in the two constitutions differs on a significant point. Under the current Constitution, the recognized minorities can only run for the minority seats. The consociational system under the current Constitution thereby establishes a roof for minority representation. Under the past Constitution, on the other hand, minority candidates could also run for the ordinary seats, and the system thus represented a minimum guarantee for representation.

Reservation of political seats based on a person's religious affiliation, although ensuring representation of minority groups, gives rise to the question of whether this, nonetheless, is compatible with constitutionalism. The fundamental democratic right to take part in the conduct of public affairs in conjunction with fundamental equality rights implies that every person, regardless of religious affiliation, should be in a position to run for public office. Moreover, the 1979 Constitution precludes non-recognized religious minorities from running for Parliament. Minorities not mentioned in Article 64 are excluded from any representation.

In the executive branch, the right to political participation is subject to strict criteria for all positions, including that of the Supreme Leader, the president and members of the cabinet. The Supreme Leader is elected among the higher clergy, to which only Muslim men of the 12-imam Shia branch of Islam can qualify.[60] Also, the President is to be elected among religious and political personalities and must fulfill the criteria set out in Article 115 of the Constitution, which includes having a convinced belief in the fundamental principles of the Islamic Republic and the official religion of the country. Article 115 of the Constitution is worded in a way that suggests an overlap between Islam on the one hand and the fundamental principles of the Islamic Republic on the other. This has an impact on the way in which political disagreement is viewed. Political dissidents or critics of the Islamic Republic as a form of republic are thus viewed to be enemies of Islam, which is a crime under the Penal Code.

There are no specific constitutional provisions about qualifications for members of cabinet, but all cabinet ministers must receive a positive vote of confidence

58 Guardian Council, Interpretative Statement 28/4/1360.

59 Constitution of Iran (1979), Article 4.

60 Constitution of Iran (1979), Articles 107 and 109.

from the Islamic Consultative Assembly. Despite the absence of an explicit constitutional ban on women cabinet ministers, Iran has had only one woman minister between 1979 and 2009. In 2009, three women were appointed by the President as ministers, but two of the three, despite their conservative profiles, were subsequently rejected by Parliament.

The criteria in the Constitution and the Electoral Law thus preclude the minimum political diversity that the State is required to promote and guarantee under its obligations pursuant to international human rights law. Through the requirement of allegiance to the ideology of the Islamic Republic, the Constitution instrumentalizes religion for the achievement of political aims and to preclude political diversity. As such, it also helps illuminate the scope of the nondiscrimination clause in Article 20. While some have argued that the non-discrimination clause, through conditioning non-discrimination with "conformity with Islamic criteria" does not necessarily contradict international standards for non-discrimination, the constitutional provisions on political participation and their interpretation by the Guardian Council show that "conformity with Islamic criteria" under the Iranian Constitution means that the exclusion of parts of the population on grounds of gender, physical abilities, education, reputation, religion, and political beliefs, is justified.

The Human Rights Committee has clarified that restricting eligibility for government service to members of the predominant religion violates the rights of members of minority religions and non-believers.[61] Commenting on this aspect of the Iranian Constitution, the Human Rights Committee pronounced that "Measures restricting eligibility for government service to members of the predominant religion ... are incompatible with the prohibition of discrimination based on religion or belief and the guarantee of equal protection under article 26 of the Covenant".[62]

5.3 Iraq

The Iraqi Constitution of 2005 includes freedom of thought beyond freedom of religion, as distinct from the Afghan and Iranian constitutions. Freedom of religion is found in Article 2(2):

> "This Constitution guarantees the Islamic identity of the majority of the Iraqi people and guarantees the full religious rights to freedom of religious belief and practice of all individuals such as Christians, Yazidis and Mandean Sabeans".

Freedom of thought is guaranteed under Article 42 which establishes that "Each individual shall have the freedom of thought, conscience and belief". The right

61 Human Rights Committee, General Comment 22, para. 9.

62 Human Rights Committee, Concluding Observations (Iran), A/48/40 vol I (1993) 44 at 269.

applies to everyone, not just to citizens. Article 43 elaborates on the content of religious freedom. The nondiscrimination provision under Article 14 explicitly includes religion as one of the grounds upon which discrimination is prohibited. Moreover, Article 37(2) protects against coercion of thought: "The State shall guarantee protection of the individual from intellectual, political and religious coercion".

Personal status is linked to thought and belief, and Article 41 does not limit personal status to religion, but also to any belief and personal choice: "Iraqis are free in their commitment to their personal status according to their religions, sects, beliefs, or choices, and this shall be regulated by law". The broad guarantees of the right to freedom of thought are nonetheless limited under the provisions on de-Ba'athification under Articles 7 and 135, which in turn have implications for the right to political participation.

The Iraqi Constitution regulates freedom of expression in Article 36:

> The State guarantees [the following] in a way that does not violate public order and morality:
>
> Freedom of expression, through all means.
> Freedom of the press, printing, advertisement, media and publication.
> Freedom of assembly and peaceful demonstration.
> Every Iraqi has the right to engage in sports, and the State should encourage its activities and promotion and will provide its necessities.
> The exercise of these freedoms shall be regulated by law.

The provision limits the scope of freedom of expression in two main ways. Firstly, by conditioning the right to expressions that do "not violate public order and morality". Secondly, by allowing for limitations through legislation. Freedom of expression is thus conditional upon non-violation of public order and morality, which opens up for the state to restrict freedom of expression based on two broad and vague terms. In addition to the limitation based on "public order and morality", freedom of expression can be limited under the general limitation clause in Article 46. Article 46 allows for restrictions to constitutional rights "by law or on the basis of it, and insofar as that limitation or restriction does not violate the essence of the right or freedom". Freedom of expression is, moreover, undefined in Article 38, and censorship is not explicitly prohibited.

While the provision does not explicitly prohibit blasphemy, attempts have been made to interpret blasphemy as a permissible limitation under "public order and morality". Article 372 of the Penal Code punishes with imprisonment of up to three years, or a fine of up to 300 dinars, "Anyone who publicly abuses the beliefs of any religious community, or insults any of its rituals ... Anyone who publicly insults a symbol or person who constitutes an object of sanctification, glorification, and respect to a religious community". During the review of Iraq by the Human Rights Committee in 2015, the authorities affirmed that persons in Iraq have the right to change their religion "but only to Islam", and the

Committee noted with concern that Law No. 105 prohibiting the practice of the Baha'i faith remains in force.[63]

The Publication Law of 1968 which also continues to be in force, prescribes up to seven years imprisonment for insulting the government, and the Penal Code of 1969, which continues to be in force, criminalizes libel, defamation, the disclosure of state secrets, and the spreading of "false news". Despite the constitutional ban on the creation of special courts (Article 95), in 2010, the Supreme Judicial Council created a special court for the prosecution of journalists.

In 2011, the Journalist Protection Law was passed, initially offering some hope of reform for freedom of expression. However, the law did not override sections of the Penal Code or the Publications Law that pertain to journalists. The Society for Defending Press Freedom in Iraq challenged the law, but its constitutionality was upheld by the Federal Supreme Court in 2012.

In Iraq, the politicization of religion in the area of political participation bears some resemblance to Iran. But while secular political views are entirely banned in Iran, in Iraq, their limitation is more indirect through the constitutionalized de-Ba'athification process. The notion of "de-Ba'athification" was introduced in Iraq shortly after the war in 2003 to describe a series of legal and administrative measures with the aim of removing the traces of the Ba'ath influence in the country.[64]

The main provision on political participation is found in Article 20 of the Iraqi Constitution which states that "The citizens – men and women – have the right to participate in public affairs and to enjoy political rights, including the right to vote, elect and to nominate". This broad provision is limited through Articles 7 and 135 of the Constitution. These two provisions on de-Ba'athification have direct impact on the right to political participation.

Article 7(1) states:

> First: Any entity or program that adopts, incites, facilitates, glorifies, promotes, or justifies racism or terrorism or accusations of being infidel (*takfir*) or ethnic cleansing, especially the Saddamist Ba'ath Party in Iraq and its symbols, under any name whatsoever, shall be prohibited. Such entities may not be part of the political pluralism in Iraq. This shall be regulated by law.

In prohibiting anything that "under any name whatsoever" can be associated with the Ba'ath party, the overbroad language can be interpreted as including programs that are secular or socialist, since these would constitute two of the features of the Ba'ath ideology. Article 135 of the Constitution bans people who have been subject to the de-Ba'athification policies from holding positions in the Presidency Council, Prime Ministership, Parliament, and, in broadly drafted language, from other equivalent judicial, provincial, and state positions.

63 CCPR/C/IRQ/CO/5, para. 37.

64 For an account of the history and ideology of the Ba'ath party in Iraq, see John Devlin, "The Baath Party: Rise and Metamorphosis", *The American Historical Review* [1991] 96:5 1396–1407.

Articles 7 and 135, together with legislation based on these provisions, limit the equal right to political participation. A significant number of Sunni Arab Iraqis were not represented in the initial formations of government because of the high number of Ba'ath party members among the Sunni Arab population. As a result, a large number of Iraqis were systematically excluded from public and political life.[65]

The de-Ba'athification policy had its roots in the regime change preceding the adoption of the new Constitution. Given the identification between Saddam Hussein and the Ba'ath party there was, from the early days of the occupation of Iraq, a strong interest in dismantling the Ba'ath party structure. The de-Ba'athification began before the adoption of the Constitution, and was based on a series of orders and the memorandums issued by the Coalition Provisional Authority (CPA) with the goal of removing the Ba'ath party's influence in the new Iraqi political system.

The first order issued by the CPA expressed this goal in clear terms. The aim of the deBa'athification policy was to "eliminate the Party's structures and remove its leadership from positions of authority and responsibility in Iraqi Society".[66] The goal was thus two-fold: eliminating the party and ensuring the exclusion of its higher members from important political posts in the future. The CPA Order no. 5 established the National De-Ba'athification Council (NDC) to identify Ba'ath Party property and assets, identify and locate former officials, and advise the CPA on the effective dismantling of the structure of the party.[67]

The issue of de-Ba'athification arose again during constitutional negotiations and resulted in two constitutional provisions: Article 7, which prohibits Ba'ath ideology and any political activity based on it, and Article 135 which recognizes the continued existence of the NDC, as well as conditions for its termination. Both provisions were controversial and subject to strong disagreement during the drafting process. The Sunni faction was concerned that the two provisions unfairly targeted Sunni Iraqis whose ties to the Ba'ath Party had been weak, or in some cases non-existent, while at the same time largely reinforcing the Shia Alliance position in the government.[68]

The de-Ba'athification policies did not only have the effect of removing past Ba'ath members; it also contributed to the sectarian divide. Although the Ba'ath ideology itself was non-religious, the de-Ba'athification resulted in removing a large number of Sunni Iraqis from the political arena. From this angle, the de-Ba'athification program following the constitutional transition was much more

65 Andrew Arato, *Constitution-Making Under Occupation: The Politics of Imposed Revolution in Iraq* (Columbia University Press, 2009); see also Ashley Deeks and Matthew Burton, "Iraq's Constitution: A Drafting History", *Cornell International Law Journal* [2007] 40.

66 CPA Order No. 1, *De-Ba'athification of Iraqi Society,* 16 May 2003.

67 The NDC was later replaced by a nominally less hostile de-Ba'athification institution called the Supreme National Commission for Accountability and Justice, following the enactment of the Accountability and Justice Act in 2008.

68 Ashley Deeks and Matthew Burton, "Iraq's Constitution: A Drafting History", *Cornell International Law Journal* [2007] 40 24–25.

than a mere dismantling of the previous regime of Saddam Hussein. It significantly contributed to leading the state towards a more religious direction and strengthened the sectarian divide. The de-Ba'athification can therefore be viewed as a measure towards the religious politicization of the political sphere. Some of the early drafts of the Constitution are clear in their pursuit of this aim. The draft of 22 July 2005 outlawed both thought and practice in relation to the Ba'ath ideology.[69] Later negotiations reflected the struggle between factions that wanted to sanction all former Ba'ath members and those who wanted the constitutional language to distinguish the Ba'ath Party from Saddam Hussein. The result ultimately went in favor of the advocates for de-Ba'athification in the broad sense. As a result of the CPA order, 30,000 ex-Ba'ath party members were fired from government posts. The second order dissolved Iraq's 500,000-member military and intelligence services.[70]

The Constitution's de-Ba'athification provisions established a division of the political scene along ethno-religious lines, where Iraqi Kurds and Iraqi Shia Muslims were represented, while Sunni Muslims, to a considerable extent, were excluded. By targeting membership, rather than acts of wrongdoings, the de-Ba'athification collectivized guilt along a sharp sectarian line.[71] As a result, it has been pointed out that the agenda was not de-Ba'athification, but de-Sunnization of Iraq.[72] To this, one can add that the policy can be described as a religionization of the political sphere. In 2004, Paul Bremer, the administrator of the CPA, admitted that the de-Ba'athification had been applied "unevenly and unjustly". However, his announcement addressed only the flaws in the application of the policy, and not the flaws inherent in the de-Ba'athification policy as such.

The de-Ba'athification process was modified through legislation enacted by the Iraqi Parliament in January 2008. The Accountability and Justice Law defines de-Ba'athification as "the procedures taken by the Commission in accordance with the provisions of the Law in order to intellectually, administratively, politically, culturally and economically dismantle the Ba'ath Party system in Iraqi society, state institutions, and civil society institution".[73]

Under this law, a member of the Ba'ath Party, subject to penalties of the law, is defined as "any individual who joined the Ba'ath Party and gave an oath of allegiance to it".[74] The law furthermore defines as a "collaborator" any individual

69 The draft provided that "Any thinking that adopts radicalism, terrorism, taqfir (labeling others as infidels), or incites, glorifies, initiates or promotes thereto, especially the Saddamist Ba'ath, shall be prohibited in thought and in practice under any name".

70 CPA Order No. 1 (2003) and No. 2, *Dissolution of Entities*, 23 May 2003.

71 Beth Dougherty, "De-Ba'athification in Iraq: How not to Pursue Transitional Justice", *Middle East Institute*, 30 January 2014. Accessible at: www.mei.edu/content/de-bathification-iraq-how-not-pursue-transitional-justice.

72 Andrew Terrill, "Lessons of the Iraqi de-Ba'athification Program for Iraq's Future and the Arab Revolutions", *Strategic Studies Institute Monograph* [2012].

73 Accountability and Justice Law, Article 1(4). Unofficial translation of the law available at: www.ictj.org/publication/unofficial-translation-iraqs-accountability-and-justice-law.

74 Accountability and Justice Law, Article 1(6).

who worked with or benefited from the party.[75] The law-makers have been criticized for failing to understand the role that party membership played in Iraq.[76]

Despite the absence of religious criteria for political participation, the constitutional ban on Ba'athism in Article 7 in effect also affects secular candidates. Although the majority of Iraqi political parties identify themselves in Islamic sectarian terms, the Iraqi National Movement (INM), commonly referred to as *al-Iraqiyya*, is explicitly established on a secular and nonsectarian platform.

In Iraq, affiliation to the state religion has historically not been a requirement for political participation under the past constitutions, and this continues to be the case under the present Constitution. Article 65, regulating the criteria for candidacy to the Presidency, requires that:

A nominee to the Presidency must meet the following conditions:

A. He must be an Iraqi by birth, born to Iraqi parents.
B. He must be fully eligible and have completed forty (40) years of age.
C. He must be of good reputation and political experience, and be known for his integrity, righteousness, fairness and loyalty to the homeland.
D. He must not have been convicted of a crime involving moral turpitude.

While the criteria are neutral with respect to religion, legislative representation on the other hand is based on a system of ethno-religious federalism. The power is divided according to ethnic and religious criteria, and the right to political participation is therefore articulated as a group right rather than as an individual right. Although not expressly prescribed by the Constitution, an informal convention since 2005 has established a system where the President is Kurdish, the Prime Minister is Shia, and the Speaker of the House of Representatives is Sunni. In addition, the Election Law of 2005 establishes a consociational system through its provisions, ensuring the representation of the major religious groups in Iraq. Christian, Yazidi, Sabean Mandean, and Shabak minorities have allocated seats in the Federal Parliament. However, unlike the quota system under the Iranian Constitution, the Iraqi model is a minimum guarantee of representation. Persons belonging to minority groups have the right to run for regular seats in the Parliament in addition to their minimum representation. In addition to the quota representation of religious minorities, the Council of Representatives has quota representation of women. Article 47 of the Constitution requires that women make up no less than one-quarter of the Council of Representatives. This is further elaborated in the Elections Law which requires that at least one woman must be among the first three nominees in a list.[77]

75 Accountability and Justice Law, Article 1(9).

76 Beth Dougherty, "De-Ba'athification in Iraq: How not to Pursue Transitional Justice", *Middle East Institute*, 30 January 2014. Accessible at: www.mei.edu/content/de-bathification-iraq-how-not-pursue-transitional-justice.

77 Constitution of Iraq (2005), Article 49(4) and Electoral Law (2005), Article 3(3).

6 Conclusions

Equal liberty, as a fundamental feature of modern constitutionalism and international human rights law, sets a certain standard for the regulation of political authority and constitutional rights and for the exercise of governance. The focus of this book has been to highlight the strengthened role of religion in constitutional desecularization as a constitutional language that alters the formal regulation of equal liberty. As such, religion performs a legal and political function, rather than merely reflecting a strengthened role of religion as such.

The phenomenon of constitutional desecularization in modern constitutions raises many questions, more than those that have been raised in this book. But by focusing on equal liberty and constitutional desecularization as a particular category, the book has aimed to say four things. Firstly, the "de" in "desecularization" signals the direction of the constitutional development and the importance of highlighting the significance of this. For there to be a constitutional approximation towards the standards of constitutionalism and international human rights law, the constitution must develop in a particular way over time. A constitutional transition that, instead of amending the weaknesses of past constitutions, introduces new weaknesses, will represent a reversal in the path of constant approximation towards the standards of constitutionalism.

Secondly, by taking the direction of the constitutional development as a starting point, the book suggests a more nuanced approach to the categorization of constitutions that are nominally religious. Instead of making religion in general, or Islam in particular, the identifying characteristic of a constitution, the account has suggested that what is relevant is the way in which religion is used, particularly the way in which it is used in a new constitutional transition seen in the light of the same country's own constitutional past.

Thirdly, and related to the previous items, the approach of the book has been to understand these constitutions, like all other constitutions, as matters of *constitutional law*. The use of religion in the constitution is thus interpreted as a form of constitutional language.

Finally, by understanding the references to Islam as a form of constitutional language, the study suggests that the concept of "Islamic law" or "Islamic constitutionalism" is not helpful as an analytical framework for the analysis of contemporary constitutional arrangements. By analyzing the constitutions as constitutions, the study takes the constitutions out of a religious framework. The constitution is a political and legal instrument. The inclusion of Islam in the constitution thus serves political and legal purposes. This reflects the distinction between, on the one hand, Islam as a religion, and on the other hand, political Islam – that is, Islam as a political ideology, as a tool for political governance. Constitutional desecularization is an outcome of political Islam and should thus be analyzed as such, not as primarily a religious or cultural product. Studying it as the latter is not only inaccurate, but often leads to reducing the level of critical scrutiny applied to the constitutions.

Obstacles to the achievement of constitutionalism and international human rights law are of various kinds. One may distinguish between obstacles in practice and obstacles through law. The extent to which practice reflects the standards set by the formal norms of the constitution will always remain an important question, subject to human and economic resources, abilities or political will. Yet, the study has sought to highlight the formal obstacles for the achievement of equal liberty that is created by constitutional desecularization. These obstacles are problematic because of the normative standard that the constitution establishes for itself, and which thereby makes infringements of equal liberty "lawful".

Constitutional desecularization represents a *formal* obstacle to the achievement of constitutionalism and international human rights law through the type of normative standards that it establishes. What makes it singular in the context of constitutional developments is that, rather than continuing the path of ongoing approximation of a legal system towards constitutionalism and international human rights law, the de-secularized constitution introduces further limitations. As a result, constitutional desecularization represents a constitutional development that moves off the path towards constitutionalism and international human rights law. This is particularly problematic when considering the political context in which constitutional desecularization takes place, which is a context of political change. None of the political changes presented in this book came about promising increased limitations to equal liberty. The explicit justifications given in support of the political regime changes have been the quest for increased democracy, political pluralism, and liberty. These arguments were not translated into the constitutional provisions, and the constitutions themselves have created weak foundations for these values to be achieved.

The issue becomes more pressing when considering the constitutional landscape against which the de-secularized constitutions are drafted and adopted. Constitution-making is not an isolated task but has always been comparative in nature. Since the Second World War, international human rights law sets particular standards for constitution-making, and constitutions created today are made against the backdrop of a different social and normative reality than that which existed at the time of the first modern constitutions. Constitutions made today are made for diverse societies. This is a change from earlier, when it was rightly or wrongly assumed that a constitution was made for people with common history, religion, and language.[1]

1 Cheryl Saunders, "Constitution-Making in the 21st Century", *International Review of Law* [2012] 4 2.

The underlying argument of this book has been that in using religion as a ground for justifying limitation to equal liberty, such constitutions depart from the standards of constitutionalism. The departure from these standards is not primarily because of the use of religion in general, or because of Islam in particular, but because constitutional desecularization represents a constitutional development that strengthens a constitutional external aim instead of a development toward its weakening. In other words, that constitutional desecularization represents a departure from the standards of constitutionalism is not merely because such constitutions privilege one religion in ways that formalize discrimination on grounds of religion. More importantly, such constitutions depart from the standards of constitutionalism because they establish religion as an external aim in a way that denies the very basis of constitutionalism itself.

Under this perspective, constitutional desecularization can therefore be seen as something more than a reaction against and a rejection of secularity or a mere strengthening of religion, which may, or may not, reflect the level of religiosity in society. In entrenching a constitutional external aim that limits equal liberty, constitutional desecularization can additionally be understood as a rejection or erosion of constitutional democracy. The discussion is thus ultimately not one of religion, but one of public law.

Through the way in which the rights to freedom of opinion, expression, and political participation is limited, the issue becomes more than a matter of religion, and becomes, ultimately, a reaction to the central features of a democratic society, even if the desecularized constitution comes about through processes that, at first glance, may look democratic, and are often characterized as such, but where the content and final result of the constitution depart from democratic standards.[2]

Modern constitutionalism and the idea of the constitution in the liberal tradition, involve both procedural and material aspects that are indivisible. These aspects are both "democracyenabling" and "democracy-constraining".[3] By democracy-enabling, one refers to the idea of participation in the direction of public policy and the capacity to act as a check on tyrannous governance.[4] The democracy-constraining feature consists of the constitution's identification and acknowledgment of certain values and rights which cannot be limited through majority decisions. Political authority cannot unconditionally deny the rights of persons in order to achieve political purposes.

Under the constitutions of Afghanistan, Iran, and Iraq, democracy is, at best, not a central concern. In the Iranian constitution, democracy is not even a factor. From a procedural point of view, the opening up of the political landscape

2 For an account of non-democratic constitutions adopted through seemingly democratic procedures, see Čarna Pištan, *Pseudo Constitutionalism in Central Asia: Curse or Cure?* Paper presented at World Congress of Constitutional Law 2014, Oslo.

3 Viki Jackson, "Paradigms of Public Law: A Review of Ruling the World?" *International Journal of Constitutional Law* [2010] 8:3 539–540.

4 Ibid. 540.

has meant a strengthening of the role of religion. Some commentators have articulated this as a democratization that has led to the inclusion of Islam, or as held by Feldman and Martinez, that "more democracy meant more Islam".[5] But is that really so? To begin with, this statement appears to reduce democracy to majority rule. To treat democracy as only one of several mechanisms by which constitutions function detracts from one of the most important sources of a constitution's political legitimacy, which is to promote democratic self-governance while at the same time sustaining effective governance and protecting individual rights. A commitment to democratic self-governance, like commitments to the protection of individual rights, are linked by a commitment to the equal liberty of individuals as constitutionalism entails.

Because religion historically has regulated private life, the use of religious rhetoric in the constitution expands political authority into areas that are considered as a matter of individual autonomy under the idea of modern constitutionalism. As such, it breaks with the development of constitutionalism towards reducing the sphere of influence of the state in the personal autonomy of persons. The conception of rights under constitutionalism consists of protecting a sphere from state interference. At the same time, the state is needed in order for such rights to be guaranteed. As such, state sovereignty and individual sovereignty engage in a relationship of mutual dependence, entailing a particular understanding of the notion of "sovereignty".

In pointing to the centrality of popular sovereignty and equality in liberty to the idea of constitutionalism as well as to international human rights law, this book identifies one form of constitutional development that forms an obstacle to the constitutional approximation to constitutionalism. Certain elements of modern constitutionalism are not simply add-ons. They are constitutive of constitutionalism. This study has highlighted equal liberty and the absence of external aims as two such features. A constitution where these two features are absent will no longer find itself under the paradigm of constitutionalism.

5 Noah Feldman and Roman Martinez, "Constitutional Politics and Text in the New Iraq: An Experiment in Islamic Democracy", *Fordham Law Review* [2006] 75 883–920.

References

1.1 National constitutions and legislation

1.1.1 Constitutions

Basic Law of Saudi Arabia (1992).
Basic Statute of the State of Oman (1996).
Constitution of Afghanistan (1923), (1931), (1964), (1976), (1987), (1990).
Constitution of Brunei Darussalam (1959).
Constitution of Iran (1906–1907).
Constitution of Iraq (1925), (1958), (2004).
Constitution of Poland (1997).
Constitution of the Islamic Republic of Afghanistan (2004).
Constitution of the Islamic Republic of Iran (1979).
Constitution of the Islamic Republic of Pakistan (1973).
Constitution for the Kingdom of Bahrain (2002).
Constitution of Malta (1964).
Constitution of the Maldives (2008).
Constitution of Mauritania (1991).
Constitution of the Kingdom of Morocco (1972).
Constitution of the Kingdom of Bahrain (2002).
Constitution of the People's Socialist Republic of Albania (1976).
Constitution of the Principality of Monaco (1962).
Constitution of the Republic of Armenia (2005).
Constitution of the Republic of Costa Rica (1949).
Constitution of the Republic of Indonesia (1945).
Constitution of the Republic of Yemen (1990).
Constitution of the United States (1787).
New Fundamental Law of the State of Vatican City (2000).
Ta'if Agreement (Document of National Accord), Lebanon (1989).

1.1.2 National legislation

Afghanistan

Mass Media Law (2006).
Penal Code (7 October 1976).

Iran

Code of Criminal Procedure for Public and Revolutionary Courts (19 September 1999).
Elections Act of the Islamic Consultative Assembly (28 November 1999).
Islamic Penal Code (2013).
Political Crimes Bill, draft (2013).
Press Law (31 January 1987).
Regulatory Code on Sentences of Qisas, Stoning, Cruxifiction, Execution and Flogging (19 September 1999).

Iraq

Accountability and Justice Law (12 January 2008).
Code of Criminal Procedure (Law No. 23, 1971).
CPA Order No. 1, *De-Ba'athification of Iraqi Society*, May 16, 2003. The Coalition Provisional Authority.
CPA Order No. 2, *Dissolution of Entities*, 23 May 2003. The Coalition Provisional Authority.
Electoral Law of 2005.
National Revolutionary Command Council Law No. 25 of 1963 and 1964.
National Revolutionary Command Council Laws No. 61 of 1964; No. 173 of 1964; No. 137 of 1965 and 1968.
Revolutionary Command Council Resolution No. 792 of 1970
Penal Code (Law No. 111, 1969).
Personal Status Act (Law No. 188, 1959).

Other

Document 19, Directive of the Chinese Communist Party (The People's Republic of China): The Basic Viewpoint and Policy on the Religious Question during our Country's Socialist Period, March 1982.

1.2 International conventions

CEDAW *Convention on the Elimination of All Forms of Discrimination Against Women*, 18 December 1979.
CERD *International Convention on the Elimination of All Forms of Racial Discrimination*, 21 December 1965.
CMW *International Convention on the Protection of the Rights of All Migrant Workers and Members of their Families*, 18 December 1990.
Convention Against Torture *Convention Against Torture and Other Cruel, Inhuman or Degrading Treatment or Punishment*, 10 December 1984.
CPPCG *Convention on the Prevention and Punishment of the Crime of Genocide*, 9 December 1948.
CRC *Convention on the Rights of the Child*, 20 November 1989.
DROB *Declaration on the Elimination of All Forms of Intolerance and of Discrimination Based on Religion or Belief*, 25 November 1981.

ECHR *European Convention for the Protection of Human Rights and Fundamental Freedoms, as amended by Protocols Nos. 11 and 14*, 4 November 1950 (European Convention on Human Rights).

ICESC *International Covenant on Economic, Social and Cultural Rights*, 16 December 1966.

ICCPR *International Covenant on Civil and Political Rights*, 16 December 1966.

Refugee Convention *Convention Relating to the Status of Refugees*, 28 July 1951.

UDHR *Universal Declaration of Human Rights*, 10 December 1948.

UN Charter *Charter of the United Nations*, 24 October 1945, 1 UNTS XVI.

VCLT *Vienna Convention on the Law of Treaties*, 23 May 1969.

1.3 UN Expert Bodies

CEDAW Committee, General Recommendation 23, A/52/38 (1997).

CEDAW Committee, General Recommendation 29, CEDAW/C/GC/29 (2013).

CEDAW Committee, Concluding Observations Iraq, CEDAW/C/IRQ/CO/4-6 (2014).

Committee on Economic, Social and Cultural Rights, E/1999/22 (1998) 43 R.

Committee on the Elimination of Racial Discrimination, A/57/18 (2002).

UN Human Rights Committee, A/46/40 (1991).

UN Human Rights Committee, CCPR/C/SR.1128 (1992).

UN Human Rights Committee, A/336/40 (1998).

UN Human Rights Commission Human Rights Resolution 1999/57 on Promotion of the Right to Democracy (1999).

UN Human Rights Committee, A/56/40 Vol. I (2001).

UN Human Rights Committee's Concluding Observations (1993) A/48/40 vol. I (1993).

UN Human Rights Committee, General Comment 22, UN Doc. CCPR/C/21/Rev.1/Add.4 (1993).

UN Human Rights Committee, General Comment 25, UN Doc. CCPR/C/21/Rev.1/Add.7 (1996).

UN Human Rights Committee, General Comment 34, UN Doc. CCPR/C/GC/34 (2011).

Report of the UN High Commissioner for Human Rights on the Situation of Human Rights in Afghanistan and on the Achievement of Technical Assistance in the Field of Human Rights. A/HRC/13/62.

Report of the Special Rapporteur on All Forms of Religious Intolerance and of Discrimination Based on Religion or Belief, Civil and Political Rights, Including Religious Intolerance. UN Doc. E/CN.4/1999/58 (1999).

Report of the Special Rapporteur on Extrajudicial, Summary, and Arbitrary Executions. A/HRC//17/28/Add.6 (2011).

Report of the Special Rapporteur on the Promotion and Protection of the Right to Freedom of Opinion and Expression. E/CN.4/2000/63 (2000).

Report of the Special Rapporteur on the Right to Freedom of Opinion and Expression. 2E/CN.4/2004/62/Add.2 (2004).

Report of the Special Rapporteur on Freedom of Religion or Belief. E/CN.4/2005/61 (2005).

Report of the Special Rapporteur on Religious Freedom. E/CN.4/2006/5 (2006).

Report of the Special Rapporteur on Groups in need of Attention, Limitations to the Right to Freedom of Expression, and Protection of Journalists. A/HRC/14/23 (2010).

Report of the Special Rapporteur in the Field of Cultural Rights. A/HRC/34/56 (2017).

1.4 Selected UN Reports

Study of Discrimination in the Matter of Religious Rights and Practices. UN Doc. E/CN.4/Sub.2/200/Rev.1 (1960). Arcot Krishnaswami.

Respect for the Principles of National Sovereignty and Non-Interference in the Internal Affairs of States in Their Electoral Processes. G.A.Res. 45/151, UN GAOR, 45th Sess., UN Doc. A/RES/45/151 (1990).

UN, Guidance Note of the Secretary-General, United Nations Assistance to Constitution-Making Processes (3 April 2009).

UN, Secretary-General, SG/SM/12585 (2009).

UN, Secretary-General, *In-Depth Study on All Forms of Violence Against Women,* 81, delivered to the General Assembly. UN Doc. A/61/122/Add.1 (6 July 2006).

1.5 Books, articles, and other literature

Abbas, Sadia. "Other People's History: Contemporary Islam and Figures of Early Modern European Dissent". *Early Modern Culture*, vol. 49 (2007). Available at: http://emc.eserver.org/1-6/abbas.html [Accessed December 2018].

Abiad, Nisrine. *Sharia, Muslim States and International Human Rights Treaty Obligations: A Comparative Study* (British Institute of International and Comparative Law, 2008).

Adamiyat, Fereydoon. *Eide-ology Nahzate Mashroutiyate Iran* (in Farsi) (Gostareh Publications, 2009).

Afary, Janet. *The Iranian Constitutional Revolution 1906–1911: Grassroots Democracy, Social Democracy and the Origins of Feminism* (Columbia University Press, 1996).

Afshari, Reza. *Human Rights in Iran* (University of Pennsylvania Press, 2001).

Ahdar, Rex and Ian Leigh. *Religious Freedom in the Liberal State* (Oxford University Press, 2005).

Al Ali, Zaid. *The Struggle for Iraq's Future* (Yale University Press, 2014).

Alexy, Robert. *A Theory of Constitutional Rights* (Oxford University Press, 2002).

Ali, Souad T. *A Religion, Not a State: Ali abd-Al Raziq's Islamic Justification for Political Secualrism* (University of Utah Press, 2009).

Al-Khalil, Samir. *The Republic of Fear: The Politics of Modern Iraq* (University of California Press, 1989).

Almond, Gabriel A., Scott Appleby and Emmanuel Sivan (eds.). *Strong Religion: The Rise of Fundamentalism around the World* (Chicago University Press, 2013).

Amanat, Abbas. *Pivot of the Universe: Nasir al-Din Shah Qajar and the Iranian Monarchy (1831–1896)* (Tauris, 1997).

Anderson, Elizabeth S. "What is the Point of Equality?" *Ethics*, vol. 109, no. 2 (1999): 287–337.

Anghie, Anthony. *Imperialism, Sovereignty and the Making of International Law* (Cambridge University Press, 2005).

An-Na'im, Abdullahi Ahmed. *Islam and the Secular State: Negotiating the Future of Shari'a* (Harvard University Press, 2008).

Ansari, Sarah and Vanessa Martin (eds.). *Women, Religion and Culture in Iran* (Routledge, 2002).

Antoun, Richard and Mary Hegland (eds.). *Religious Resurgence: Contemporary Cases in Islam, Christianity, and Judaism* (Syracuse University Press, 1987).

Appelby, R. Scott. *The Ambivalence of the Sacred: Religion, Violence, and Reconciliation* (Rowman & Littlefield, 2000).

Arato, Andrew. *Constitution-Making under Occupation: The Politics of Imposed Revolution in Iraq* (Columbia University Press, 2009).

Arendt, Hannah. *The Origins of Totalitarianism* (Harcourt, Brace, 1951).

Arjomand, Said A. "The Ulama's Traditionalist Opposition to Parliamentarianism: 1907–1909". *Middle Eastern Studies*, vol. 17, no. 2 (1981): 174–190.

Arjomand, Said A. *The Turban for the Crown: The Islamic Revolution in Iran* (Oxford University Press, 1988).

Arjomand, Said A. (ed.). *Constitutional Politics in the Middle East* (Hart Publishing, 2008).

Arjomand, Saïd A. and Nathan J. Brown (eds.). *The Rule of Law, Islam and Constitutional Politics in Egypt and Iran* (SUNY Press, 2013).

Arneson, Richard. "Equality and Equality of Opportunity for Welfare". In Louis Pjman and Robert Westmoreland (eds.). *Equality: Selected Readings* (Oxford University Press, 1997) 229–241.

Asad, Talal. *Formations of the Secular: Christianity, Islam, Modernity* (Stanford University Press, 2003).

Averroes. *Averroes, The Decisive Treatise* (Brigham Young University, 2002).

Babie, Paul. "Synthesis or Separation? Church, State and Marriage in Byzantine Law". *Journal of Law and Religion*, vol. 26, no. 2 (2010): 585–594.

Babie, Paul. "Religion and Constitutionalism: Oscilliations along a Continuum". *Journal of Religious History*, vol. 39, no. 1 (2015): 123–146.

Baderin, Mashood A. *International Human Rights and Islamic Law* (Oxford University Press, 2003).

Bahlul, Raja. "Is Constitutionalism Compatible with Islam?" In Pietro Costa and Danilo Zolo (eds.). *The Rule of Law: History, Theory and Criticism* (Springer, 2007) 515–542.

Bangstad, Sindre. *Sekularismens ansikter* (Universitetsforlaget, 2009).

Barak, Aharon. *Proportionality: Constitutional Rights and Their Limitations* (Cambridge University Press, 2012).

Barak, Aharon. *Human Dignity: The Constitutional Value and the Constitutional Right* (Cambridge University Press, 2016).

Barfield, Thomas. *Afghanistan: A Cultural and Political History* (Princeton University Press, 2010).

Barro, Robert J. and Rachel M. McCleary. "Which Countries Have State Religions?" *The Quarterly Journal of Economics*, vol. 120, no. 4 (2005): 1331–1370.

Barros, Robert. *Constitutionalism and Dictatorship: Pinochet, the Juna, and the 1980 Constitution* (Cambridge University Press, 2002).

Batau, Hanna. *The Old Social Classes and the Revolutionary Movements of Iraq: A Study of Iraq's Old Landed and Commercial Classes and of its Communists, Ba'thists and Free Officers* (Princeton Studies on the Near East, 1978).
Battaglia, Gino. "Neo-Hindu Fundamentalism Challenging the Secular and Pluralistic Indian State". *Religions*, vol. 8 (2017): 10.
Bauer, Joanne R. and Daniel A. Bell (eds.). *The East Asian Challenge for Human Rights* (Cambridge University Press, 1999).
Bechir, Saleh and Hazem Saghieh. "The Muslim Community: A European Invention". *OpenDemocracy*, 17 October (2005).
Beinin, Joel and Joe Stork. *Political Islam* (University of California Press, 1997).
Benhabib, Seyla. "Unholy Wars". In Betsy Reed (ed.). *Nothing Sacred* (Nation Books, 2002) 397–412.
Bennoune, Karima. "Remembering the Other's Others". *Columbia Human Rights Law Review*, vol. 49 (2010): 635–638.
Bennoune, Karima. *Your Fatwa Does Not Apply Here: Untold Stories from the Fight against Muslim Fundamentalism* (Norton and Company, 2015).
Berger, Peter L. *The Sacred Canopy: Elements of a Sociological Theory of Religion* (Doubleday, 1967).
Berger, Peter L. (ed.). *The Desecularization of the World: Resurgent Religion and World Politics* (Ethics and Public Policy Center and Wm. B. Eerdmans Publishing Co., 1999).
Berger, Peter L., Grace Davie and Effie Fokas. *Religious America, Secular Europe? A Theme and Variations* (Ashgate Publishing Limited, 2008).
Bernstein, Alyssa. "A Human Right to Intervention? Legitimacy and Intervention". In Rex Martin and David Reidy (eds.). *Rawls's Law of Peoples: A Realistic Utopia?* (Blackwell Publishing Ltd, 2006) 278–298.
Bertram, Christopher. *Rousseau and the Social Contract* (Routledge, 2004).
Bickel, Alexander M. *The Least Dangerous Branch: The Supreme Court at the Bar of Politics* (Bobbs-Merrill, 1962).
Bielskis, Andrius. "Multiculturalism and the Politics of Recognition: Jacques Derrida and James Tully". *Sociologija. Mintis ir Veiksmas*, vol. 02 (2009): 40–52.
Bonakdarian, Mansour. *Britain and the Iranian Constitutional Revolution of 1906–1911: Foreign Policy, Imperialism and Dissent* (Syracuse University Press, 2006).
Boozari, Amirhassan. *Shi'I Jurisprudence and Constitution: Revolution in Iran* (Palgrave, 2011).
Borer, Tristan Anne. "A Taxonomy of Victims and Perpetrators. Human Rights and Reconciliation in South Africa". *Human Rights Quarterly*, vol. 25 (2003): 1088–1116.
Brannan, Patrick. "Herodotus and History: The Constitutional Debate Preceding Darius' Accession". *Traditio*, vol. 19 (1963): 427–438.
Brown, Nathan J. *Constitutions in a Nonconstitutional World* (State University of New York Press, 2002).
Browne, Edward. *Press and Poetry in Modern Persia* (Cambridge University Press, 1914).
Bruce, Steve. *Fundamentalism* (Polity, 2000).
Brunkhorst, Hauke. "Constitutionalism and Democracy in the World Society". In Petra Dobner and Martin Loughlin (eds.). *The Twilight of Constitutionalism?* (Oxford University Press, 2010) 179–200.

Burns, James (ed.). *The Cambridge History of Medieval Political Thought 350–1450* (Cambridge University Press, 1988).
Casanova, José. *Public Religions in the Modern World* (University of Chicago Press, 1994).
Caspar, Gerhard. "Constitutionalism". University of Chicago Occasional Paper, No. 22 (1987): 2–20.
Castiglione, Dario. "The Political Theory of the Constitution". *Political Studies*, vol. 33 (1996): 417–435.
Chalmers, David J. "Verbal Disputes". *Philosophical Review*, vol. 120, no. 4 (2011): 515–566.
Chaves, Mark. "Secularization as Declining Religious Authority". *Social Forces*, vol. 72, no. 3 (1994): 749–774.
Cheibub, José A. and Fernando Limongi. "Democratic Institutions and Regime Survival: Presidentialism and Parliamentarism Reconsidered". *Annual Review of Political Science*, vol. 5 (2002): 151–179.
Chelkowski, Peter J. and Robert J. Pranger (eds.). *Ideology and Power in the Middle East: Studies in Honor of George Ienczowski* (Duke University Press, 1988).
Chehabi, Houchang and Vanessa Martin (eds.). *Iran's Constitutional Revolution: Popular Politics, Cultural Transformations and Transnational Connections* (Bloomsbury Academic, 2010).
Chen, Albert H.Y. "The Achievement of Constitutionalism in Asia". In Albert H.Y. Chen (ed.). *Constitutionalism in Asia in the Early 21st Century* (Cambridge University Press, 2014).
Chisti, Nighat M. *Constitutional Development in Afghanistan* (Royal Book Co., 1998).
Choudry, Sujit (ed.). *The Migration of Constitutional Ideas* (Cambridge University Press, 2006).
Cohen, Jean. *Globalization and Sovereignty: Rethinking Legality, Legitimacy and Constitutionalism* (Cambridge University Press, 2012).
Cohen, Jean. "Political Religion vs Non-Establishment". *Philosophy and Social Criticism*, vol. 39, no. 4–5 (2013): 443–469.
Cohen, Jean and Cécile Laborde (eds.). *Religion, Secularism and Constitutional Democracy* (Columbia University Press, 2015).
Cohen, Joshua. "Is there a Human Right to Democracy?" In Christine Sypnowich (ed.). *The Egalitarian Conscience: Essays in Honour of G.A. Cohen* (Oxford University Press, 2006) 226–248.
Cohen-Eliya, Moshe and Iddo Porat. *Proportionality and Constitutional Culture* (Cambridge University Press, 2013).
Coleman, Isobel. "Women, Islam, and the New Iraq". *Foreign Affairs*, vol. 85, no. 1 (2006): 24–38.
Costa, Pietro and Danilo Zolo (eds.). *The Rule of Law: History, Theory and Criticism* (Springer, 2007).
Cotran, Eugene and Adel Sherif (eds.). *Democracy, the Rule of Law and Islam* (Kluwer Law International, 1999).
Cristi, Marcela. *From Civil to Political Religion: the Intersection of Culture, Religion and Politics* (Wilfrid Laurier University Press, 2001).
Cronin, Stephanie (ed.). *The Making of Modern Iran* (Routledge, 2003).
Daudelin, Jean and W.E. Hewitt. "Churches and Politics in Latin America: Catholicism at the Crossroads". *Third World Quarterly*, vol. 16, no. 4 (1995): 221–236.

Davis, Eric. *Memories of State: Politics, History, and Collective Identity in Modern Iraq* (University of California Press, 2005).

Dawisha, Adeed. *Iraq: A Political History from Independence to Occupation* (Princeton University Press, 2009).

Dawn, Ernest C. "The Formation of Pan-Arab Ideology in the Inter-war Years". *International Journal of Middle East Studies*, vol. 20, no. 1 (1988): 67–91.

Dawood, Ahmad I. and Tom Ginsburg, "Constitutional Islamization and Human Rights: The Surprising Origin and Spread of Islamic Supremacy in Constitutions". University of Chicago Public Law & Legal Theory Working Paper, No. 477 (2014).

De Carvalho, Benjamin. "The Confessional State in International Politics: Tudor England, Religion and the Eclipse of Dynasticism". *Diplomacy & Statecraft*, vol. 25, no. 3 (2014): 407–431.

Deeks, Ashley S. and Matthew Burton. "Iraq's Constitution: A Drafting History". *Cornell International Law Journal*, vol. 40 (2007): 2–84.

Devlin, John F. "The Baath Party. Rise and Metamorphosis". *The American Historical Review*, vol. 96, no. 5 (1991): 1396–1407.

Dobner, Petra and Martin Loughlin (eds.). *Twilight of Constitutionalism?* (Oxford University Press, 2010).

Dougherty, Beth. "De-Ba'athification in Iraq: How not to Pursue Transitional Justice". *Middle East Institute*, 30 January 2014. Available at: www.mei.edu/content/de-bathification-iraq-how-not-pursue-transitional-justice (last accessed on 16 July 2019).

Dressler, Markus and Arvind-Pal S. Mandair (eds.). *Secularism and Religion-Making* (University Press, 2011).

Dunoff, Jeffrey L. and Joel P. Trachtman (eds.). *Ruling the World? Constitutionalism, International Law, and Global Governance* (Cambridge University Press, 2009).

Durham, W. Cole. "Perspectives on Religious Liberty: A Comparative Framework". In Johan Van der Vyver and John Witte (eds.). *Religious Human Rights in Global Perspective: Legal Perspectives* (Martinus Nijhoff Publishers, 1996) 1–44.

Dworkin, Ronald. "What is Equality? Part II: Equality of Resources". *Philosophy and Public Affairs*, vol. 10, no. 4 (1981): 283–345.

Dworkin, Ronald. *Freedom's Law: The Moral Reading of the Constitution* (Harvard University Press, 1996).

Dyzenhaus, David. *Hard Cases in Wicked Legal Systems: Pathologies of Legality* (Oxford University Press, 2010).

Ehsani, Kaveh. "The Politics of Property in Post-Revolutionary Iran". In Saïd A. Arjomand and Nathan J. Brown (eds.). *The Rule of Law, Islam and Constitutional Politics in Egypt and Iran* (SUNY Press, 2013) 154–178.

Eisgruber, Christopher L. *Constitutional Self-Government* (Princeton University Press, 2001).

Elster, J. *Ulysses Unbound: Studies in Rationality, Precommitment, and Constraints* (Cambridge University Press, 2000).

Elster, Jon and Rune Slagstad. *Constitutionalism and Democracy* (Cambridge University Press, 1988).

Endress, Gerhard. *An Introduction to Islam* (Edinburgh University Press, 1994).

Esbeck, Carl H. "1987 Survey of Trends and Developments on Religious Liberty in the Courts". *Journal of Law and Religion*, vol. 6 (1988): 145–200.

Evans, Malcolm. *Religious Liberty and International Law in Europe* (Cambridge University Press, 1997).

Fadel, Mohammed. "Judicial Institutions, the Legitimacy of Islamic State Law and Democratic Transition in Egypt: Can a Shift toward a Common Law Model of Adjudication Improve the Prospects of a Successful Democratic Transition?" *International Journal of Constitutional Law*, vol. 11, no. 3 (2013): 646–665.

Farzaneh, Mateo Mohammad. *The Iranian Constitutional Revolution and the Clerical Leadership of Khurasani* (Syracuse University Press, 2015).

Fassbender, Bardo. "Rediscovering a Forgotten Constitution: Notes on the Place of the UN Charter in the International Legal Order". In Jeffrey L. Dunoff and Joel P. Trachtman (eds.). *Ruling the World? Constitutionalism, International Law and Global Governance* (Cambridge University Press, 2009) 133–148.

Fawcett, Liz. *Religion, Ethnicity, and Social Change* (St. Martin's, 2000).

Feldman, Noah. "The Democratic Fatwa: Islam and Democracy in the Realm of Constitutional Politics". *Oklahoma Law Review*, vol. 58 (2005): 1–9.

Feldman, Noah. *The Fall and Rise of the Islamic State* (Princeton, NJ: Princeton University Press, 2008).

Feldman, Noah and Roman Martinez. "Constitutional Politics and Text in the New Iraq: An Experiment in Islamic Democracy". *Fordham Law Review*, vol. 75 (2006): 883–920.

Ferrari, Alessandr and James Toronto (eds.). *Religions and Constitutional Transitions in the Muslim Mediterranean* (Routledge, 2018).

Forst, Rainer. "The Justification of Human Rights and the Basic Right to Justification: A Reflexive Approach". *Ethics*, vol. 120, no. 4 (2010): 711–740.

Forst, Rainer. *Toleration in Conflict: Past and Present* (Cambridge University Press, 2013).

Fox, Gregory H. "The Right to Political Participation in International Law". *Yale Journal of International Law*, vol. 17, no. 2 (1992): 539–607.

Fox, Gregory H. and Brad R. Roth (eds.). *Democratic Governance and International Law* (Cambridge University Press, 2000).

Fox, Gregory H. and Brad R. Roth. "Democracy and International Law". *Review of International Studies*, vol. 27 (2001): 327–352.

Fox, Jonathan. "World Separation of Religion and State Into the 21st Century". *Comparative Political Studies*, vol. 39, no. 5 (2006): 537–569.

Fox, Jonathan. *A World Survey of Religion and the State* (Cambridge University Press, 2008).

Fox, Jonathan and Shmuel Sandler. *Bringing Religion into International Relations* (Palgrave Macmillan, 2004a).

Fox, Jonathan and Shmuel Sandler. "World Separation of Religion and State in the Twenty First Century". *Comparative Political Studies*, vol. 39, no. 5 (2006): 537–569.

Franck, Thomas M. "The Emerging Right to Democratic Governance". *American Journal of International Law*, vol. 86, no. 1 (1992): 46–91.

Franklin, Julian (ed.). *Bodin on Sovereignty* (Cambridge University Press, 1992).

Fuller, Lon L. *The Morality of Law* (Yale University Press, 1964).

Galston, William. *The Practice of Liberal Pluralism* (Cambridge University Press, 2005).

Gardbaum, Stephen. "The New Commonwealth Model of Constitutionalism". *American Journal of Comparative Law*, vol. 49, no. 4 (2001): 707–760.

Gardbaum, Stephen. "Limiting Constitutional Rights". *UCLA Law Review*, vol. 54 (2007): 789–854.

Gardbaum, Stephen. "Human Rights as International Constitutional Rights". *European Journal of International Law*, vol. 19, no. 4 (2008): 749–768.

Gardbaum, Stephen. "Human Rights and International Constitutionalism". In Jeffrey L. Dunoff and Joel P. Trachtman (eds.). *Ruling the World? Constitutionalism, International Law and Global Governance* (Oxford University Press, 2009) 233–257.

Gardbaum, Stephen. "A Democratic Defense of Constitutional Balancing". *Law and Ethics of Human Rights*, vol. 4 (2010): 79–106.

Garlicki, Lech. "Backsliding into Authoritarianism in Europe? Reflections on Hungary and Romania". *Constitutional Transitions and Global Comparative Law Colloquium, NYU School of Law*, 6 November 2013.

Garlicki, Lech and Zofia A. Garlicka. "External Review of Constitutional Amendments? International Law as a Norm of Reference". *Israel Law Review*, vol. 44, no. 2 (2011): 343–368.

Gauchet, Marcel. *The Disenchantment of the World: A Political History of Religion* (Princeton University Press, 1997).

Gearon, Liam. *Freedom of Expression and Human Rights: Historical, Literary and Political Contexts* (Sussex Academic Press, 2006).

Germino, Dante. *Machiavelli to Marx: Modern Western Political Thought* (University of Chicago Press, 1972).

Gheissari, Ali. "Constitutional Rights and the Development of Civil Law in Iran, 1907–41". In Houchang E. Chehabi and Vanessa Martin (eds.). *Iran's Constitutional Revolution: Popular Politics, Cultural Transformations and Transnational Connections* (I.B. Tauris, 2010) 69–79.

Gill, Anthony. *Rendering unto Caesar: The Catholic Church and the State in Latin America* (University of Chicago Press, 1998).

Ginsburg, Tom (ed.). *Comparative Constitutional Design* (Cambridge University Press, 2012).

Ginsburg, Tom and Alberto Simpser (eds.). *Constitutions in Authoritarian Regimes* (Cambridge University Press, 2014).

Glendon, Mary Ann. *A World Made New: Eleanor Roosevelt and the Universal Declaration of Human Rights* (Random House, 2001).

Gray, Matthew. "Islam in the Iraqi and Afghan Constitutions: A Comparative Perspective". *Global Peace, Change and Security*, vol. 19, no. 1 (2007): 17–34.

Grewe, Constance and Michael Riegner. "International Constitutionalism in Ethnically Divided Societies: Bosnia-Herzegovina and Kosovo Compared". In Armin Von Bogdandy and Rüdiger Wolfrum (eds.). *Max Planck Yearbook of United Nations Law* (Max Planck Institute for Comparative Public Law and International Law, 2011) 1–64.

Grimm, Dieter. "The Achievement of Constitutionalism". In Petra Dobner and Martin Loughlin (eds.). *The Twilight of Constitutionalism?* (Oxford University Press, 2010) 3–22.

Grimm, Dieter. "Types of Constitutions". In Michel Rosenfeld and Andràs Sajó (eds.). *Oxford Handbook of Comparative Constitutional Law* (Oxford University Press, 2012) 98–132.

Grote, Rainer and Tilmann Röder (eds.). *Constitutionalism in Islamic Countries: Between Upheaval and Continuitiy* (Oxford University Press, 2012).

Grote, Rainer, Tilmann Röder and Ali El-Haj (eds.). *Constitutionalism, Human Rights and Islam after the Arab Spring* (Oxford University Press, 2016).

Habermas, Jürgen. *Between Facts and Norms. Contributions to a Discourse Theory of Law and Democracy* (MIT Press, 1996).

Habermas, Jürgen. *The Postnational Constellation: Political Essays 127*, Max Pensky (ed.). (MIT Press, 2001).

Halbertal, Moshe. *Maimonides: Life and Thought* (Princeton University Press, 2014).

Hall, Thomas. *The British Occupation of Iraq, 1915–1948* (University of Vermont Press, 2008).

Halmai, Gábor, Kim Lane Scheppele and Miklós Bánkuti. "Hungary's Illiberal Turn: Disabling the Constitution". *Journal of Democracy*, vol. 23, no. 3 (2012) 138–146.

Halper, Stephan and Jonathan Clark. *America Alone: The Neo-Conservatives and the Global Legal Order* (Cambridge University Press, 2004).

Hamoudi, Haider A. *Judicial Review of Islamic Law under Iraq's Constitution*, JURIST-Forum, 26 April 2011.

Hamoudi, Haider A. "Repugnancy in the Arab World". *Willamette Law Review*, vol. 48 (2012): 427–450.

Hariri, Abdul-Hadi. "Shaykh Fazl Allah Nuri's Refutation of the Idea of Constitutionalism". *Middle Eastern Studies*, vol. 13, no. 3 (1977): 327–335.

Harris, William F. II. *The Interpretable Constitution* (Johns Hopkins University Press, 1992).

Haynes, Jeffrey. *Democracy and Civil Society in the Third World: Politics and New Political Movements* (Polity Press, 1997).

Hélie-Lucas, Marieme A. "What is Your Tribe?: Women's Struggles and the Construction of Muslimness". *Dossier 23/24*, vol. 49, no. 54 (2009). http://www.wluml.org/node/343

Herodotus, Histories, III.

Herrin, J. *Byzantium: The Surprising Life of a Medieval Empire* (Princeton University Press, 2008).

Hibbard, Scott W. *Religious Politics and Secular States: Egypt, India and the United States* (Johns Hopkins University Press, 2012).

Hirschl, Ran. *Constitutional Theocracy* (Harvard University Press, 2010).

Hirschl, Ran. "The Political Economy of Constitutionalism in a Non-Secularist World". In Tom Ginsburg (ed.). *Comparative Constitutional Design* (Cambridge University Press, 2012) 164–191.

Holmes, Stephen. "What Russia Teaches Us Now: How Weak States Threaten Freedom". *The American Prospect*, 30 June 1997.

Holmes, Stephen. "Constitutions and Constitutionalism". In Michel Rosenfeld and Andras Sájò (eds.). *The Oxford Handbook of Comparative Constitutional Law* (Oxford University Press, 2012).

Hopkins, Benjamin D. *The Making of Modern Afghanistan* (Basingstoke, UK: Palgrave McMillan, 2011).

Hsia, Ronnie Po-Chia. *Social Discipline in the Reformation: Central Europe 1550–1750* (London, UK: Routledge, 1992).

Huntington, Samuel. *The Clash of Civilizations and the Re-making of the World Order* (Simon and Schuster, 2002).

Hurd, Elizabeth S. "The Political Authority of Secularism in International Relations". *European Journal of International Relations*, vol. 10, no. 2 (2004): 235–262.

Inglehart, Ronald and Wayne E. Baker. "Modernization, Cultural Change, and the Persistence of Traditional Values". *American Sociological Review*, vol. 65, no. 1 (2000): 19–51.

Israel, Jonathan. *Radical Enlightenment: Philosophy and the Making of Modernity 1650–1750* (Oxford University Press, 2001).

Israel, Jonathan. *Democratic Enlightenment: Philosophy, Revolution and Human Rights 1750–1790* (Oxford University Press, 2011a).

Israel, Jonathan. “Libertas Philosophandi in the Eighteenth Century: Radical Enlightenment versus Moderate Enlightenment (1775–1776)”. In Elizabeth Powers (ed.). *Freedom of Speech: The History of an Idea* (Bucknell University Press, 2011b) 1–17.

Jackson, Vicki C. “Paradigms of Public Law: A Review of Ruling the World?” *International Journal of Constitutional Law*, vol. 8, no. 3 (2010): 517–562.

Jackson, Vicki C. and Mark Tushnet. *Comparative Constitutional Law* (Foundation Press, 2006).

Jakobsen, Janet R. and Ann Pellegrini. *Secularisms* (Duke University Press, 2008).

Janis, Mark and Carolyn Evans (eds.). *Religion and International Law* (Martinus Nijhoff Publishers, 1999).

Jawad, Saad. *The Iraqi Constitution: Structural Flaws and Political Implications*, LSE Middle Eastern Centre Paper Series/ 01, 2013.

Joetgen, Miranda. “Learning from Mistakes of the Past: Christianity, Apartheid and Social Movement Framing”. *Bridge/Work*, vol. 2, no. 1, article 6.

Johnson, James Turner. *Sovereignty: Moral and Historical Perspectives* (Georgetown University Press, 2014).

Juergensmeyer, Mark. *The New Cold War?* (University of California Press, 1993).

Kamali, Masoud. *Revolutionary Iran: Civil Society and State in the Modernization Process* (Aldershot, UK: Ashgate Publishers, 1998).

Kamali, Mohammad H. *Law in Afghanistan: A Study of the Constitutions, Matrimonial Law and the Judiciary* (Brill Academic Publishers, 1985).

Karpov, Vyacheslav. “Desecularization: A Conceptual Framework”. *Journal of Church and State*, vol. 52, no. 2 (2010): 232–270.

Karsh, Efraim. *Islamic Imperialism: A History* (Yale University Press, 2006).

Kasravi, Ahmad. *Tarikh-e Mashrute-ye Iran* (Sepehr, 1991).

Katouzian, Homa. *State and Society in Iran* (I.B. Tauris, 2000).

Kay, Richard S. “American Constitutionalism”. In Larry Alexander (ed.). *Constitutionalism* (Cambridge University Press, 1998) 16–62.

Keane, John. “The Limits of Secularism”. In Jon L. Esposito and Azzam Tamimi (eds.). *Islam and Secularism in the Middle East* (New York University Press, 2000) 29–37.

Keddi, Nikki R. “Iranian Revolutions in Comparative Perspective”. *American Historical Review*, vol. 88 (1983): 579–598.

Ketscher, Kirsten. “Cultural Rights and Religious Rights”. In M.L.P. Loenen and J.E. Goldschmidt (eds.). *Religious Pluralism and Human Rights in Europe: Where to Draw the Line?* (Intersentia Uitgevers, 2007) 219–237.

Ketscher, Kirsten. *Socialret: Principper, Rettigheder*, Værdier (Karnov Group, 2008).

Khadduri, Majid. *Republican Iraq: A Study in Iraqi Politics since the Revolution of 1958* (Oxford University Press, 1969).

Khatab, Sayed and Gary D. Bouma. *Democracy in Islam* (Routledge, 2007).

Khomeini, Ruhollah. “Islamic Government” translated to English. In Hamid Algar (ed.). *Khomeini: Islam and Revolution* (Mizan Press, 1981).

Kim Lane Scheppele. “Autocratic Legalism”, *University of Chicago Law Review*, vol. 85, no. 2 (March 2008): 545–583.

Kinross, Patrick. *The Ottoman Centuries: The Rise and Fall of the Turkish Empire* (Morrow Quill, 1977).

Koselleck, Reinhart. *The Practice of Conceptual History: Timing History, Spacing Concepts* (Stanford University Press, 2002).

Koskenniemi, Martti. "Constitutionalism as Mindset: Reflections on Kantian Themes about International Law and Globalization". *Theoretical Inquiries in Law*, vol. 8, no. 1 (2006): 9–36.

Kosmin, Barry. "Contemporary Secularity and Secularism". In Barry Kosmin and Ariela Keysar (eds.). *Secularism and Secularity: Contemporary International Perspectives* (Taylor Francis, 2007) 1–13.

Kramer, Larry D. *The People Themselves: Popular Constitutionalism and Judicial Review* (Oxford University Press, 2004).

Krasner, Stephan D. "Problematic Sovereignty". In Stephen D. Krasner (ed.). *Problematic Sovereignty: Contested Rules and Political Possibilities* (Columbia University Press, 2001) 1–23.

Krindatch, Alexey. "Changing Relationships between Religion, the State, and Society in Russia". *GeoJournal*, vol. 67, no. 4 (2006): 267–282.

Kuhonta, Erik. "Towards Responsible Sovereignty: The Case for Intervention". In Donald K. Emmerson (ed.). *Hard Choices: Security, Democracy, and Regionalism in Southeast Asia* (Walter H. Shorenstein Asia-Pacific Research Center Books, 2008) 292–314.

Kumm, Mattias. "Democratic Constitutionalism Encounters International Law: Terms of Engagement". In Sujit Choudry (ed.). *The Migration of Constitutional Ideas* (Cambridge University Press, 2006) 256–293.

Kumm, Mattias. "Political Liberalism and the Structure of Rights: On the Place and Limits of the Proportionality Requirement". In George Pavlakos (ed.). *Law, Rights, and Discourse: The Legal Philosophy of Robert Alexy* (Hart Publishing, 2007) 131–166.

Kumm, Mattias. "The Cosmopolitan Turn in Constitutionalism: On the Relationship between Constitutionalism in and beyond the State". In Jeffrey L. Dunoff and Joel P. Trachtman (eds.). *Ruling the World? Constitutionalism, International Law and Global Governance* (Cambridge University Press, 2009) 258–325.

Kumm, Mattias. "The Best of Times and the Worst of Times: Between Constitutional Triumphalism and Nostalgia". In Petra Dobner and Martin Loughlin (eds.). *The Twilight of Constitutionalism?* (Oxford University Press, 2010) 201–219.

Kumm, Mattias. "Institutionalising Socratic Contestation: The Rationalist Human Rights Paradigm, Legitimate Authority and the Point of Judicial Review". *European Journal of Legal Studies*, vol. 1, no. 2 (2011): 1–32.

Künkler, Mirjam. "The Special Court of the Clergy and the Repression of Dissident Clergy in Iran". In Said Arjomand and Nathan Brown (eds.). *The Rule of Law, Islam and Constitutional Politics in Egypt and Iran* (SUNY Press, 2013) 57–100.

Kuru, Ahmet T. *Secularism and State Policies Toward Religion: The United States, France and Turkey* (Cambridge University Press, 2009).

Lapidus, Ira M. "The Separation of State and Religion in the Development of Early Islamic Society". *International Journal of Middle East Studies*, vol. 6, no. 4 (1975): 363–385.

Larsen, Kjetil. *The European Convention on Human Rights and UN-Mandated Peace Operations: A Square Peg in a Round Hole?* (Faculty of Law, University of Oslo, 2010).

Lauterpacht, Hersch. *An International Bill of the Rights of Man* (Oxford University Press, 1945).
Levitsky, Steven and Lucan A. Way. *Competitive Authoritarianism: Hybrid Regimes After the Cold War* (Cambridge University Press, 2010).
Lewis, Bernard. *The Shaping of the Modern Middle East* (Oxford University Press, 1994).
Lidén, Kristoffer and Henrik Syse. "The Politics of Peace and Law: Realism, Internationalism and the Cosmopolitan Challenge". In Cecilia M. Bailliet and Kjetil M. Larsen (eds.). *Promoting Peace Through International Law* (Oxford University Press, 2015) 21–42.
Lisovskaya, Elena and Vyacheslav Karpov. "Orthodoxy, Islam, and Desecularization of Russia's State Schools". *Politics and Religion*, vol. 3, no. 2 (2010): 276–302.
Lloyd, Howell. "Sovereignty: Bodin, Hobbes, Rousseau". *Revue Internationale de Philosophie*, vol. 45, no. 179 (1991): 353–379.
Lombardi, Clark B. *State Law as Islamic Law in Modern Egypt: The Incorporation of the Shari'a into Egyptian Constitutional Law* (Brill, 2006).
Lombardi, Clark B. "Can Islamizing a Legal System Ever Help Promote Liberal Democracy? A View from Pakistan". *University of St. Thomas Law Journal*, vol. 7 (2010): 649–691.
Lombardi, Clark B. "Designing Islamic Constitutions: Past Trends and Options for a Democratic Future". *International Journal of Constitutional Law*, vol. 11 (2013): 615–645.
Lombardi, Clark B. and Nathan J. Brown. "Do Constitutions Requiring Adherence to Shari'a Threaten Human Rights? Egypt's Constitutional Court Reconciles Islamic Law with the Liberal Rule of Law". *American University International Law Review*, vol. 21 (2006): 379–435.
Loughlin, Martin. "What is Constitutionalism?" In Petra Dobner and Martin Loughlin (eds.). *The Twilight of Constitutionalism?* (Oxford University Press, 2010a) 47–72.
Loughlin, Martin. *Foundations of Public Law* (Oxford University Press, 2010b).
Loughlin, Martin and Neil Walker (eds.). *The Paradox of Constitutionalism: Constituent Power and Constitutional Form* (Oxford University Press, 2007).
Madeley, John. "A Framework for the Comparative Analysis of Church-State Relations in Europe". *West European Politics*, vol. 26, no. 1 (2003): 23–50.
Madeley, John. "Unequally Yoked: The Antinomies of Church-State Separation in Europe and the USA". *European Political Science*, vol. 8, no. 3 (2009): 273–288.
Madsen, Mikael R. "Transnational Fields: Elements of a Reflexive Sociology of the Internationalisation of Law". *Retferd*, vol. 29, no. 3/114 (2006): 23–41.
Malik, Yogendra and Dhirendra Vajpeyi. "The Rise of Hindu Militancy: India's Secular Democracy at Risk". *Asian Survey*, vol. 29 (1989): 3.
Malloy, James. "Authoritarianism and Corporatism in Latin America: The Modal Pattern". In James M. Malloy (ed.). *Authoritarianism and Corporatism in Latin America* (University of Pittsburgh Press, 1977) 3–20.
Mancini, Susanna and Michel Rosenfeld (eds.). *Constitutional Secularism in an Age of Religious Revival* (Oxford University Press, 2014).
Mango, Andrew. *Atatürk* (John Murray Publishers, 1999).
March, Andrew. *Islam and Liberal Citizenship* (Oxford University Press, 2009).
Martin, David. *On Secularization: Towards a Revised General Theory* (Ashgate, 2005).

Martin, Vanessa. *Islam and Modernism: The Iranian Revolution of 1906* (Syracuse University Press, 1989).

Martinich, A.P. *Hobbes* (Routledge, 2005).

Mayer, Ann Elizabeth. "Law and Religion in the Muslim Middle East". *American Journal of Comparative Law*, vol. 35, no. 1 (1987): 127–184.

Mayer, Ann Elizabeth. "Universal Versus Islamic Human Rights: A Clash of Cultures or a Clash with a Construct?" *Michigan Journal of International Law*, vol. 15 (1994): 307–379.

Mayer, Ann Elizabeth. "Religious Reservations to the Convention on the Elimination of All Forms of Discrimination against Woman: What do They Really Mean?" In Courtney W. Howland (ed.). *Religious Fundamentalisms and the Human Rights of Women* (Palgrave, 1999) 105–116.

Mayer, Ann Elizabeth. "Challenging the Universality of International of Human Rights Law". In Andras Sajo (ed.). *Human Rights with Modesty: The Problem of Universality* (Springer, 2004) 349–374.

McDonald, Ronald St. John and Douglas M. Johnston (eds.). *Towards World Constitutionalism: Issues in the Legal Ordering of the World Community* (Martinus Nijhoff, 2005).

Merry, Sally Engle. "Human Rights Law and the Demonization of Culture (and Anthropology along the Way)". *Political and Legal Anthropology Review*, vol. 55, no. 1 (2003): 55–76.

Metz, Helin Chapin. "Iraq, A Country Study". In Leon Jeffries (ed.). *Iraq: Issues, Historical Background, Bibliography* (Nova Science Publishers, 2003) 141ff.

Michalsen, Dag. *Rett en internasjonal historie* (Pax Forlag, 2011).

Mill, John S. *Utilitarianism* (Hackett Publishing, 2001).

Moeckli, Daniel and Nigel White. "Treaties as 'Living Instruments". In Dino Kritsiotis and Michael Bowman (eds.). *Conceptual and Contextual Perspectives on the Modern Law of Treaties* (Cambridge University Press, 2016) 136–171.

Moschtaghi, Ramin. "Structure and Principles of the State". In Tilmann Röder (ed.). *Max Planck Manual on Afghan Constitutional Law*, vol. 1, 3rd ed., (Max Planck Institute for Comparative Public and International Law, 2009).

Möller, Kai. *The Global Model of Constitutional Rights* (Oxford University Press, 2012).

Müller, Jan-Werner. *Contesting Democracy: Political Ideas in Twentieth-Century Europe* (Yale University Press, 2011).

Müller, Jan-Werner. *What is Populism?* (University of Pennsylvania Press, 2016).

Mutua, Makau Wa. "The Problem of Universalism; The Ideology of Human Rights". *Virginia Journal of International Law*, vol. 36 (1996): 589–657.

Nederman, Cary. *Community and Consent: The Secular Political Thought of Marsiglio of Padua's Defensor Pacis* (Rowman and Littlefield Publishers, 1995).

Neff, Stephen C. "An Evolving International Legal Norm of Religious Freedom: Problems and Prospects". *California Western International Law Journal*, vol. 7, no. 3 (1977): 543–590.

Neuman, Gerald L. "Human Rights and Constitutional Rights: Harmony and Dissonance?" *Stanford Law Review*, vol. 55, no. 5 (2003): 1863–1900.

Nighat, Mehroze C. *Constitutional Development in Afghanistan* (Royal Book, 1998).

Nino, Carlos Santiago. "Transition to Democracy, Corporatism, and Presidentialism with Special Reference to Latin America". In Douglas Greenberg, Stanley N.

Katz, Melanie Beth Olivero, and Steven C. Wheatley (eds.). *Constitutionalism and Democracy: Transitions in the Contemporary World* (American Council of Learned Societies Comparative Constitutionalism Papers, 1993) 46–64.

Norris, Pippa and Ronald Inglehart. *Sacred and Secular: Religion and Politics Worldwide* (Cambridge University Press, 2004).

Norton, Anne. *Republic of Signs: Liberal Theory and American Popular Culture* (University of Chicago Press, 1993).

Nowak, Manfred. *U.N. Covenant on Civil and Political Rights: CCPR Commentary* (Engel, 2005).

Oakeshott, Michael. *On History and Other Essays* (Basil Blackwell, 1983).

Okoth-Ogendo, H.W.O. "Constitutions without Constitutionalism: An African Political Paradox". In Douglas Greenberg, S.N. Kartz, B. Oliviero and S.C. Wheatley (eds.). *Constitutionalism and Democracy: Transitions in the Contemporary World* (Oxford University Press, 1993).

Olsen, Henrik P. "The Right to Freedom of Religion: A Critical Review". *Scandinavian Studies in Law*, vol. 52 (2007): 227–254.

Perry, Michael. "Why Political Reliance on Religiously Grounded Morality is not Illegitimate in a Liberal Democracy". *Wake Forrest Law Review*, vol. 36 (2001): 217.

Peters, Anne. "Compensatory Constitutionalism: The Functions and Potential of Fundamental International Norms and Structures". *Leiden Journal of International Law*, vol. 19 (2006): 579–610.

Pirimäe, Pärtel. "The Westphalian Myth and the Idea of External Sovereignty". In Quentin Skinner and Kalmo Hent (eds.). *Sovereignty in Fragments: The Past, Present and Future of a Contested Concept* (Cambridge University Press, 2010) 64ff.

Pištan, Čarna. *Pseudo Constitutionalism in Central Asia: Curse or Cure?* Paper presented at World Congress of Constitutional Law 2014, Oslo.

Pitkin, Hanna. "The Idea of a Constitution". *Journal of Legal Education*, vol. 37 (1987): 2.

Pocock, J.G.A. *The Machiavellian Moment, Florentine Political Thought and the Atlantic Republican Tradition* (Princeton University Press, 1975).

Post, Robert C. and Reva B. Siegel. "Roe Rage: Democratic Constitutionalism and Backlash". *Harvard Civil Rights-Civil Liberties Law Review*, vol. 42, no. 2 (2007): 373–434.

Poulat, Émile. *Notre Laïcité Public* (Berg International, 2013).

Poulson, Stephen. *Social Movements in Twentieth Century Iran: Culture, Ideology and Mobilizing Frameworks* (Lexington Books, 2006) 103ff.

Preuss, Ulrich K. "Disconnecting Constitutions from Statehood: Is Global Constitutionalism a Viable Concept?" In Petra Dobner and Martin Loughlin (eds.). *The Twilight of Constitutionalism?* (Oxford University Press, 2010) 23–46.

Pullada, Leon B. *Reform and Rebellion in Afghanistan, 1919–1929: King Amanullah's Failure to Modernize a Tribal Society* (Cornell University Press, 1973).

Questier, Michael C. *Conversion, Politics and Religion in England, 1580–1625* (Cambridge University Press, 1996).

Rabb, Intisar. "'We the Jurists': Islamic Constitutionalism in Iraq". *University of Pennsylvania Journal of Constitutional Law*, vol. 10, no. 3 (2008): 527–579.

Raday, Frances. "Constitutional Secularism Vindicated. (Constitutionalism and Secularism in an Age of Religious Revival: The Challenge of Global and Local Fundamentalisms)". *Cardozo Law Review*, vol. 30, no. 6 (2009): 2769–2798.

Rajagopal, Balakrishnan. *International Law from Below: Development, Social Movements and Third World Resistance* (Cambridge University Press, 2003).

Rakel, Eva P. *Power, Islam, and Political Elite in Iran: A Study on the Iranian Political Elite from Khomeini to Ahmadinejad* (Brill, 2009).

Rawls, John. *Political Liberalism* (Columbia University Press, 1993).

Rawls, John. *A Theory of Justice*, rev. ed. (Harvard University Press, 1999).

Rawls, John. *Justice as Fairness: A Restatement* (Harvard University Press, 2001).

Raz, Joseph. "On the Authority and Interpretation of Constitutions: Some Preliminaries". In Larry Alexander (ed.). *Constitutionalism: Philosophical Foundations* (Cambridge University Press, 1998) 152–193.

Raz, Joseph. *The Authority of the Rule of Law* (Oxford University Press, 2002).

Reed, Douglas S. "Popular Constitutionalism: Toward a Theory of State Constitutional Meanings". *Rutgers Law Journal*, vol. 30 (1999): 871–932.

Rehman, Javaid and Susan C. Breau (eds.). *Religion, Human Rights and International Law: A Critical Examination of Islamic State Practices* (Martinus Nijhoff Publishers, 2007).

Rieff, Philip. *My Life among the Deathworks* (University of Virginia Press, 2006).

Ripstein, Arthur. *Force and Freedom* (Harvard University Press, 2009).

Romero, Juan. *The Iraqi Revolution of 1958: A Revolutionary Quest for Unity and Security* (University Press of America, 2010).

Rosenfeld, Michel. "Modern Constitutionalism as Interplay between Identity and Diversity". In Michel Rosenfeld (ed.). *Constitutionalism, Identity, Difference, and Legitimacy: Theoretical Perspectives* (Duke University Press, 1994) 3–38.

Rosenfeld, Michel. "A Pluralist Critique of the Constitutional Treatment of Religion". In András Sájo and Sholomo Avineri (eds.). *The Law of Religious Identity: Models for Post-Communism* (Springer, 1998) 39–40.

Rubin, Barry. "Religion and International Affairs". In Douglas Johnston and Cynthia Sampson (eds.). *Religion, the Missing Dimension of Statecraft* (Oxford University Press, 1994) 20–36.

Rutherford, Bruce K. "What do Egypt's Islamists Want? Moderate Islam and the Rise of Islamic Constitutionalism". *Middle East Journal*, vol. 60, no. 4 (2006): 707–731.

Rutledge, Ian. *Enemy on the Euphrates: The British Occupation of Iraq and the Great Arab Revolt, 1914–1921* (Saqi Books, 2014).

Ruud, Morten and Geir Ulfstein. *Innføring i folkerett* (Universitetsforlaget, 2006).

Sachedina, Abdulaziz. *Islam and the Challenge of Human Rights* (Oxford University Press, 2009).

Sachs, Albie. *The Sacred and the Secular: South Africa's Constitutional Court Rules on Same-Sex Marriages*. 2013 Ray Distinguished Lecture. Available at: http://law-apache.uky.edu/wordpress/wp-content/uploads/2014/01/8-Sachs.pdf (accessed 16 July 2019).

Sadurski, Wojciech. *Equality and Legitimacy* (Oxford University Press, 2008).

Said, Edward W. *Orientalism* (Pantheon Books, 1978).

Saikal, Amin, Ravan Farhadi and Kirill Norzhanov. *Modern Afghanistan: A History of Struggle and Survival* (I.B. Taurus, 2004).

Sajo, Andras. *Limiting Government: An Introduction to Constitutionalism* (Central European University Press, 1999).

Sájo, Andras. "Preliminaries to a Concept of Constitutional Secularism". *International Journal of Constitutional Law*, vol. 6, no. 3–4 (2008): 605–629.

Sajo, Andras. "Constitutionalism and Secularism: The Need for Public Reason?" *Cardozo Law Review*, vol. 30 (2008–2009): 2401–2430.

Samuels, David J. and Matthew S. Shugart. "Presidentialism, Elections and Representation". *Journal of Theoretical Politics*, vol. 15, no. 1 (2003): 33–60.

Sartori, Giovanni. "Constitutionalism: A Preliminary Discussion". *American Political Science Review*, vol. 56, no. 4 (1962): 853–864.

Sartori, Giovanni. "Constitutionalism: A Preliminary Discussion". In Wojciech Sadurski (ed.). *Constitutional Theory* (Dartmouth/Ashgate, 2005) 3–14.

Saunders, Cheryl. "Constitution-making in the 21st Century". *International Review of Law*, vol. 4 (2012) 1–10.

Scheinin, Martin. *An Introduction to the International Protection of Human Rights: A Textbook* (Åbo Akademi Univesity Institute for Human Rights, 1999).

Scheppele, Kim L. "Aspirational and Aversive Constitutionalism: The Case of Studying Cross-Constitutional Influence Through Negative Models". *International Journal of Constitutional Law*, vol. 1 (2003): 269.

Scheppele, Kim L., Gàbor Halmai and Miklós Bánkuti. "Hungary's Illiberal Turn: Disabling the Constitution". *Journal of Democracy*, vol. 23, no. 3 (2012): 138–146.

Schilling, Heinz. *Religion, Political Culture and the Emergence of Early Modern Societies: Essays in German and Dutch History* (Leiden, the Netherlands: E.J. Brill, 1992).

Schmitt, Carl. *Constitutional Theory* (Duke University Press, 2008).

Schoiswohl, Michael. "Linking the International Legal Framework to Building the Formal Foundations of a "State at Risk": Constitution-Making and International Law in Post-Conflict Afghanistan". *Vanderbilt Journal of Transnational Law*, vol. 39 (2006): 819–863.

Scott, Joan W. "Multiculturalism and the Politics of Identity". *October*, vol. 61 (1992): 12–19.

Sellin, Volker. "Restorations and Constitutions". In Kelly L. Grotke and Markus J. Prutsch (eds.). *Constitutionalism, Legitimacy and Power* (Oxford University Press, 2014) 84–106.

Serrano, Vicente. "Freedom of Thought as Radical Freedom in Spinoza's Critique of Religion". *Reformation and Renaissance Review*, vol. 14, no. 1 (2012): 23–39.

Seyed-Gohrab, Ali-Asghar (ed.). *Literature of the Early Twentieth Century: From the Constitutional Period to Reza Shah* (I.B. Tauris, 2015).

Shirazi, Asghar. *The Constitution of Iran: Politics and State in the Islamic Republic* (I.B. Tauris, 1998).

Shweder, Richard. "Moral Realism without the Ethnocentrism: Is It Just a List of Empty Truisms?" In András Sajó (ed.). *Human Rights with Modesty: The Problem of Universalism* (Nijhoff, 2004) 65–102.

Skinner, Quentin. "Hobbes on Sovereignty: An Unknown Discussion". *Political Studies*, vol. 13, no. 2 (1965): 213–218.

Skinner, Quentin. *Foundations of Modern Political Thought*, vol. 2 (Cambridge University Press, 1978).

Skinner, Quentin. "The Sovereign State: A Geneology". In Quentin Skinner and Kalmo Hent (eds.). *Sovereignty in Fragments: The Past, Present and Future of a Contested Concept* (Cambridge University Press, 2010).

Smart, Ninian. *The World's Religions* (Cambridge University Press, 1992).

Smith, Christian (ed.). *The Secular Revolution: Power, Interests, and Conflict in the Secularization of American Public Life* (University of California Press, 2003).

Smith, Graeme. *A Short History of Secularism* (I.B. Tauris, 2008).

Sorokin, Pitirim. *Social and Cultural Dynamics: A Study of Change in Major Systems of Art, Truth, Law, and Social Relationships* (Transaction Publishers, 2006).

Sow, Fatou (ed.). *Gender and Fundamentalisms* (CODESIRA, 2018).

Spencer, William. *Iraq: Old Land, New Nation in Conflict* (Twenty-First Century Books, 2000).

Stepan, Alfred. "Religion, Democracy and the 'Twin Tolerations'". *Journal of Democracy*, vol. 11, no. 4 (2000): 37–57.

Stigen, Anfinn. *Tenkningens historie* (Ad Notam Gyldendal, 1993).

Stilt, Kristen A. "Islamic Law and the Making and Remaking of the Iraqi Legal System". *The George Washington International Law Review*, vol. 36, no. 4 (2004): 695–756.

Stone Sweet, Alec and Jud Mathews. "Proportionality Balancing and Global Constitutionalism". *Columbia Journal of Transnational Law*, vol. 47, no. 1 (2008): 68–149.

Strauss, Leo. *The Political Philosophy of Hobbes: Its Basis and Its Genesis* (University of Chicago Press, 1963).

Sultany, Nimer. "Against Conceptualism: Islamic Law, Democracy and Constitutionalism in the Aftermath of the Arab Spring". *Boston University International Law Journal*, vol. 31 (2013): 435–464.

Sunstein, Cass R. "Beyond the Republican Revival". *Yale Law Journal*, vol. 97 (1988): 1539–1590.

Swatos, William and Daniel Olson (eds.). *The Secularization Debate* (Rowman and Littlefield Publishers, 2010).

Tayler, Wilder. "Notes on the Human Rights Movement and the Issue of Terrorism". *International Council on Human Rights Policy*, 2005.

Taylor, Charles. *A Secular Age* (Belknap Press of Harvard University Press, 2007).

Taylor, Paul. *Freedom of Religion* (Cambridge University Press, 2005).

Teitel, Ruti. "Critique of Religion as Politics in the Public Sphere". *Cornell Law Review*, vol. 78, no. 5 (1993): 747–821.

Teitel, Ruti. *Transitional Justice* (Oxford University Press, 2000).

Teitel, Ruti. "Transitional Justice and the Transformation of Constitutionalism". In Tom Ginsburg and Rosalind Dixon (eds.). *Comparative Constitutionalism* (Edward Elgar, 2011) 57–76.

Temperman, Jeroen. "The Neutral State: Optional or Necessary? A Triangular Analysis of State-Religion Identification, Democratisation & Human Rights Compliance". *Religion and Human Rights: An International Journal*, vol. 1, no. 3 (2006): 269–303.

Temperman, Jeroen. *State-Religion Relationships and Human Rights Law: Towards a Right to Religiously Neutral Governance* (Martinus Nijhoff Publishers, 2010).

Terrill, W. Andrew. "Lessons of the Iraqi de-Ba'athification Program for Iraq's Future and the Arab Revolutions". Strategic Studies Institute Monograph, 2012.

Thomas, Scott (ed.). *The Global Resurgence of Religion and the Transformation of International Relations: The Struggle for the Soul of the Twenty-First Century* (Palgrave MacMillan, 2005).

Thornhill, Chris. *A Sociology of Constitutions: Constitutions and State Legitimacy in Historical-Sociological Perspective* (Cambridge University Press, 2011).

Tóth, Gábor Attila. *Constitution for a Disunited Country: on Hungary's 2011 Fundamental Law* (Central European University Press, 2013).

Travis, Hannibal. "Freedom or Theocracy: Constitutionalism in Afghanistan and Iraq". *Northwestern University Journal of International Human Rights*, vol. 4, no. 3 (2005): 1–52.

Tripp, Charles. *A History of Iraq* (Cambridge University Press, 2000).

Tsakyrakis, Stavros. "Proportionality: An Assault on Human Rights". *International Journal of Constitutional Law*, vol. 7, no. 3 (2009): 468–493.

Tully, James. *Strange Multiplicity: Constitutionalism in an Age of Diversity* (Cambridge University Press, 1995).

Tushnet, Mark. *Taking the Constitution Away from the Courts* (Princeton University Press, 1999).

Tushnet, Mark. "Authoritarian Constitutionalism". *Cornell Law Review*, vol. 100, no. 2 (2015): 391–461.

Van der Vyver, Johan D. "Legal Dimensions of Religious Human Rights; Constitutional Texts". In Johan D. Van der Vyver and John Witte (eds.). *Religious Human Rights in Global Perspective: Legal Perspectives* (Martinus Nijhoff Publishers, 1996) XI–XLVII.

Vikør, Knut. *Mellom Gud og stat. Ei historie om islamsk lov og rettsvesen* (Spartacus Forlag, 2003).

Vikør, Knut. "The Origins of the Shari'a". In P. Bearman and R. Peters (eds.). *The Ashgate Research Companion to Islamic Law*.

Vikør, Knut. *Ei Verd Bygd på islam: oversikt over midtaustens historie* (Det norske samlaget, 2010).

Volpi, Frédéric. *Political Islam: A Critical Reader* (Routledge, 2011).

Von Bogdandy, Armin and Rüdiger Wolfrum (eds.). *Max Planck Yearbook of United Nations Law*, vol. 15 (Max Planck Institute for Comparative Public Law and International Law, 2011).

Wærstad, Tone. *Protecting Muslim Minority Women's Human Rights at Divorce: Application of the Protection against Discrimination Guarantee in Norwegian Domestic Law, Private International Law and Human Rights Law* (Faculty of Law, 2015).

Waldron, Jeremy. *Law and Disagreement* (Oxford University Press, 1999).

Weber, Max. *Economy and Society* (Berkeley University Press, 1978).

Webber, Gregoire. "Proportionality, Balancing and the Cult of Constitutional Rights Scholarship". *Canadian Journal of Law and Jurisprudence*, vol. 23, no. 1 (2010): 179–202.

Weinrib, Ernest J. "Legal Formalism". In Dennis M. Patterson (ed.). *A Companion to Philosophy of Law and Legal Theory* (Blackwell, 1996) 332–342.

Weinrib, Jacob. "Authority, Justice, and Public Law: A Unified Theory". *University of Toronto Law Journal*, vol. 64, no. 5 (2014): 703–735.

Weinrib, Jacob. *Dimensions of Dignity: The Theory and Practice of Modern Constitutional Law* (Cambridge University Press, 2016).

Weinrib, Lorraine E. "Constitutional Conceptions and Constitutional Comparativsm". In Vicki C. Jackson and Mark Tushnet (eds.). *Defining the Field of Comparative Constitutional Law* (ABC-CLIO, 2002) 23–81.

Weinrib, Lorraine E. "The Postwar Paradigm and American Exceptionalism". In Sujit Choudry (ed.). *The Migration of Constitutional Ideas* (Cambridge University Press, 2006) 84–112.

Whelan, Frederick. *Hume and Machiavelli: Political Realism and Liberal Thought* (Lexington Books, 2001).
Whittington, Keith E. "Extrajudicial Constitutional Interpretation: Three Objections and Responses". *North Carolina Law Review*, vol. 80, no. 3 (2002): 773–851.
Whittington, Keith E., R. Daniel Kelemen and Gregory A. Caldeira (eds.). *The Oxford Handbook of Law and Politics* (Oxford University Press, 2010).
Wilson, Bryan. *Religion in Secular Society: A Sociological Comment* (Watts, 1966).
Witte, John and Christian Green. *Religion and Human Rights: An Introduction* (Oxford University Press, 2011).
Wolff, Jonathan. *An Introduction to Political Philosophy* (Oxford University Press, 1996, revised ed. 2006).
Wolfgang, Reinhard. "Reformation, Counter-Reformation, and the Early Modern State: A Reassessment". *Catholic Historical Review*, vol. 75, no. 3 (1989): 383–404.
Wyatt, Christopher. *Afghanistan and the Defence of Empire: Diplomacy and Strategy during the Great Game* (I.B. Tauris, 2011).
Zakariya, Fouad. *Laïcité ou islamisme: Les Arabes à l'heure du choix* (La Découverte/ Al-Fikr, 1991).
Zeidel, Ronen, Amatzia Baram, and Achim Rohde. *Iraq Between Occupations: Perspectives from 1920 to the Present* (Palgrave MacMilllan, 2010).
Zucca, Lorenzo. *A Secular Europe: Law and Religion in the European Constitutional Landscape* (Oxford University Press, 2012).

1.6 Encyclopedia

Miller, Fred. "Aristotle's Political Theory" in *Stanford Encyclopedia of Philosophy*.
Longstaff, Aline Marie and Tara Fitzgerald. "Iraq" in Gerhard Robbers and Cole Durham (eds). *Encyclopedia of Law and Religion* (Brill, 2015).

1.7 Reports

Bechir, Saleh and Hazem Saghieh. "The "Muslim Community": A European Invention", openDemocracy. Available at: www.opendemocracy.net/conflict-terrorism/community_2928.jsp [Accessed 17 October 2018].
Freedom House. "Freedom in the world 2014". Available at: https://freedomhouse.org/sites/default/files/Freedom%20in%20the%20World%202014%20Booklet.pdf [Accessed 29 April 2018].
Pew Research Centre, *In 30 countries, heads of state must belong to a certain religion*, Available at: www.pewresearch.org/fact-tank/2014/07/22/in-30-countries-heads-of-state-must-belong-to-a-certain-religion/?moderated#comment-494879 [Accessed 20 May 2018].
Journalists and Writers Foundation. "Assault on Education in Turkey and Abroad" (2017).

Index